VITAL STATISTICS

Everything a Man Needs to Know

Chris Wood

summersdale

VITAL STATISTICS
Copyright © Chris Wood 2008

Summersdale Publishers Ltd
46 West Street
Chichester
West Sussex
PO19 1RP
UK

www.summersdale.com

Printed and bound in Great Britain

ISBN: 978-1-84024-694-0

HOW TO USE THIS BOOK

In this book you will find tables containing vital information on everything from sport to the sex industry, cars to music and beer to films, plus a miscellany of other information that every man should know. The tables aren't grouped in any particular order, but you will find a handy alphabetised list of tables with page references at the back.

PUBS ON TV

TV SHOW	PUB	LOCATION	SHOW RUN
Angel (US)	Caritas	Los Angeles, California	1999–2004
Brookside	Bar Brookie	Liverpool	1982–2003
Cheers (US)	Cheers	Boston, Massachusetts	1982–1993
Coronation Street	The Rovers Return	Coronation Street (F), Manchester	1960–present
Crossroads	Cat in the Moon	King's Oak (F), Birmingham	1964–1988; 2001–2003
The Dukes of Hazzard (US)	The Boar's Nest	Hazzard County (F), Georgia	1979–1985
EastEnders	The Queen Victoria	Albert Square (F), Walford (F), London	1985–present
Emmerdale	The Woolpack	Emmerdale (F), Yorkshire	1972–present
Family Guy (US)	The Drunken Clam	Quahog (F), Providence County, Rhode island	1999–present
Futurama (US)	O'Zorgnax's Pub	'New' New York City (F)	1999–2003
Goodnight Sweetheart	The Royal Oak	London	1993–1999
Hollyoaks	The Dog in the Pond	Chester	1995–present
Home & Away (Aus)	Noah's Bar	Summer Bay (F), New South Wales	1988–present
I Love Lucy (US)	Club Babalu (originally Tropicana)	New York City	1951–1957
The Jeffersons (US)	Charlie's	New York City	1975–1985
Last of the Summer Wine	The White Horse	Holmfirth, West Yorkshire	1973–present
*M*A*S*H (US)*	Rosie's	South Korea	1972–1983
Men Behaving Badly	The Crown	London	1992–1998
Neighbours (Aus)	Charlie's (formerly The Waterhole; Chez Chez; Lou's Place; Scarlet Bar)	Ramsay Street (F), Erinsborough (F), Melbourne	1985–present
Northern Exposure (US)	The Brick	Cicely (F), Alaska	1990–1995
The Office	Chasers	Slough	2001–2003
Only Fools and Horses	The Nag's Head	Peckham, London	1981–2003
Phoenix Nights	The Phoenix Club	Bolton	2001–2002
Queer As Folk (US)	Babylon	Pittsburgh, Pennsylvania	2000–2005
Rab C. Nesbitt	Two Ways	Govan, Glasgow	1988–1997

TV SHOW	PUB	LOCATION	SHOW RUN
Shameless	The Jockey	Chatsworth Estate (F), Manchester	2004–present
The Simpsons (US)	Moe's Tavern	Springfield (F)	1989–present
Star Trek: Deep Space Nine (US)	Quark's	Deep Space Nine Space Station (F)	1993–1999
Still Game	The Clansman	Craiglang (F), Glasgow	2002–present
Two Pints of Lager and a Packet of Crisps	Mayhew; The Archer Hotel	Runcorn, Cheshire	2001–2006
The Young Ones	The Kebab and Calculator	London	1982–1984
Key: (F) = denotes fictional location.			

HOW BEER IS PRODUCED

	YEAST	TYPE OF FERMENTATION	STORAGE PERIOD	SERVING TEMPERATURE
Ale	Made with yeast that floats on the top of the fermenting wort.	Quickly at 15–25°C	May be served within days of fermentation.	Warmer (10–19°C)
Lager	Made with yeast that sinks to the bottom of the fermenting wort.	Slowly at 5–9°C	Must be stored at freezing point for 21–90 days after initial fermentation.	Chilled (7–10°C)

THE BREWING PROCESS

Stage 1: barley is malted, ground, then mixed with hot water.

Stage 2: flavourings (hops, spices etc.) are added to the fermenting wort, and the wort is boiled.

Stage 3: extra sugar may be added (to increase alcohol content).

Stage 4: the wort is cooled and then the yeast is added.

Stage 5: the wort is fermented, filtered, aged (to carbonate), and pasteurised (to kill off the last of the yeast).

Stage 6: ale is ready for distribution; lager is stored at 0–5°C for further maturation (during which time yeast and protein sediment settles, and is extracted).

GRAND NATIONAL

YEAR	HORSE	AGE	JOCKEY	TRAINER	ODDS
1990	Mr Frisk	11	Marcus Armytage	Kim Bailey	16/1
1991	Seagram	11	Nigel Hawke	David Barons	12/1
1992	Party Politics	8	Carl Llewellyn	Nick Gaselee	14/1
1993	Race made void. A proportion of runners ignored officials signalling for a false start because they thought they were protesters.				
1994	Miinnehoma	11	Richard Dunwoody	Martin Pipe	16/1
1995	Royal Athlete	12	Jason Titley	Jenny Pitman	40/1
1996	Rough Quest	10	Mick Fitzgerald	Terry Casey	7/1 F
1997	Lord Gyllene	9	Tony Dobbin	Steve Brookshaw	14/1
1998	Earth Summit	10	Carl Llewellyn	Nigel Twiston-Davies	7/1 F
1999	Bobbyjo	9	Paul Carberry	Tommy Carberry	10/1
2000	Papillon	9	Ruby Walsh	Ted Walsh	10/1
2001	Red Marauder	11	Richard Guest	Norman Mason	33/1
2002	Bindaree	8	Jim Culloty	Nigel Twiston-Davies	20/1
2003	Monty's Pass	10	Barry Geraghty	Jimmy Mangan	16/1
2004	Amberleigh House	12	Graham Lee	Ginger McCain	16/1
2005	Hedgehunter	9	Ruby Walsh	Willie Mullins	7/1 F
2006	Numbersixvalverde	10	Niall Madden	Martin Brassil	11/1
2007	Silver Birch	10	Robbie Power	Gordon Elliott	33/1
2008	Comply Or Die	9	Timmy Murphy	David Pipe	7/1 F

F = favourite.

First Ever Winner: the first Grand National was run in 1836 and was won by The Duke. He won again in 1837. In those days the race was called the 'Great Liverpool Steeplechase'.

Longest Winning Odds: in the 1967 race, two of the leaders pulled up just before the 23rd fence. Chaos ensued with horses refusing to jump and riders unseated. The outsider, Foinavon, was at the back of the field and his jockey, Johnny Buckingham, saw the disruption from behind and managed to pull his horse to the other side of the fence. He jumped safely and won at odds of 100/1.

Greys: the last grey to win was Nicolaus Silver in 1961. The only other grey winner was The Lamb (1868 and 1871).

Mares: in total 12 mares have won the National. The last mare to win was Nickel Coin in 1951.

Most Successful Horse: Red Rum is by far the most successful National winner. He won three times (1973, 1974 and 1977), and came second in 1975 and 1976.

SCHMIDT STING PAIN INDEX

RATING	INSECT	SENSATION	STRENGTH
1.0	Sweat bee	Light, ephemeral, almost fruity.	A tiny spark has singed a single hair on your arm.
1.2	Fire ant	Sharp, sudden, mildly alarming.	Like walking across a shag carpet and reaching for the light switch.
1.8	Bullhorn acacia ant	A rare, piercing, elevated sort of pain.	Someone has fired a staple into your cheek.
2.0	Bald-faced hornet	Rich, hearty, slightly crunchy.	Similar to getting your hand mashed in a revolving door.
2.0	Yellowjacket	Hot and smoky, almost irreverent.	Imagine W. C. Fields extinguishing a cigar on your tongue.
3.0	Red harvester ant	Bold and unrelenting.	Somebody is using a drill to excavate your ingrown toenail.
3.0	Paper wasp	Caustic and burning, distinctly bitter aftertaste.	Like spilling a beaker of hydrochloric acid on a paper cut.
4.0	Pepsis wasp	Blinding, fierce, shockingly electric.	A running hairdryer has been dropped into your bubble bath (if you get stung by one you might as well lie down and scream).
4.0+	Bullet ant	Pure, intense, brilliant pain.	Like walking over flaming charcoal with a 3-inch rusty nail in your heel.

From the work of Carl Hayden Bee Research Centre entomologist, Justin O. Schmidt. Schmidt's original paper was published in 1984 and updated in 1990. The index of 78 species rates human pain from sting from 0 (completely ineffective) to 4 (most painful).

UK CHAMPIONS OF EUROPEAN CLUB COMPETITIONS

YEAR	WINNER	CAPTAIN	RUNNERS-UP/SCORE	CUP
1963	Tottenham Hotspur	Danny Blanchflower	Atlético de Madrid (5–1)	Cup Winners'
1965	West Ham United	Bobby Moore	1860 Munich (2–0)	Cup Winners'
1967	Celtic	Billy McNeill	Inter Milan (2–1)	Champions'
1968	Man Utd	Bobby Charlton	Benfica (4–1) [aet]	Champions'
1968	Leeds United	Willie Bremner	Ferencváros (0–0, 1–0) [1–0 agg.]	Fairs
1969	Newcastle Utd	Robert Moncur	Újpest (2–3, 3–0) [6–2 agg.]	Fairs
1970	Man City	Tony Book	Górnik Zebrze (2–1)	Cup Winners'
1970	Arsenal	Frank McLintock	Anderlecht (3–0, 3–1) [4–3 agg.]	Fairs
1971	Chelsea	Ron Harris	Real Madrid (1–1) [aet] [2–1 replay]	Cup Winners'
1971	Leeds United	Willie Bremner	Juventus (1–1, 2–2) [agg. 3–3] [away goals]	Fairs
1972	Rangers	John Greig	Dynamo Moscow (3–2)	Cup Winners'
1972	Tottenham Hotspur	Alan Mullery	Wolverhampton W (1–1, 1–2) [3–2 agg.]	UEFA
1973	Liverpool	Emlyn Hughes	Borussia Mönchengladbach (2–0, 3–0) [3–2 agg.]	UEFA
1976	Liverpool	Emlyn Hughes	Club Brugge (1–1, 3–2) [4–3 agg.]	UEFA
1977	Liverpool	Emlyn Hughes	Borussia Mönchengladbach (3–1)	Champions'
1978	Liverpool	Emlyn Hughes	Club Brugge (1–0)	Champions'
1979	Nottingham Forest	John McGovern	Malmö (1–0)	Champions'
1980	Nottingham Forest	John McGovern	Hamburg (1–0)	Champions'
1981	Liverpool	Phil Thompson	Real Madrid (1–0)	Champions'
1981	Ipswich Town	Mick Mills	AZ Alkmaar (4–2, 3–0) [5–4 agg.]	UEFA
1982	Aston Villa	Dennis Mortimer	Bayern Munich (1–0)	Champions'

YEAR	WINNER	CAPTAIN	RUNNERS-UP/SCORE	CUP
1983	Aberdeen	Willie Miller	Real Madrid (2–1) [aet]	Cup Winners'
1984	Liverpool	Graeme Souness	Roma (1–1) [aet] [4–2 pens]	Champions'
1984	Tottenham Hotspur	Steve Perryman	Anderlecht (1–1, 1–1) [agg. 2–2] [4–3 pens]	UEFA
1985	Everton	Kevin Ratcliffe	Rapid Vienna (3–1)	Cup Winners'
1991	Man Utd	Bryan Robson	Barcelona (2–1)	Cup Winners'
1994	Arsenal	Tony Adams	Parma (1–0)	Cup Winners'
1998	Chelsea	Steve Clarke	VfB Stuttgart (1–0)	Cup Winners'
1999	Man Utd	Peter Schmeichel	Bayern Munich (2–1)	Champions' League
2001	Liverpool	Sami Hyypia	Alavés (5–4) [aet] [golden goal]	UEFA
2005	Liverpool	Steven Gerrard	AC Milan (3–3) [4–3 pens]	Champions' League
2008	Man Utd	Rio Ferdinand	Chelsea (1–1) [4–3 pens]	Champions' League

aet = after extra time, pens = penalties, agg = aggregate

WORLD'S HIGHEST MOUNTAINS

	NAME	LOCATION	HEIGHT ABOVE SEA LEVEL IN M (FT)
1	Mount Everest	Himalayan range, Nepal-Tibet border	8,850 (29,035)
2	K2	Karakorum range, Pakistan-China border	8,611 (28,251)
3	Känchenjunga	Himalayan range, Nepal-India border	8,598 (28,209)
4	Lhotse	Himalayan range, Nepal-Tibet border	8,516 (27,940)
5	Makalu	Himalayan range, Nepal-Tibet border	8,481 (27,824)
EU	Mont Blanc	Graian Alps, France/Italy border	4,807 (15,771)
UK	Ben Nevis	Fort William, Scotland	1,343 (4,406)
US	Mount McKinley (aka Denali)	Alaska	6,194 (20,320)

Source: Encarta Encyclopedia

CHRONOLOGY OF EAST COAST HIP HOP ARTISTS

RAPPER	ORIGIN OF STAGE NAME	BIRTH NAME	HOME CITY	DEBUT ALBUM
Kurtis Blow (1959–)	From his first name and the boxing punch – body blow	Curtis Walker	Harlem, NY	*Kurtis Blow* (1980)
Schoolly D (1966–)	His nickname as a kid	Jesse B. Weaver	Philadelphia, PE	*Schoolly D* (1986)
ODB (1968–04)	From the 1980 kung fu film *Ol' Dirty & The Bastard*	Russell Jones	Brooklyn, NY	*Return to the 36 Chambers: The Dirty Version* (1995)
LL Cool J (1968–)	From the acronym of 'Ladies Love Cool James'	James Smith III	Queens, NY	*Radio* (1985)
Jay-Z (1969–)	From his nickname, Jazzy. Also a homage to his mentor, Jaz-O	Shawn Carter	Brooklyn, NY	*Reasonable Doubt* (1996)
P. Diddy (1969–)	Suggested by his friend Notorious B.I.G.	Sean Combs	Mount Vernon, NY	*No Way Out* (1997)
Fat Joe (1970–)	He chose the stage name 'Fat Joe Da Gangster', and later shortened it	Joseph Cartagena	Bronx, NY	*Represent* (1993)
DMX (1970–)	After the Oberheim DMX drum machine	Earl Simmons	Yonkers, NY	*It's Dark and Hell is Hot* (1998)
AZ (1972–)	From the first and last letters of his name	Anthony Cruz	Brooklyn, NY	*Doe or Die* (1995)
Notorious B.I.G. (1972–97)	From the acronym 'Business Instead of Game'	Chris Wallace	Brooklyn, NY	*Ready To Die* (1994)
Nas (1973–)	Shortening of his first name	Nasir Jones	Queens, NY	*Illmatic* (1994)
50 Cent (1975–)	Chosen by himself as a metaphor for 'change'	Curtis Jackson	Queens, NY	*Get Rich or Die Tryin'* (2003)
Ja Rule (1976–)	From his initials and the mantra 'Real Unconditional Love Exists'	Jeffrey Atkins	Queens, NY	*Venni Vetti Vecci* (1999)
Cam'ron (1976–)	Shortening of his first name	Cameron Giles	Harlem, NY	*Confessions of Fire* (1998)
Ludacris (1977–)	Chosen by himself, based on the word 'ludicrous'	Christopher Bridges	Atlanta, GE	*Incognegro* (2000)

RAPPER	ORIGIN OF STAGE NAME	BIRTH NAME	HOME CITY	DEBUT ALBUM
Ma$e (1977–)	From his first name	Mason Betha	Harlem, NY	*Harlem World* (1997)
Tony Yayo (1978–)	Tony is an acronym for his nickname 'Talk Of New York', and 'yayo' is a street name for cocaine	Marvin Bernard	Queens, NY	*Thoughts of a Predicate Felon* (2005)
Young Buck (1981–)	Given to him by older gang members because he was good at making money	David Brown	Nashville, TE	*Straight Outta Ca$hville* (2004)
Lloyd Banks (1982–)	From his last name (Lloyd), and his great grandfather's last name (Banks)	Christopher Lloyd	Queens, NY	*The Hunger For More* (2004)

PROFESSIONAL BOXING WEIGHT DIVISIONS

DIVISION	UPPER LIMIT
Flyweight	112 lb = 50.8 kg
Bantamweight	118 lb = 53.5 kg
Featherweight	126 lb = 57.1 kg
Lightweight	135 lb = 61.2 kg
Welterweight	147 lb = 66.7 kg
Middleweight	160 lb = 72.6 kg
Light heavyweight	175 lb = 79.4 kg
Heavyweight	200 lb = 90.7 kg and over

There are 17 recognised weight divisions in boxing; however, the majority of professional fights are fought within the eight traditional classes.

CONDOM ADVERTISING SLOGANS

BRAND (BRAND ORIGIN)	SLOGAN
Beyond Seven (Japan)	'Safe, Sensitive, Strong'
Condomi (Germany)	'Virtual Skinwear'
Durex (UK)	'For A Hundred Million Reasons'
EXS (UK)	'Enhancing Your Pleasure'
Harmony (India)	'Try Something New Tonight! Harmony. Safe Love.'
Jiffi (Australia)	'The Thinking Man's Condom'
Jimmie Hatz (US)	'The Official Condom Of The Hip Hop Kulture.'
Joy (Brazil)	'The Safest Love'
KamaSutra (US)	'Kamasutra. For The Pleasure Of Sensual Living'
LifeStyles Brand (US)	'Proven Protection That Feels Really Good! Feel Good. Play Safe.'
Manix (France)	'The World's Thinnest Condom. Less Latex, More Sex.'
Mates (UK)	'Have A Good Time With Your Mates'
Night Light (US)	'Rise And Shine With Night Light Glow-In-The-Dark Condoms'
Okamoto (Japan)	'Okamoto. Super Fine!'
Trojan (US)	'Trojan. Pleasure You Want. Protection You Trust.'

Condom Chronology:

Circa 1,000 BC – ancient cave drawings show forms of sheath contraceptive.

1855 – first rubber condoms were produced. At 1–2 mm thick and with seams down the sides, early condoms were expensive but reusable.

1912 – German inventor Julius Fromm created the first seamless (latex) condom. Fromm became the first recognised condom brand.

1994 – first polyurethane (PU) types were introduced. PU has the advantage of being thinner (as thin as 0.02 mm), has better heat conduction and a longer shelf life.

The future – tests are in progress on future condom types that may be made from quick-hardening gels and/or spray-on liquids.

SCOVILLE SCALE

SCOVILLE HEAT UNITS	PEPPER	ORIGIN
0	Bell	Latin America
100–500	Pepperoncini (aka banana; golden Greek; Tuscan; sweet Italian)	Greece; Italy
100–500	Pimento	Latin America
400–700	Santa Fe Grande	Santa Fe, New Mexico
500–1,000	New Mexico	New Mexico
500–2,500	Anaheim	Anaheim, California
1,000–2,000	Poblano	Puebla, Mexico
2,500–5,000	Jalapeño	Xalapa, Mexico
5,000–10,000	Chipotle (a smoked-dried jalapeño)	Mexico
8,000–22,000	Serrano	Hidalgo, Mexico; Puebla, Mexico
30,000–50,000	Tabasco	Tabasco, Mexico
30,000–50,000	Cayenne	Cayenne, French Guiana
30,000–60,000	Pequin	Mexico
50,000–100,000	Chiltepin	Mexico
100,000–200,000	Jamaican Hot	Jamaica
100,000–225,000	Piri Piri (aka African Birdseye; African Devil)	Africa
0.1–0.32 million	Scotch Bonnet	Caribbean
0.1–0.35 million	Habanero	South America
0.35–0.58 million	Red Savina	California
0.86–1.04 million	Naga Jolokia	Bangladesh; North-east India; Sri Lanka

Man-Made Products: pure capsaicin extract (16 m); Blair's 16 Million Reserve brand sauce additive (around £250/ml) (16 m); Nordihydrocapsaicin extract (9.1 m); Homodihydrocapsaicin and Homocapsaicin (8.6 m); US police grade pepper spray (5.3 m); pepper spray (2 m); Tabasco Habanero brand sauce (7 k–8 k); Tabasco brand pepper sauce (2.5 k–5 k).

The Scoville Organoleptic Test: the scale is named after the American chemist, Wilbur Scoville, who developed the heat intensity test in 1912. The test works by diluting the pepper in a water-sugar solution and physically tasting it to determine if heat is detectable. The number of times this has to be done before no heat is detected whatsoever determines how many Scoville Heat Units (SHU) a pepper has.

POST-WAR ENGLAND FOOTBALL CAPTAINS

	PERIOD*	CAPS (AS CAPTAIN)	CAPS (GOALS)	POSITION	NATURAL FOOT	PLACE OF BIRTH	CLUB(S) WHEN ENGLAND CAPTAIN	NUMBER OF CLUBS	TEAM HONOURS	PERSONAL HONOURS
George Hardwick	1946–1948	13	13 (0)	LB	L	Middlesbro'	Middlesbro'	2	-	-
Billy Wright	1948–1959	90	105 (3)	CB	R	Telford	Wolves	1	EL(3); FA	FWA
Johnny Haynes	1960–1962	22	56 (18)	ST	R	Camden, London	Fulham	2	-	-
Jimmy Armfield	1962–1964	15	43 (0)	RB	R	Manchester	Blackpool	1	WC	-
Bobby Moore	1964–1973	90	108 (2)	CB	R	Barking, London	West Ham	4	WC; CW; FA	FWA; BBC
Emlyn Hughes	1974; 1977–1979	23	62 (1)	LB; CB; DM	R	Sheffield	Liverpool	7	EC(2); UE(2); EL(4); FA; LC	FWA
Gerry Francis	1975–1976	8	12 (3)	CM	R	Chiswick, London	QPR	8	-	-
Kevin Keegan	1976–1977; 1979–1982	31	63 (21)	ST	R	Doncaster	Liverpool; Hamburg; S'hampton	6	EC; UE(2); EL(3); GL; FA	EF(2); FWA; PFA
Bryan Robson	1982–1990	65	90 (26)	CM	R	Chester-le-Street	Man Utd	3	CW; EL(2); FA(3)	-
Gary Lineker	1990–1992	18	80 (48)	ST	R	Leicester	Tottenham	5	CWC; FA; SC	PFA; FWA(2)
David Platt	1993–1995	19	62 (27)	CM	R	Oldham	Sampdoria	7	EL; FA	PFA

	PERIOD*	CAPS (AS CAPTAIN)	CAPS (GOALS)	POSITION	NATURAL FOOT	PLACE OF BIRTH	CLUB(S) WHEN ENGLAND CAPTAIN	NUMBER OF CLUBS	TEAM HONOURS	PERSONAL HONOURS
Tony Adams	1996	15	66 (5)	CB	R	Romford, London	Arsenal	1	CW; EL(4); FA(3); LC(2)	PFY
Alan Shearer	1997–2000	34	63 (30)	ST	R	Newcastle	Newcastle	3	EL	PFA(2); FWA
David Beckham	2000–2006	59	102 (17)	RM	R	Waltham Forest, London	Man Utd; Real Madrid; LA Galaxy	3	CL; EL(6); SL; FA(2)	PFY; BBC
John Terry	2006–	14	44 (4)	CB	R	Barking, London	Chelsea	1	EL(2); FA(2); LC(2)	PFA

Key: * = For the period 2/9/1945 to 1/7/2008. During this time 26 other players started matches as captain but were never actual incumbents of the role (they were filling in because the present incumbent was unavailable). In chronological order with caps as captain and total caps records these were:

Frank Swift (2/19); Alf Ramsey (3/32); Ron Clayton (5/35); Ron Flowers (3/49); Bobby Charlton (3/106); Alan Mullery (1/35); Martin Peters (4/67); Colin Bell (1/48); Alan Ball (6/72); Mick Channon (2/46); Mick Mills (8/42); Phil Thompson (6/42); Trevor Cherry (1/27); David Watson (3/65); Ray Clemence (1/61); Peter Shilton (15/125); Phil Neal (1/50); Ray Wilkins (10/84); Terry Butcher (10/77); Peter Beardsley (1/59); Mark Wright (1/43); Stuart Pearce (10/78); Paul Ince (7/53); David Seaman (1/75); Sol Campbell (3/73); Martin Keown (1/43); Michael Owen (8/89); Steven Gerrard (7/67), and Rio Ferdinand (1/68). Other players have been passed the armband during matches but only players who start matches as team captain are recognised by the FA as 'official' England captains.

Team Honours Key: WC = World Cup; EC = European Cup; CL = Champions League; CW = Cup Winners Cup; UE = Uefa Cup; EL = English League; SL = Spanish League; GL = German League; FA = FA Cup; SC = Spanish Cup; LC = League Cup.

Personal Football Honours Key: EF = European Footballer of the Year (aka Ballon d'Or); PFA = Players Footballers Association Players' Player of the Year; PFY = Players Footballers Association Players' Young Player of the Year; FWA = Football Writers Association Player of the Year; BBC = BBC Sports Personality of the Year.

Positions: LB = left back; CB = centre back; RB = right back; DM defensive midfielder; CM = centre midfielder; RM = right midfielder; ST = striker.

GLOSSARY OF US/UK PORN INDUSTRY TERMS

Ass to mouth (A2M)	Removing the penis from a partner's anus then immediately inserting it into their mouth.
Balsa boy	A male actor who can't be relied upon to get and/or maintain an erection.
Bear	A male actor with a great deal of body hair.
Brown eye	Anal sex.
Brown wings	An actor is said to have gained them after they have given anal sex for the first time.
Butterfly	When fingers are used to spread the vagina wide. Also sometimes called 'split beaver'.
Cocksucker red	Bright red lipstick.
Cook book	A porn magazine for male homosexuals. Also sometimes called a 'fag mag' or 'butt book'.
Cowgirl	Sexual position where the woman sits atop and facing the man. Also sometimes called 'top jock'.
Clam dive	Cunnilingus. Also sometimes called 'muff dive' or 'lick-out'.
Creampie	Ejaculation into a partner's vagina or anus.
Cum dodger	An actress who tries to avoid being ejaculated on.
Cum shot	The shot in pornography with the man ejaculating. Also called the 'money shot'.
Deadwood	A flaccid penis on a porn set. Also sometimes called 'Mr Softy'.
Deepthroating	The act of taking the full erect penis into the mouth during fellatio.
Downblouse	Photos or video taken looking down the blouse of a woman, and showing underwear or breasts.
E-coli pie	Oral stimulation of the anus.
Facial	Ejaculating onto a partner's face.
Felching	Sucking semen out of another person's vagina or anus.
Fence painting	Close-up of cunnilingus.
Fisting	Insertion of a fist into a vagina or anus.
Fluffer	A member of a pornographic video team whose job it is to arouse (fluff) male performers prior to filming.
Gang bang	One person having sexual intercourse with a group.
Gay-for-pay	Male or female (usually male) pornographic actors who identify themselves as 'straight' but who are still prepared to perform gay scenes.
Giggler	Girl-on-girl porn scene.
Glory hole	A hole between two booths that allows anonymous sex.

Gonzo	Porn video where the cameraman participates in the action.
Gyno shot	Vaginal close-up.
Hummer	A blowjob.
King triad	A ménage à trois involving one man and two women.
Klondike	A large black penis.
Leather film	A porn video that focuses on leather fetishes.
Pinch	A technique whereby the male actor pinches the base of the penis (to make it look more erect).
Piston Shot	Close-up shots of the moment of actual genital penetration that prove the scene is real.
Plumber	Male porn actor.
Popping	Ejaculating.
Queen triad	A ménage à trois involving one woman and two men.
Reverse cowgirl	Sex with the woman on top, where the woman is sitting facing away from the man.
Riding the cotton pony	Menstruating.
Sandwich	When the woman is penetrated by two men simultaneously: one in the vagina and one in the anus.
Spit roast	When the woman is penetrated by two men simultaneously: one in the vagina (from behind) and one in the mouth.
Stickspin	A scene in which the woman changes position (e.g. from cowgirl to reverse cowgirl) whilse the man's penis stays inside her.
Transwoman	An actor who looks feminine and has breasts but also has male genitalia. The term 'she-male' is also used but is usually considered derogatory. In Thailand these male to female transsexuals may also be called 'ladyboys' or kathoey.
Stovepipe	An anus with an extended opening after a sex scene.
Snowballing	Passing semen from one mouth to another.
Stunt cock	A secondary actor who is used to replace a male actor for a cum shot.
Triple play	A sexual position where the woman is penetrated in the anus, mouth and vagina simultaneously.
Upskirt	Photos or video taken looking up the skirt of a woman, showing either underwear or the vagina.

VEHICLE REGISTRATION LETTERING SCHEME IN GREAT BRITAIN (POST 2001)

A	East Anglia	**H**	Hampshire/Dorset	**P**	Preston/Pennines
B	Birmingham	**HW**	Isle of Wight	**R**	Reading
C	Wales	**K**	Kettering/Luton	**S**	Scotland
D	Deeside	**L**	London	**T**	Scotland
E	Essex/Hertfordshire	**M**	Manchester/Merseyside	**V**	Vale of Severn
F	Forest and Fens	**N**	North east	**W**	West Country
G	Garden of England (Kent)	**O**	Oxford	**Y**	Yorkshire

For most areas the second letter indicates the DVLA office where the plate was registered. For example in Scotland, A–J = Glasgow; K–O = Edinburgh; P–T = Dundee; U–W = Aberdeen; X–Y = Inverness. For B, E, M, O, R and V, a single office administers the whole area and registrations are not fragmented any further than the initial letter. Age Identifier: The third and fourth digits indicate the age of the vehicle. These change for vehicles registered each year from the first of March (last two digits of the year), and the first of September (last two digits of the year plus 50). The current system began with '51' (September 2001).

FA CUP WINS

	CLUB	LAST WIN	WINS	RUNNERS-UP
1	**Manchester United**	2004	11	7
2	**Arsenal**	2005	10	7
3	**Tottenham Hotspur**	1991	8	1
4=	**Liverpool**	2001	7	6
4=	**Aston Villa**	1957	7	3
6=	**Newcastle United**	1955	6	7
6=	**Blackburn Rovers**	1928	6	2
8=	**Everton**	1995	5	7
8=	**West Bromwich Albion**	1968	5	5
8=	**The Wanderers**	1878	5	0

Inception: 1871/1872.

Most Finals Without Winning: Leicester City (4); Birmingham City (2).

LAUREUS WORLD SPORTS AWARDS

YEAR	SPORTSMAN	SPORTSWOMAN	TEAM	BREAKTHROUGH	LIFETIME ACHIEVEMENT
2000	Tiger Woods (US) Golf	Marion Jones (US) Athletics	Manchester United (Football)	Sergio Garcia (Spa) Golf	Pelé (Brazil) Football
2001	Tiger Woods (US) Golf	Cathy Freeman (Aus) Athletics	France (Football)	Marat Safin (Rus) Tennis	Sir Steve Redgrave (UK) Rowing
2002	Michael Schumacher (Ger) F1	Jennifer Capriati (US) Tennis	Australia (Cricket)	Juan Pablo Montoya (Col) F1	Sir Peter Blake (NZ) Yachting
2003	Lance Armstrong (US) Cycling	Serena Williams (US) Tennis	Brazil (Football)	Yao Ming (Chi) Basketball	Gary Player (SA) Golf
2004	Michael Schumacher (Ger) F1	Annika Sörenstam (Swe) Golf	England (Rugby Union)	Michelle Wie (US) Golf	Arne Naess (Norway) Climbing
2005	Roger Federer (Swi) Tennis	Kelly Holmes (UK) Athletics	Greece (Football)	Liu Xiang (Chi) Athletics	None
2006	Roger Federer (Swi) Tennis	Janica Kostelić (Cro) Skiing	Renault (F1)	Rafael Nadal (Spa) Tennis	Johan Cruyff (Net) Football
2007	Roger Federer (Swi) Tennis	Yelena Isinbayeva (Rus) Athletics	Italy (Football)	Amélie Mauresmo (Fra) Tennis	Franz Beckenbauer (Ger) Football
2008	Roger Federer (Swi) Tennis	Justin Henin (Bel) Tennis	South Africa (Rugby Union)	Lewis Hamilton (UK) F1	Sergey Bubka (Ukr) Pole Vault

Note: Awards are made to mark achievements in the calendar year prior to the ceremony.

Voting: votes are cast by leading sports editors, writers and broadcasters from over 80 countries. The two-phase process is overseen by independent auditors at PricewaterhouseCoopers.

Ceremony: the ceremony is held between February and April at a different venue each year.

Prize: winners receive a 30 cm-high silver/gold Laureus statuette, weighing 2.5 kg. The statuettes are produced by the French jeweller, Cartier.

Other Awards: Comeback of the Year, Sportsperson with a Disability, Alternative Sportsperson, Spirit of Sport, and Sports for Good.

UK TOY CRAZES

YEAR	TOY / GAME	DESCRIPTION	YEAR	TOY / GAME	DESCRIPTION
1970	Hot Wheels/ Sindy	Die-cast toy cars / dolls for girls	1983	My Little Pony/ He-Man	Figures based on the popular cartoons
1971	Space Hoppers	Inflatable orange bouncer	1984	Care Bears/ Trivial Pursuit	More cartoon figures / the general knowledge board game
1972	Klackers	Plastic 'klacking' marbles on strings	1985	Transformers	Cartoon action figures
1973	Mastermind	Peg-based board game	1986	Panini World Cup Stickers	Football player stickers and album
1974	Magna Doodle	Magnetic drawing board	1987	Sylvanian Families	Collectible toy figures
1975	Wombles	TV merchandise	1988	Ghostbusters	Movie action figures
1976	Raw Power	Bike handle add-on that makes a 'revving' sound	1989	Batman	Movie action figures
1977	Slime/ skateboards	Mouldable goo / four-wheeled platforms	1990	Teenage Mutant Hero Turtles	Comic book / cartoon action figures
1978	Simon/Star Wars	Lights and audio sequence game / licensed toys and figures from the movie	1991	Game Boy	Handheld Nintendo console
1979	Space Lego	Space editions of the building block sets	1992	Thunderbirds	Toys inspired from BBC repeats of the 1960s sci-fi series
1980	Rubik's Cube	Mechanical hand puzzle	1993	Power Rangers	Cartoon action figures
1981	Lego Train	Lego electric train set	1994	Magic Eye Pictures	Autostereogram image books and posters
1982	BMX Bikes/ZX Spectrum	Stunt bikes called 'Bicycle Motocross' / the original gaming computer.	1995	POGS	Playground cardboard disc game

YEAR	TOY / GAME	DESCRIPTION	YEAR	TOY / GAME	DESCRIPTION
1996	Toy Story/ Corinthian Figures	Movie figures / small football player figurines	2002	Beyblades/ Bratz Dolls	Customisable spinning tops / dolls
1997	Tamagotchi/ Teletubbies	Pocket e-pets / TV series cuddly toys	2003	Yucky Yo Balls	Fluid filled balls on elastic (later banned)
1998	Furby/Yo-Yo	Interactive pet / 1950s string toy	2004	RoboSapien/ trampolines	Biomorphic robot toy / elasticised bounce mats
1999	Pokémon	Trading cards and computer games	2005	Tamagotchi Connexion	Interactive virtual pet
2000	Scooters	Aluminium folding scooters	2006	Shoot Out Cards	Football trading cards
2001	Bob the Builder/pogo Sticks	Cartoon related toys / bouncing platforms	2007	Dr Who Dalek Sec Hybrid Mask	Voice changer mask

CAR MANUFACTURER ENGINE/ TRANSMISSION LAYOUTS

Front-wheel drive	Rear-wheel drive
Audi, Citroën, Ford, Honda, Kia, Mazda (except RX-7, RX-8), Mitsubishi, Peugeot, Saab, Subaru, Suzuki, Toyota, Vauxhall, and Volkswagen.	BMW (except Mini), Jaguar (except X-Type), Lexus (except ES), Lotus, Mercedes-Benz and TVR. Plus the vast majority of non-4x4 sports cars and SUVs.

THE KENNEDY 'CURSE'

DATE	AGE	FAMILY MEMBER	INCIDENT
12/8/1944	29	Joseph P. Kennedy Jr (JFK's oldest sibling)	Killed in a plane crash over the English Channel whilst fighting in WW2.
10/9/1944	26	William Cavendish (husband of JFK's sister Kathleen)	Killed by a sniper in Belgium while in service for Britain during WW2.
13/5/1948	28	Kathleen Kennedy Cavendish (JFK's second eldest sister)	Died in a civilian plane crash in southern France.
23/8/1956	27	Jacqueline Kennedy (JFK's wife)	Gave birth to a stillborn daughter.
9/8/1963	0	Patrick Bouvier Kennedy (second son of JFK and Jacqueline)	After being born five weeks prematurely, died of RDS two days after birth.
22/11/1963	46	John F. Kennedy (35th US President)	Assassinated during a motorcade on a political visit to Dallas, Texas.
19/6/1964	32	Ted Kennedy (JFK's second youngest brother)	Spent weeks in hospital after a plane crash in which the pilot and an aide were killed.
5/6/1968	42	Robert F. Kennedy (JFK's youngest brother)	While involved in a Presidential election campaign, was shot by a Palestinian gunman in the Ambassador Hotel, LA. He died the next day.
18/7/1969	28	Mary Jo Kopechne (Secretary to Robert F. Kennedy)	Died after a car driven by Ted Kennedy careered off a bridge into water on Chappaquiddick Island, Martha's Vineyard, MA.
23/2/1972	39	Joseph P. Kennedy II (eldest son and second of eleven children of RFK and Ethel Kennedy)	Passenger on a Lufthansa plane that was hijacked over India by Palestinians and flown to South Yemen.
23/1/1973	24	Alexander Onassis (stepson of Jacqueline Kennedy)	Died in a plane crash at a Greek airport.
17/11/1973	12	Edward Kennedy Jr (elder son of Ted Kennedy)	Had to have right leg amputated after bone cancer was discovered.
13/8/1973	18	Pam Kelley (then girlfriend of David Kennedy)	Passenger when a car driven by Joseph F. Kennedy crashed on Nantucket island. The crash left her permanently paralysed.
25/4/1984	28	David Kennedy (fourth of eleven children of RFK and Ethel)	Suffered a fatal overdose after taking a mixture of cocaine, Demerol and Mellaril.

DATE	AGE	FAMILY MEMBER	INCIDENT
19/11/1988	37	Christina Onassis (stepdaughter of Jacqueline Kennedy)	Suffered a fatal overdose while staying at a country club near Buenos Aires, Argentina.
19/5/1994	64	Jacqueline Kennedy Onassis (JFK's wife)	Died at her Manhattan penthouse, four months after being diagnosed with cancer.
31/12/1997	39	Michael Kennedy (sixth of eleven children of RFK and Ethel)	Died in a skiing accident in Aspen, Colorado.
16/7/1999	38	John F. Kennedy Jr (son of JFK and Jacqueline)	Died when a plane piloted by JFK Jr crashed into the Atlantic on route between Essex, NJ and a Kennedy family home on Martha's Vineyard, MA.
16/7/1999	33	Carolyn Bessette-Kennedy (wife of John F Kennedy Jr)	
16/7/1999	34	Lauren Bessette (John F. Kennedy Jr's wife's sister)	

PRECIOUS METALS

SILVER PRODUCERS		GOLD PRODUCERS		PLATINUM PRODUCERS		RHODIUM PRODUCERS	
Peru	3,184	China	276	S. Africa	156.6	S. Africa	21.6
Mexico	2,812	S. Africa	272	Russia	28.3	Russia	2.8
China	2,336	US	255	N. America	10.1	N. America	0.5
Chile	1,758	Australia	251	Zimbabwe	5.3	Zimbabwe	0.4
Australia	1,712	Indonesia	171	Others	3.4	Others	0.2
AVERAGE PRICES FOR 2007*							
$13.37		$696.95		$1,304		$6,191	

Figures in metric tonnes and relate to 2007. *Values per troy ounce (ozt). One ozt = 31.103 g = 1.097 oz. The troy ounce is the international standard unit for expressing the mass of precious metals.

Sources: Silver – www.silverinstitute.org; Gold – www.goldsheetlinks.com; Platinum and Rhodium – www.matthey.com

BRITAIN'S FAVOURITE SITCOMS

	SHOW	VOTES	SERIES/EPISODES (RUN)
1	*Only Fools and Horses*	**342,426**	**7/64 (1981–2003)**
2	*Blackadder*	**282,106**	**4/27 (1983–1989)**
3	*The Vicar of Dibley*	**212,927**	**3/20 (1994–2007)**
4	Dad's Army	174,138	9/80 (1968–1977)
5	Fawlty Towers	172,066	2/12 (1975–1979)
6	Yes Minister / Yes, Prime Minister	123,502	5/38 (1980–1988)
7	Porridge	93,902	3/20 (1973–1977)
8	Open All Hours	67,237	4/26 (1976–1985)
9	The Good Life	40,803	4/30 (1975–1978)
10	One Foot in the Grave	31,410	6/42 (1990–2000)

Compiled by the British Film Institute in 2004. Top ten from a top 100 chosen by the public through phone, text and web voting.

TEN PIN BOWLING - ODDS OF BOWLING A PERFECT 300 GAME

AVERAGE STRIKE FREQUENCY	APPROXIMATE ODDS
10%	1 in a trillion
18%	1 in a billion
32%	1 in a million
46%	1 in ten thousand
68%	1 in a hundred
82%	1 in ten

First Person Ever to Score Three Perfect Games in a Three Game Series: Jeremy Sonnenfeld in Lincoln, Nebraska (2/2/1997).

Youngest Person Ever to Score a Perfect Game: Chaz Dennis (10 y 2 m 27 d) in Columbus, Ohio (16/12/2006).

Youngest Person in the UK to Score a Perfect Game: Elliot Crosby (12 y 2 m 10 d) at the AMF Purley, London (7/1/2006).

TYRE WALL CODING

ELEMENT	MEANING	EXAMPLE
Tyre Type	This is optional lettering and is not present on all tyres: P=Passenger; LT=Light Truck; T=Temporary.	P
Nominal Section Width	The width of the tyre from sidewall edge to sidewall edge (in millimetres).	255
Aspect Ratio	The height of the tyre as a percentage of the nominal section width.	40
Construction	Radial (modern tyres) = R Run flat (designed to keep going after a puncture) = RF or RSC Cross-ply (original tyres on vehicles circa 20+ years old) = C	R
Inner Diameter	The diameter of the inner rim of the metal wheel that the tyre is designed to fit to (in inches).	18
Load Capacity	The code for the maximum load capacity each tyre can take when driven at maximum speed. The code ranges from 71 = 345 kg, to 110=1060 kg.	95
Speed Rating	The code for the maximum safe speed of the tyre at full load. Generally the higher the rated speed, the better the tyre quality. A tyre with a high-rated speed should never be replaced with one of a lower-rated speed. The code ranges from A1=3 mph, to (Y)=over 186 mph.	Y
EXAMPLE: Ferrari Enzo (front) 255/40 R18 95Y		

ALL-TIME BEST-SELLING COMPUTER GAMES AND CONSOLES

	GAMES			FRANCHISES		CONSOLES		
1	The Sims	PC	50 m	Mario	200 m	Sony	PS2	120 m
2	Super Mario Bros.	NES	40.2 m	Pokémon	175 m	Nintendo	Game Boy / GB Colour	119 m
3	Tetris	Game Boy	33 m	The Sims	100 m	Sony	Playstation	102.5 m
4	Wii Sports	Wii	21.6 m	Final Fantasy	80 m	Nintendo	Game Boy Advance	81 m
5	Super Mario World	SNES	20 m	Grand Theft Auto	70 m	Nintendo	DS	70.6 m
6	Pokémon Red, Blue, and Green	Game Boy	20 m	Madden NFL	70 m	Nintendo	NES	61.9 m
7	Nintendogs	DS	18.7 m	Tetris	70 m	Nintendo	SNES	49.1 m
8	Super Mario Bros. 3	NES	18 m	FIFA Soccer	65 m	Nintendo	N64	32.9 m
9	GTA: Vice City	PS2 PC Xbox	17.5 m	The Legend of Zelda	52 m	Atari	Atari 2600	30 m
10	Pokémon Diamond and Pearl	DS	14.8 m	Donkey Kong	48 m	Sega	Mega Drive	29 m

List is compiled from figures published in media reports and released company statistics up to the end of 2007.

TRI-NATIONS SERIES – RUGBY UNION

YEAR	WINNER	RUNNERS-UP	LEADING POINTS SCORER(S)	LEADING TRY SCORER(S)
1996	New Zealand*	South Africa	A. Mehrtens (NZ) 69	J. Marshall (NZ) 2
1997	New Zealand*	South Africa	C. Spencer (NZ) 84	C. Cullen (NZ) 4
1998	South Africa*	Australia	M. Burke (Aus) 50	M. Burke (Aus) 3
1999	New Zealand	Australia	A. Mehrtens (NZ) 68	C. Cullen (NZ) 3
2000	Australia	New Zealand	S. Mortlock (Aus) 71	C. Cullen (NZ) 7
2001	Australia	New Zealand	M. Burke (Aus) 53	P. Alatini (NZ) 2
2002	New Zealand	Australia	A. Mehrtens (NZ) 47	M. Joubert (SA) 3
2003	New Zealand*	Australia	C. Spencer (NZ) 60	J. Rokocoko (NZ) 6
2004	South Africa	Australia	P. Montgomery (SA) 45	M. Joubert (SA); L. Tuqiri (Aus); J. de Villiers (SA) 3
2005	New Zealand	South Africa	P. Montgomery (SA) 52	B. Habana (SA); D. Howlett (NZ); J. Rokocoko (NZ) 3
2006 ^	New Zealand	Australia	D. Carter (NZ) 99	J. Fourie (SA); L. Tuqiri (Aus) 3
2007	New Zealand	Australia	D. Carter (NZ) 62	M. Giteau (Aus); T. Woodcock (NZ) 2
2008	New Zealand	Australia	D. Carter (NZ) 82	J. Nokwe (SA) 4

Key: * = Denotes Grand Slam win (the team won all of their Tri-Nations matches).

^ = In 2006 SANZAR first adopted a six match per side season. In 2007 (a World Cup year), SANZAR returned to the four match format; in 2008 the six match per side schedule was reintroduced.

Organising Body: SANZAR, a consortium of the unions from South Africa, New Zealand and Australia.

Bledisloe Cup: awarded to the winner of the most matches between Australia and New Zealand in any year. If tied, the trophy remains with the previous year's winners. New Zealand has won 36 times, Australia 12.

Mandela Challenge Plate: awarded since 2000, to the winner of the most matches between South Africa and Australia in any Tri-Nations Series. Australia has won the plate three times, South Africa twice.

Most Appearances: 48 – G. Gregan (SA) 1996–2007.

Most Points: 328 – A. Mehrtens (NZ) 1996–2004.

Most Tries: 16 – C. Cullen (NZ) 1996–2002.

MODERN HISTORY OF NBA FINALS

YEAR	WESTERN CHAMPIONS	SCORE	EASTERN CHAMPIONS	MOST VALUABLE PLAYER
1990	Portland Trail Blazers	1–4	Detroit Pistons	Magic Johnson (LA Lakers)
1991	LA Lakers	1–4	Chicago Bulls	Michael Jordan (Chicago Bulls)
1992	Portland Trail Blazers	2–4	Chicago Bulls	Michael Jordan (Chicago Bulls)
1993	Phoenix Suns	2–4	Chicago Bulls	Charles Barkley (Phoenix Suns)
1994	Houston Rockets	4–3	New York Knicks	Hakeem Olajuwon (Houston Rockets)
1995	Houston Rockets	4–0	Orlando Magic	David Robinson (San Antonio Spurs)
1996	Seattle Super Sonics	2–4	Chicago Bulls	Michael Jordan (Chicago Bulls)
1997	Utah Jazz	2–4	Chicago Bulls	Karl Malone (Utah Jazz)
1998	Utah Jazz	2–4	Chicago Bulls	Michael Jordan (Chicago Bulls)
1999	San Antonio Spurs	4–1	New York Knicks	Karl Malone (Utah Jazz)
2000	LA Lakers	4–2	Indiana Pacers	Shaquille O'Neal (LA Lakers)
2001	LA Lakers	4–1	Philadelphia 76ers	Allen Iverson (Philadelphia 76ers)
2002	LA Lakers	4–0	New Jersey Nets	Tim Duncan (San Antonio Spurs)
2003	San Antonio Spurs	4–2	New Jersey Nets	Tim Duncan (San Antonio Spurs)
2004	LA Lakers	1–4	Detroit Pistons	Kevin Garnett (Minnesota Timberwolves)
2005	San Antonio Spurs	4–3	Detroit Pistons	Steve Nash (Phoenix Suns)
2006	Dallas Mavericks	2–4	Miami Heat	Steve Nash (Phoenix Suns)

YEAR	WESTERN CHAMPIONS	SCORE	EASTERN CHAMPIONS	MOST VALUABLE PLAYER
2007	San Antonio Spurs	4–0	Cleveland Cavaliers	Dirk Nowitzki (Dallas Mavericks)
2008	LA Lakers	2–4	Boston Celtics	Paul Pierce (Boston Celtics)

First Ever Finals: 1947 - Philadelphia Warriors (East) beat Chicago Stags (West) 4–1.

Most Times Winners: 17 – Boston Celtics (East), 14 – LA Lakers (West).

Most Times Losers: 15 – LA Lakers (West), six – Philadelphia 76ers (East), New York Knicks (East).

Most Valuable Player (MVP): the Maurice Podoloff Trophy is awarded to the player voted by US and Canadian sportswriters and broadcasters as being the outstanding player of that season.

Most Times MVP Winner: six – Joe Montana (1971, 1972, 1974 Milwaukee Bucks, 1976, 1977, 1980 LA Lakers) San Francisco 49ers).

Overseas Born MVP Winners: Hakeem Olajuwon (Nigeria) 1994; Tim Duncan (US Virgin Islands) 2002, 2003; Steve Nash (South Africa/Canada) 2005, 2006.

'BIG FOUR' COFFEE CHAINS IN THE UK

COFFEE CHAIN	YEAR FOUNDED	NUMBER OF UK OUTLETS (2008)	MAIN MARKETING COLOUR(S)
Caffè Nero	1997	330	Blue and black
Coffee Republic	1995	173	Black and red
Costa	1995	655	Maroon
Starbucks	1971	660	Green and black

MOST PREVALENT SCOTTISH CUP WINNERS

	CLUB	LAST WIN	WINS	RUNNERS-UP
1	Celtic	2007	34	19
2	Rangers	2008	32	18
3	Queens Park	1893	10	2
4 =	Aberdeen	1990	7	8
4 =	Hearts	2006	7	6
6 =	Kilmarnock	1997	3	5
6 =	Vale of Levan	1879	3	4
6 =	Clyde	1958	3	3
6 =	St Mirren	1987	3	3
10 =	Hibernian	1902	2	9
10 =	Motherwell	1991	2	4
10 =	Third Lanark	1905	2	4
10 =	Renton	1888	2	3
10 =	Dunfermline	1968	2	3
10 =	Falkirk	1957	2	1

Inception: 1873/1874. One-Time Winners: Airdrieonians, Dumbarton, Dundee, Dundee Utd, East Fife, Greenock Morton, Partick Thistle, St Bernard's.

Most Finals Without Winning: Hamilton Academical (2).

US BANK NOTES

BILL	FRONT DESIGN	REVERSE DESIGN
$1	**George Washington** (1st President 1789–1797)	Great Seal of the United States – a seal used to authenticate certain US government documents.
$2	**Thomas Jefferson** (3rd President 1801–1809)	Declaration of Independence – the document that signalled the end of British control over 13 North American British colonies, signed on 4th July 1776.
$5	**Abraham Lincoln** (16th President 1861–1865)	Lincoln Memorial – 107 acres (45ha) of parkland in Potomac Park, Washington DC encircle the 36 Greek Doric columns of the Lincoln Memorial.
$10	**Alexander Hamilton** (1st US Secretary of State (1789–1795)	Treasury Building – 1500 Pennsylvania Avenue NW, Washington D.C, home of the US Treasury Dept since 1789.
$20	**Andrew Jackson** (7th President 1829–1837)	The White House – 1600 Pennsylvania Avenue, Washington DC and home of the US President.
$50	**Ulysses S. Grant** (18th President 1869–1877)	Capitol Hill – the building in Washington DC that is home to The Senate (north wing) and House of Representatives (south wing).
$100	**Benjamin Franklin** (multi-talented statesman whose inventions included the bifocal lens and the lightning rod. Also served as US postmaster and US ambassador to France)	Independence Hall – Pennsylvania State House, the original home of the Liberty Bell. This is where the Declaration of Independence was signed on 4 July 1776.

BRITISH FOOTBALL RIVALRIES

CLUBS (YEAR EST)	HEAD-TO-HEAD*	HIGHEST-SCORING WIN**	NAME	NATION
Aston Villa (1874) v Birmingham City (1875)	49–37 (29)	7–3 (1895/96); 4–0 (1968/69)	The Birmingham Derby	England
West Bromwich Albion (1878) v Wolverhampton Wanderers (1877)	62–52 (42)	8–0 (1893/94); 7–0 (1962/63)	The Black Country Derby	England
Bristol City (1897) v Bristol Rovers (1883)	42–28 (33)	5–0 (1926/27); 5–1 (1933/34)	The Bristol Derby	England
Ipswich Town (1878) v Norwich City (1902)	39–33 (17)	5–0 (1997/98); 4–2 (1968/69)	The East Anglian Derby	England
Blackburn Rovers (1875) v Burnley (1882)	39–37 (15)	8–3 (1929/30); 6–0 (1895/96)	The East Lancashire Derby	England
West Ham Utd (1895) v Millwall (1885)	8–5 (10)	4–1 (1929/30); 4–1 (2003/04)	The East London Derby	England
Nottingham Forest (1865) v Derby County (1884)	33–27 (19)	5–1 (1903/04); 5–0 (1897/98)	The East Midlands Derby	England
Manchester Utd (1878) v Manchester City (1880)	59–41 (49)	6–1 (1925/26); 5–0 (1994/95)	The Manchester Derby	England
Liverpool (1892) v Everton (1878)	79–64 (62)	5-0 (1914/15); 7–4 (1932/33)	The Merseyside Derby	England
Arsenal (1886) v Chelsea (1905)	68–49 (51)	5–2 (1978/79); 5–0 (1998/99)	The New London Derby	England
Arsenal (1886) v Tottenham Hotspur (1892)	67–50 (42)	6–0 (1934/35); 5–1 (2007/08)	The North London Derby	England
Manchester Utd (1878) v Liverpool (1892)	68–57 (50)	7–1 (1895/96); 6–1 (1927/28)	The North West Derby	England
Southampton (1885) v Portsmouth (1898)	19–8 (8)	4–1 (2004/05); 5–2 (1965/66)	The South Coast Derby	England

CLUBS (YEAR EST)	HEAD-TO-HEAD*	HIGHEST-SCORING WIN**	NAME	NATION
Sheffield Utd (1889) v Sheffield Wednesday (1867)	44–38 (38)	7–3 (1951/52); 5–2 (1928/29)	The Steel City Derby	England
Newcastle Utd (1892) v Sunderland (1879)	51–43 (45)	6–1 (1955/56); 9–1 (1908/09)	The Tyne & Wear Derby	England
Manchester Utd (1878) v Leeds Utd (1919)	45–25 (35)	5–0 (1930/31); 6–0 (1959/60)	The War of the Roses	England
Preston North End (1881) v Blackpool (1887)	43–29 (17)	6–2 (1955/56); 7–0 (1947/48)	The West Lancashire Derby	England
Chelsea (1905) v Fulham (1879)	38–9 (20)	5–3 (1983/84); 3–1 (1976/77)	The West London Derby	England
Dundee Utd (1909) v Dundee (1893)	71–45 (37)	6–4 (1971/72); 5–0 (1965/66)	The Dundee Derby	Scotland
Hearts (1874) v Hibernian (1875)	124–74 (81)	8–3 (1934/35); 7–0 (1972/73)	The Edinburgh Derby	Scotland
Aberdeen (1903) v Dundee Utd (1909)	84–67 (60)	6–0 (1967/68); 5–0 (1997/98)	The New Firm Derby	Scotland
Rangers (1873) v Celtic (1888)	151–136 (92)	6–2 (2001/02); 5–0 (1893/94)	The Old Firm Derby	Scotland
Swansea City (1912) v Cardiff City (1899)	23–19 (15)	5–0 (1964/65); 5–1 (1949/50)	The South Wales Derby	Wales

Key: * = Number of head-to-head draws in brackets.

** = The first scoreline is the most goals ever scored in a rivalry win by the team on the left; the second scoreline is the most goals ever scored in a rivalry win by the team on the right.

Statistics are accurate up to the end of the 2007/08 season. Source: www.soccerbase.com

RADIO 1

BREAKFAST SHOW PRESENTER	SPAN	BORN
Tony Blackburn	9/1967–6/1973	Guildford, Surrey
Noel Edmonds	6/1973–4/1978	Ilford, London
Dave Lee Travis	5/1978–1/1981	Buxton, Derbyshire
Mike Read	1/1981–4/1986	Manchester
Mike Smith	5/1986–5/1988	Hornchurch, London
Simon Mayo	5/1988–9/1993	Southgate, London
Mark Goodier	10/1993–12/1993	Rhodesia [Zimbabwe]
Steve Wright	1/1994–4/1995	Greenwich, London
Chris Evans	4/1995–1/1997	Warrington, Cheshire
Mark and Lard (aka Mark Radcliffe and Marc Riley)	2/1997–10/1997	Bolton/Manchester
Kevin Greening and Zoë Ball	10/1997–8/1998	Bristol/Blackpool
Zoë Ball	8/1998–3/2000	Blackpool
Sara Cox	3/2000–12/2003	Bolton
Chris Moyles	1/2004–present	Leeds

First Show: Tony Blackburn presented the station's first ever show. It commenced at 7 a.m. on 30/9/1967. The first words spoken were '... and good morning everyone! Welcome to the exciting new sound of Radio 1!'

First Song: the first complete record played on Radio 1 was 'Flowers in the Rain' by The Move. It was preceded by a broadcast of part of 'Beefeaters (on Parade)' by Johnny Dankworth (this was Blackburn's signature tune carried over from pirate radio). The second single played was 'Massachusetts' by The Bee Gees.

Frequencies: 1967–1978 – 1214 kHz MW (referred to as '247 metres' at the time); 1978–1988 – 1053/1089 kHz (275/285 m); 1988–present – 97–99 MHz.

Last MW Broadcast: MW frequencies were reallocated to commercial stations in 1994. Radio 1's last MW broadcast was on 1/7/1994, Stephen Duffy's 'Kiss Me' was the last record played.

US ALL-TIME BEST-SELLING ALBUMS

YEAR RELEASED	TITLE	RECORD LABEL	BAND / ARTIST	SALES*
1976	*Their Greatest Hits (1971–1975)*	Asylum	The Eagles	29 m
1982	*Thriller*	Epic	Michael Jackson	27 m
1971	*Led Zeppelin IV*	Atlantic	Led Zeppelin	23 m
1979	*The Wall*	Columbia	Pink Floyd	23 m
1980	*Back in Black*	Epic	AC/DC	22 m
1985	*Greatest Hits (Volumes 1 & 2)*	Columbia	Billy Joel	21 m
1998	*Double Live*	Capitol Nashville	Garth Brooks	21 m
1997	*Come on Over*	Mercury Nashville	Shania Twain	20 m
1968	*The White Album*	Capitol	The Beatles	19 m
1977	*Rumours*	Warner Bros	Fleetwood Mac	19 m
1976	*Boston*	Epic	Boston	17 m
1990	*No Fences*	Capitol Nashville	Garth Brooks	17 m
1992	*The Bodyguard (Original Soundtrack)*	Arista	Whitney Houston et al	17 m

*Total sales up to the end of 2007 (to nearest million). Source: www.infoplease.com

LADIES' GRAND SLAM
TENNIS CHAMPIONS

	AUSTRALIAN OPEN	FRENCH OPEN	WIMBLEDON	US OPEN
1990	Graf (Ger) bt Fernández (US)	Seles (Yug) bt Graf (Ger)	Navrátilová (Cze) bt Garrison (US)	Sabatini (Arg) bt Graf (Ger)
1991	Seles (Yug) bt Novotná (Cze)	Seles (Yug) bt Sánchez-Vicario (Spa)	Graf (Ger) bt Sabatini (Arg)	Seles (Yug) bt Navrátilová Navratilova (Cze)
1992	Seles (Yug) bt Fernández (US)	Seles (Yug) bt Graf (Ger)	Graf (Ger) bt Seles (Yug)	Seles (Yug) bt Sánchez-Vicario (Spa)
1993	Seles (Yug) bt Graf (Ger)	Graf (Ger) bt Fernández (US)	Graf (Ger) bt Novotná (Cze)	Graf (Ger) bt Sukova (Cze)
1994	Graf (Ger) bt Sánchez-Vicario (Spa)	Sánchez-Vicario (Spa) bt Pierce (Can)	Martinez (Spa) bt Navrátilová (Cze)	Sánchez-Vicario (Spa) bt Graf (Ger)
1995	Pierce (Can) bt Sánchez-Vicario (Spa)	Graf (Ger) bt Sánchez-Vicario (Spa)	Graf (Ger) bt Sánchez-Vicario (Spa)	Graf (Ger) bt Seles (Yug)
1996	Seles (Yug) bt Huber (Ger)	Graf (Ger) bt Sánchez-Vicario (Spa)	Graf (Ger) bt Sánchez-Vicario (Spa)	Graf (Ger) bt Seles (Yug)
1997	Hingis (Swi) bt Pierce (Can)	Majoli (Cro) bt Hingis (Swi)	Hingis (Swi) bt Novotná (Cze)	Hingis (Swi) bt V Williams (US)
1998	Hingis (Swi) bt Martínez (Spa)	Sánchez-Vicario (Spa) bt Seles (Yug)	Novotná (Cze) bt Tauziat (Fra)	Davenport (US) bt Hingis (Swi)
1999	Hingis (Swi) bt Mauresmo (Fra)	Graf (Ger) bt Hingis (Swi)	Davenport (US) bt Graf (Ger)	S. Williams (US) bt Hingis (Swi)
2000	Davenport (US) bt Hingis (Swi)	Pierce (Can) bt Martínez (Spa)	V. Williams (US) bt Davenport (US)	V. Williams (US) bt Davenport (US)
2001	Capriati (US) bt Hingis (Swi)	Capriati (US) bt Clijsters (Bel)	V. Williams (US) bt Henin (Bel)	V. Williams (US) bt S. Williams (US)
2002	Capriati (US) bt Hingis (Swi)	S. Williams (US) bt V Williams (US)	S. Williams (US) bt V Williams (US)	S. Williams (US) bt V. Williams (US)
2003	S. Williams (US) bt V. Williams (US)	Henin-Hardenne (Bel) bt Clijsters (Bel)	S. Williams (US) bt V. Williams (US)	Henin-Hardenne (Bel) bt Clijsters (Bel)

	AUSTRALIAN OPEN	FRENCH OPEN	WIMBLEDON	US OPEN
2004	Henin-Hardenne (Bel) bt Clijsters (Bel)	Myskina (Rus) bt Dementieva (Rus)	Sharapova (Rus) bt S. Williams (US)	Kuznetsova (Rus) bt Dementieva (Rus)
2005	S. Williams (US) bt Davenport (US)	Henin-Hardenne (Bel) bt Pierce (Can)	V. Williams (US) bt Davenport (US)	Clijsters (Bel) bt Pierce (Can)
2006	Mauresmo (Fra) bt Henin-Hardenne (Bel)	Henin-Hardenne (Bel) bt Kuznetsova (Rus)	Mauresmo (Fra) bt Henin-Hardenne (Bel)	Sharapova (Rus) bt Henin-Hardenne (Bel)
2007	S. Williams (US) bt Sharapova (Rus)	Henin (Bel) bt Ivanović (Ser)	V. Williams (US) bt Bartoli (Fra)	Henin (Bel) bt Kuznetsova (Rus)
2008	Sharapova (Rus) bt Ivanović (Ser)	Ivanović (Ser) bt Safina (Rus)	V. Williams (US) bt S. Williams (US)	S. Williams (US) bt Jankovic (Ser)

Key: bt=beat.

TOP SPENDERS ON COSMETIC SURGERY IN EUROPE

	COUNTRY	ANNUAL SPEND
1	UK	£497 m
2	Italy	£160 m
3	France	£141 m
4	Germany	£128 m
5	Spain	£70 m
6	Netherlands	£28 m
7	Sweden	£12 m
	Europe	£1,251 m
	US	£5,792 m

Figures relate to 2006. Of the 32,453 procedures carried out in the UK, 91 per cent were for women. Source: Datamonitor

ANIMAL AND BIRD NOMENCLATURE

SPECIES	MALE	FEMALE	OFFSPRING	COLLECTIVE
Alligator	Bull	Cow	Hatchling	Congregation or pod (young)
Ape	Male	Female	Baby	Shrewdness
Ass/donkey	Jack	Jenny	Foal	Herd or pace
Badger	Boar	Sow	Cub	Cete
Bear	Boar	Sow	Cub	Sleuth or sloth
Bee	Drone	Queen (producer) or worker (non-producer)	Larva	Hive or swarm (in flight)
Cat	Tom	Queen	Kitten	Clowder or pounce
Cattle	Bull	Cow	Calf or heifer (F), or bull (M) or bullock (castrated M)	Herd
Chicken	Rooster	Hen	Chick	Brood
Crocodile	Bull	Cow	Crocklet	Congregation
Crow	Cock	Hen	Chick	Murder
Deer	Buck or stag	Doe	Fawn	Herd or leash
Dinosaur	Bull	Cow	Juvenile	Herd (herbivore) or pack (carnivore)
Dog	Dog	Bitch	Puppy	Pack
Dolphin	Bull	Cow	Calf or pup	Pod
Duck	Drake	Duck	Duckling	Paddling
Elephant	Bull	Cow	Calf	Herd
Fly	Male	Female	Maggot	Cloud or swarm
Fox	Dog	Vixen	Cub	Skulk
Giraffe	Bull	Cow or doe	Calf, cub or whelp	Tower
Goat	Billy or buck	Doe or nanny	Kid	Herd or tribe
Goose	Gander	Goose	Gosling	Flock, gaggle or skein (in flight)
Hare	Jack	Jill	Leveret	Down, drove or husk

SPECIES	MALE	FEMALE	OFFSPRING	COLLECTIVE
Hedgehog	Boar	Sow	Piglet or pup	Array
Horse	Stallion or stud	Mare or dam	Foal, colt (M) or filly (F)	Team, stud or string (racehorses)
Kangaroo	Buck or boomer	Flyer or jill	Joey	Troop, herd or mob
Lion	Lion	Lioness	Cub	Pride
Monkey	Male	Female	Infant or suckling	Troupe
Mouse	Buck	Doe	Kitten, pinkie or pup	Mischief
Owl	Male	Female	Owlet	Parliament
Panda	Boar	Sow	Cub	Pandemonium
Parrot	Cock	Hen	Chick	Company
Peafowl	Peacock	Peahen	Peachick	Ostentation
Penguin	Male	Female	Chick	Huddle or rookery
Pig	Boar	Sow	Piglet	Herd
Pheasant	Cock	Hen	Chick	Brood (family) or nye (adult group)
Rabbit	Buck	Doe	Kit or bunny	Nest or warren
Rhinoceros	Bull	Cow	Calf	Crash
Sheep	Ram	Ewe	Lamb	Flock
Swan	Cob	Pen	Cygnet	Bevy or wedge (flying in 'V' formation)
Tiger	Tiger	Tigress	Cub	Ambush or swift
Wasp	Drone	Queen (producer) or worker (non-producer)	Larva	Colony
Whale	Bull	Cow	Calf	School (large group) or pod (small group)
Wolf	Dog	Bitch	Puppy	Pack
Zebra	Stallion	Mare	Foal or colt (M)	Zeal

FA PREMIER LEAGUE RECORDS

RECORD	HOLDER	DETAILS	SEASON
WINS AND LOSSES			
Most Wins in a Season	Chelsea	29 in 38	2004/2005; 2005/2006
Fewest Wins in a Season	Derby County	1 in 38	2007/2008
Most Losses in a Season	Ipswich Town; Sunderland; Derby County	29 in 42; 29 in 38; 29 in 38	1994/1995; 2005/2006; 2007/2008
Fewest Losses in a Season	Arsenal	0 in 38	2003/2004
GOALS			
First Premier League Goal	Brian Deane (Sheffield Utd)	(vs Man Utd)	1992/1993
Most PL Goals in a Career	Alan Shearer (Southampton; Blackburn; Newcastle)	260	1992–2006
Fastest Goal	Ledley King (Tottenham)	10 seconds (vs Bradford)	2000/2001
Fastest Goal by a Substitute	Nicklas Bendtner (Arsenal)	6 seconds (vs Tottenham)	2007/2008
Fastest Hat-trick	Robbie Fowler (Liverpool)	4 m 32 s (time between 1st and 3rd goals) (vs Arsenal)	1994/1995
Biggest Home Win	Man Utd	9–0 (vs Ipswich Town)	1994/1995
Biggest Away Win	Man Utd	1–8 (vs Nottingham Forest)	1998/1999
Most Goals Scored in a Season	Man Utd	97	1999/2000
Least Goals Scored in a Season	Derby County	20	2007/2008
Most Goals Conceded in a Season	Swindon Town	100	1993/1994
Least Goals Conceded in a Season	Chelsea	15	2004/2005
Most Clean Sheets in a Season	Chelsea	25	2004/2005
Least Failures to Score in a Season	Arsenal	0	2001/2002

RECORD	HOLDER	DETAILS	SEASON
APPEARANCES			
Most Appearances	Ryan Giggs (Man Utd)	495	1992/1993– present
Youngest Player	Matthew Briggs (Fulham)	16 y 2 m 4 d vs Middlebrough)	2006/2007
Oldest Player	John Burridge (Man City)	43 y 4 m 26 d (vs Newcastle Utd)	1994/1995
GOALKEEPERS			
Goal scoring Goalkeepers	Peter Schmeichel (Aston Villa)	(vs Everton)	2001/2002
	Brad Friedel (Blackburn)	(vs Charlton)	2003/2004
	Paul Robinson (Tottenham)	(vs Watford)	2006/2007
Statistics accurate up to end of 2007/2008 season.			

UK GEOGRAPHICAL FEATURES

	ENGLAND	NORTHERN IRELAND	SCOTLAND	WALES
Largest Island	Isle of Wight 147 m (381 km)	Rathlin Island 8 m (21 km)	Lewis and Harris 841 m (2,180 km)	Anglesey 276 m (715 km)
Largest Lake (Area)	Windermere 5.7 m (14.8 km)	Lough Neagh 147.4 m (381.8 km)	Loch Lomond 27.5 m (71.2 km)	Lake Vyrnwy 3.2 m (8.3 km)
Highest Mountain	Scafell Pike 978 m (3,209 ft)	Slieve Donard 852 m (2,795 ft)	Ben Nevis 1,344 m (4,408 ft)	Snowdon 1,085 m (3,560 ft)
Longest River	Thames* 215 m (346 km)	Bann 76 m (122 km)	Tay 117 m (188 km)	Tywi* 64 m (103 km)
Highest Waterfall	Cautley Spout 76 m (249 ft)	Ness Wood 9 m (30 ft)	Eas a' Chual Aluinn 200 m (656 ft)	Pistyll Rhaeadr 75 m (246 ft)

*Although the Severn is the longest river in Britain (220 m (34 km)), it rises in Wales and discharges in England and therefore can't be said to be the longest river in either country.

ENGLAND CRICKET CAPTAINS
(64TH TO 78TH)

NAME	PLACE OF BIRTH	PERIOD AS CAPTAIN	TESTS (W-L-D RECORD) AS CAPTAIN	1ST CLASS CLUB(S)	OVERALL TESTS	ROLE (BOWLING STYLE)
David Gower*	Tunbridge Wells, Kent	1982–1989	32 (5-18-9)	Le; H	117	Ba (ROS)
Mike Gatting	Kingsbury, London	1986–1988	23 (2-5-16)	M	79	Ba (RM)
John Emburey	Peckham, London	1988	2 (0-2-0)	B; M; WP; N	64	Bo (RO)
Chris Cowdrey	Farnborough, London	1988	1 (0-1-0)	K; Gn	6	A (RM)
Graham Gooch	Leytonstone, London	1988–1993	34 (10-12-12)	E; WP	118	Ba (RM)
Allan Lamb	Cape Province, SA	1989–1991	3 (0-3-0)	WP; Or; N	79	Ba (RM)
Alec Stewart	Merton, London	1992–2001	15 (4-8-3)	Sy	133	W (RM)
Michael Atherton	Oldham	1993–2001	54 (13-21-20)	La	115	Ba (RLS)
Nasser Hussein	Chennai, India	1999–2003	45 (17-15-13)	E	96	Ba (RLB)
Mark Butcher*	Croydon, London	1999	1 (0-1-0)	Sy	71	A (RM)
Michael Vaughan	Manchester	2003–2007	37 (22-6-9)	Y	73	Ba (RO)
Marcus Trescothick*	Keynsham, Somerset	2004–2006	2 (1-1-0)	So	76	Ba (RM)

NAME	PLACE OF BIRTH	PERIOD AS CAPTAIN	TESTS (W-L-D RECORD)	1ST CLASS CLUB(S)	OVERALL TESTS	ROLE (BOWLING STYLE)
Andrew Flintoff	Preston	2006–2007	11 (2-7-2)	La		A (RF)
Andrew Strauss*	Johannesburg, SA	2006–2007	5 (3-0-2)	M		Ba (LM)
Kevin Pietersen	Natal, SA	2008–		KN; N; H		Ba (ROS)

Key: * = Left-handed (as a batsman); ** = Also recorded 14 stumpings.

Delivery Key: L = left-arm bowler; R = right-arm bowler; F = Fast; M = medium; LS = leg spin; LB = leg break; LS = leg spin; O = off break; OS = off spin.

Clubs Key: B = Berkshire; E = Essex; Gn = Glamorgan; Ge = Gloucestershire; H = Hampshire; K = Kent; KN = KwaZulu Natal (SA); La = Lancashire; Le = Leicestershire; M = Middlesex; N = Northamptonshire; Or = Orange Free State (SA); So = Somerset; Sy = Surrey; WP = Western Province (SA); Y = Yorkshire.

Role Key: A = All-Rounder (adept at batting and bowling); Ba = Batsman; Bo = Bowler; W = Wicket Keeper.

TEN PIN BOWLING TERMINOLOGY

TERM	MEANING
Big Ears	A 4, 6, 7, 10 split (the far left and right pins in the two back rows).
Blowout	Downing all of the pins but one.
Choke	Failure (in a shot or game) due to nerves.
Clean Game	Scoring a strike or spare in each frame.
Creeper	Slow bowl.
Double	Two strikes in a row (scores 20 plus the number of pins knocked down with the next bowl).
Drying	Advanced players dry their bowls with a cloth before every shot. This is done to remove any oil that the bowl may have picked up off the wooden alley floor. A greasy bowl won't roll or turn as well.
Frame	1/10th of each game for each player.
Goal	Ball rolling between two pins in a wide split and knocking neither down.
Goal Posts	A 7–10 split (the left and right pins of the back four).
Grandma's Teeth	An obscure, random array of standing pins.
Gutter Ball	A bowl bowled into the gutter.
Hard Way	Scoring 200 with an alternation of strikes and spares (aka Sandwich game; Dutch 200).
Head Pin	The first pin in triangle (aka No.1 pin).
King Pin	The centre pin (aka No.5 pin).
Late [number]	When a pin wobbles and is the last to go down, e.g. late ten.
Leave	Number of pins left standing after the first bowl.
Lofting	When the bowl is thrown/dropped onto the lane, rather than being bowled smoothly. A bad delivery.
Miss	A missed spare (aka a 'blow').
Nose Hit	A first ball hitting the pins dead centre.
Open	A frame in which neither a strike nor a spare is hit.
Par	In professional bowling a score of 200 is considered 'par'; any points over 200 are called 'over' or 'in the black'.
Perfect Game	The rare feat of hitting continuous strikes and scoring 300 points in a single game (12 strikes in a row, and subsequently a count of 30 per frame).

TERM	MEANING
Pocket	The ideal place to hit the pins in order to score a strike (between pins 1–3 for right-handers; between 1–2 for left-handers).
Return	The conveyor mechanism that returns the bowl to the players.
Sixpack	Six strikes in a row.
Split	When, after the first bowl, two or more pins are standing with more than the width of a bowl between them.
Triple/Turkey	Scoring three strikes in a row.

BUSINESS BRANDS

	MOST VALUABLE GLOBAL BRANDS		MOST VALUABLE GLOBAL SPORTS BRANDS	
1	Google	$66 bn	ESPN	$7.5 bn
2	GE	$62 bn	Nike	$5.6 bn
3	Microsoft	$55 bn	Adidas	$2.4 bn
4	Coca-Cola	$44 bn	Under Armour	$2.2 bn
5	China Mobile	$41 bn	EA Sports	$2.0 bn
6	Marlboro	$39 bn	Sky Sports	$1.3 bn
7	Wal-Mart	$37 bn	Reebok	$0.9 bn
8	Citi	$34 bn	YES Network	$0.5 bn
9	IBM	$34 bn	IMG	$0.45 bn
10	Toyota	$33 bn	MSG Network	$0.4 bn

Sources: UK – Superbrands Council survey 2008; Global – Millard Brown survey 2007; Sports – www.forbes.com 2007. Values are estimates of the worth of the brand, not the business as a whole.

TOP TEN FOOTBALL PLAYERS/TEAMS HONOURED AS 'BEST OF THE TWENTIETH CENTURY'

	WORLD SOCCER MAGAZINE[1]	FRANCE FOOTBALL MAGAZINE[2]	PLACAR MAGAZINE[3]	FIFA MAGAZINE[4]
1	Pelé (Bra)	Pelé (Bra)	Pelé (Bra)	Real Madrid (Spa)
2	D. Maradona (Arg)	D. Maradona (Arg)	D. Maradona (Arg)	Manchester Utd (Eng)
3	J. Cruyff (Net)	J. Cruyff (Net)	J. Cruyff (Net)	Bayern Munich (Ger)
4	F. Beckenbauer (Ger)	A. Di Stéfano (Arg/Spa)	E. Garrincha (Bra)	Barcelona (Spa)
5	M. Platini (Fra)	M. Platini (Fra)	F. Beckenbauer (Ger)	(5=) Ajax (Net)
6	A. Di Stéfano (Arg/Spa)	F. Beckenbauer (Ger)	A. Di Stéfano (Arg/Spa)	(5=) Santos (Bra)
7	F. Puskás (Hun)	F. Puskás (Hun)	F. Puskás (Hun)	Juventus (Ita)
8	G. Best (NI)	M. Van Basten (Net)	M. Platini (Fra)	Peñarol (Uru)
9	M. Van Basten (Net)	Zico (Bra)	Eusébio (Por)	(9=) AC Milan (Ita)
10	Eusébio (Por)	(9=) G. Müller (Ger) (9=) Yashin (Rus)	Romàrio (Bra)	(9=) Flamengo (Bra) (9=) River Plate (Arg)

[1]Voted for by readers of World Soccer Magazine in 1999.

[2]Voted for in 1999 by 30 of the 34 former Ballon d'Or award winners of the twentieth century (Best, Matthews, and Sivori chose not to vote and Yashin died in 1990).

[3]Published in the Brazilian football magazine Placar. Voted for by Placar journalists in 1999.

[4]Voted for by readers of FIFA magazine in 2000.

EURO BANK NOTE DESIGNS

NOTE	ARCHITECTURE	ARCHITECTURAL PERIOD	COLOUR
€5	Classical	< Fifth century	Grey
€10	Romanesque	Eleventh–twelfth century	Red
€20	Gothic	Thirteenth–fourteenth century	Blue
€50	Renaissance	Fifteenth–sixteenth century	Orange
€100	Baroque & Rococo	Seventeenth–eighteenth century	Green
€200	Iron & Glass	Nineteenth–twentieth century	Yellow/brown
€500	Modern	Twentieth–twenty-first century	Purple

Paper Composition: 100 per cent pure cotton fibre.

Design Features: the bridges, windows and gateways featured on the notes are entirely fictional.

On the front, windows and gateways were chosen to symbolise the openness of the Union.

On the reverse, bridge designs were chosen to symbolise the connectedness of the Union.

LONGEST RIVERS

	NAME	COURSE	LENGTH KM (MILES)
1	Nile	Burundi > Mediterranean Sea	6,695 (4,160)
2	Amazon	Peru > South Atlantic Ocean	6,400 (4,000)
3	Yangtze	China > Yellow Sea	6,300 (3,900)
4	Mississippi	Montana, US > Gulf of Mexico	5,970 (3,710)
5	Yenisey-Angara	Mongolia > Kara Sea	5,550 (3,450)
EU	Danube (29th)	Germany > Black Sea	2,850 (1,770)
UK	Severn	Central Wales > Bristol Channel	354 (220)

Source: Encarta Encyclopedia

BRITISH & IRISH LIONS
TOUR RESULTS

YEAR	TOUR	CAPTAIN	COACH	RESULT	RECORD	TEST RESULTS
1983	New Zealand	Ciaran Fitzgerald (Ire)	Jim Telfer (Sco)	Lost	0–4	12–16 (C); 0–9 (W); 8–15 (D); 6–38 (A)
1986	Rest of World XV	Colin Deans (Sco)	Mick Doyle (Ire)	Lost	0–1	7–15 (CA)
1989	Australia	Finlay Calder (Sco)	Ian McGeechan (Sco)	Won	2–1	12–30 (S); 19–12 (B); 19–18 (S)
1993	New Zealand	Gavin Hastings (Sco)	Ian McGeechan (Sco)	Lost	1–2	18–20 (C); 20–7 (W); 13–30 (A)
1997	South Africa	Martin Johnson (Eng)	Ian McGeechan (Sco)	Won	2–1	25–16 (CT); 18–15 (DU); 16–35 (J)
2001	Australia	Martin Johnson (Eng)	Graham Henry (NZ)	Lost	1–2	29–13 (B); 14–35 (M); 23–29 (S)
2005	New Zealand	Brian O'Driscoll (Ire); Gareth Thomas (Wal)	Sir Clive Woodward (Eng)	Lost	0–3	21–3 (C); 48–18 (W); 38–19 (A)

Match Venue Key: A= Auckland; B=Brisbane; C= Christchurch; CA= Cardiff; CT= Cape Town; D= Dunedin; DU= Durban; J= Johannesburg; M= Melborune; S= Sydney.

MOST POPULOUS NATIONS
OF THE WORLD

RANK	COUNTRY	CAPITAL	CURRENCY	AREA (000 km²) [rank]	POPULATION
1	China	Beijing	Chinese renminbi yuan	9,598 [4]	1,273 m
2	India	Delhi	Indian rupee	3,166 [7]	1,029 m
3	US	Washington	US dollar	9,629 [3]	278 m
4	Indonesia	Jakarta	Indonesian rupiah	1,905 [16]	228 m
5	Brazil	Brasilia	Brazilian real	8,515 [5]	174 m
6	Russia	Moscow	Russian ruble	17,098 [1]	146 m
7	Pakistan	Islamabad	Pakistani rupee	796 [36]	145 m
8	Bangladesh	Dhaka	Bangladeshi taka	144 [94]	131 m
9	Japan	Tokyo	Japanese yen	378 [62]	127 m
10	Nigeria	Abuja	Nigerian naira	924 [32]	126 m
11	Mexico	Mexico City	Mexican peso	1,958 [15]	102 m
12	Germany	Berlin	Euro	357 [63]	83 m
22	UK	London	British pound	243 [79]	61 m
WORLD				Land: 148,940; Water: 361,132	6,671 m

GOAL CELEBRATIONS

ORIGIN	CELEBRATION	DESCRIPTION
Faustino Asprilla	The 'Asprilla'	The player runs and performs a cartwheel, followed by three underarm punches.
Archie Thompson	The 'Boxer'	The player throws a string of pretend punches at the corner flag.
Eric Cantona	The 'Cantona'	The player stands in the same spot, slowly rotates 360 degrees, and then raises his arms.
Dennis Law	The 'Dennis Law'	The player runs toward the crowd with one arm outstretched and with one finger in the air.
Papa Bouba Diop	The 'Diop'	The player hangs his shirt on the corner flag, then he and his team mates dance around it.
Paul Gascoigne	The 'Gazza'	The scorer lies on his back with his mouth open. A teammate then squirts water from a drinks bottle down his throat.
Emile Heskey	The 'Heskey'	The player holds one hand to his ear and spins an imaginary record with the other.
Unknown	The 'I love my club'	The player kisses the badge on his shirt.
Luis Garcia	The 'I love my kid(s)'	The player sucks his thumb.
Raúl	The 'I love my wife'	The player kisses the ring finger of his left hand.
Kaká	The 'Kaká'	The player stands and points to the sky in thanks to God.
Jürgen Klinsmann	The 'Klinsmann'	The player sprints away (usually toward the corner flag) and dives on their chest and knees with arms outstretched in front of them.
Bernardo Coraddi	The 'Knighthood'	The scorer picks up the corner flag and touches a kneeling teammate with it on both shoulders.
Marcelo Salas	The 'Matador'	The player kneels, bows his head and points to the sky.
Roger Milla	The 'Milla'	The player 'dances' with the corner flag.
Pelé	The 'Punch'	The player punches the air with his fist.
Fabrizio Ravanelli	The 'Ravanelli'	The player runs along lifting the front of his shirt up and tucking it behind his head.
Rio Ferdinand	The 'Rio'	The player (usually not the scorer) jumps onto the celebrating group, propelling himself above them and cheering with the crowd.

ORIGIN	CELEBRATION	DESCRIPTION
Robbie Keane	The 'Robbie Keane'	The player does a forward roll, then crouches and mimics the firing of an arrow from a bow.
Peter Crouch	The 'Robokop'	The player stands and, with joints bent and movements jerky, dances like a robot.
Bebeto	The 'Rock-a-bye Baby'	To celebrate the recent birth of a child, the scorer cups his hands and rocks his arms from side to side, as if rocking an imaginary baby.
Hugo Sanchez	The 'Sanchez Somersault'	The player performs a back flip.
Alan Shearer	The 'Shearer'	The player runs along adjacent to the crowd, and raises his right arm with palm open.
Ole Gunnar Solksjær	The 'Solksjær'	The player sprints in the direction of a camera, dives onto his knees and puts his arms in the air in the shape of a star.
Ronaldinho	The 'Surfer'	The player mimics a surfing motion toward the crowd with arms and hands outstretched.

Celebrations are a chance for a player to release some of their emotions for a few moments after a goal. In certain circumstances players may choose not to celebrate, e.g. in a friendly match, when playing against a still-liked former club, when losing heavily, when winning easily, when another goal is needed urgently, or when unhappy at their club.

'BIG FOUR' UK SUPERMARKETS

SUPERMARKET	HQ	UK MARKET SHARE (2008)	HOW NAME WAS DERIVED
ASDA	Leeds	16.7%	Combined abbreviation of previously separate companies: Asquith/ Associated Dairies & Farm Stores Ltd.
Morrisons	Bradford	11.4%	Founder's name: William Morrison.
Sainsbury's	London	16.4%	Founder's name: John James Sainsbury.
Tesco	Cheshunt	31.5%	Label from the first stock shipment: tea from T. E. Stockwell (TES), plus the first two letters of (founder) Jack Cohen's surname.

MALE BAND MEMBERS WHO ACHIEVED MAJOR SOLO SUCCESS

NAME (BORN)	BIRTHPLACE	TALENT	GROUP (FORMED)	FIRST SOLO HIT
John Lennon (1940-1980)	Liverpool	Vocals; Keyboard; Guitar	The Beatles (1962)	'Give Peace a Chance' (1969)
Mick Jagger (1943)	Dartford, Kent	Vocals; Keyboard; Guitar	The Rolling Stones (1963)	'Memo From Turner' (1970)
Paul McCartney (1942)	Liverpool	Vocals; Guitar	The Beatles (1962); Wings (1971)	'Another Day' (1971)
Michael Jackson (1958)	Gary, Indiana	Vocals	The Jackson 5 (1966)	'Got To Be There' (1971)
Rod Stewart (1945)	London	Vocals	The Faces (1969)	'Maggie May' (1971)
Lou Reed (1942)	New York	Vocals; Guitar	Velvet Underground (1965)	'Walk on the Wild Side' (1972)
Eric Clapton (1945)	Ripley, Surrey	Vocals; Guitar	Yardbirds (1962); Cream (1966); Derek and the Dominos (1970)	'I Shot the Sheriff' (1974)
Bob Marley (1945-1981)	St Anne's, Jamaica	Vocals; Guitar	The Wailers (1963)	'No Woman, No Cry' (1974)
Peter Gabriel (1950)	Cobham, Surrey	Vocals; Keyboard; Flute	Genesis (1966)	'Solsbury Hill' (1977)
Iggy Pop (1947)	Muskegon, Michigan	Vocals	The Stooges (1967)	'Lust For Life' (1977)
Phil Collins (1951)	London	Vocals; Drums	Genesis (1966)	'In the Air Tonight' (1980)
Pete Townshend (1945)	London	Vocals; Guitar	The Who (1964)	'Let My Love Open the Door' (1980)
Billy Idol (1955)	London	Vocals; Guitar; Keyboards; Piano	Generation X (1976)	White Wedding (1982)
Lionel Richie (1949)	Tuskegee, Alabama	Vocals; Piano; Saxophone	The Commodores (1968)	'Truly' (1982)

NAME (BORN)	BIRTHPLACE	TALENT	GROUP (FORMED)	FIRST SOLO HIT
Sting (Gordon Sumner) (1951)	Wallsend, Northumberland	Vocals; Bass	The Police (1977)	'Spread a Little Happiness' (1982)
George Michael (1963)	London	Vocals; Guitar	Wham! (1981)	'Careless Whisper' (1984)
Ice Cube (1969)	LA, California	Vocals	NWA (1986)	'AmeriKKKa's Most Wanted' (1990)
Jools Holland (1958)	London	Keyboard; Piano	Squeeze (1974)	'The Full Compliment' (1990)
Paul Weller (1952)	Woking, Surrey	Vocals; Keyboard; Guitar	The Jam (1975); The Style Council (1983)	'Into Tomorrow' (1991)
Dr Dre (Andre Young) (1965)	LA, California	Vocals; Keyboard	NWA (1986)	'Nuthin' But a 'G' Thang' (1993)
Shane MacGowan (1957)	Tunbridge Wells, Kent	Vocals; Guitar	The Nipple Erectors (1977); The Pogues (1982)	'That Woman's Got Me Drinking' (1994)
Mark Knopfler (1949)	Glasgow	Vocals; Guitar	Dire Straits (1977)	'Darling Pretty' (1996)
Robbie Williams (1974)	Stoke-on-Trent	Vocals	Take That (1990)	'Freedom' (1996)
Fatboy Slim (Norman Cook) (1963)	London	Mixing Decks; Keyboard; Bass guitar	The Housemartins (1983)	'The Rockafeller Skank' (1998)
Ian Brown (1963)	Warrington	Vocals; Guitar; Bass guitar	Stone Roses (1985)	'My Star' (1998)
Richard Ashcroft (1971)	Billinge, Lancashire	Vocals; Guitar	The Verve (1989)	'A Song For the Lovers' (2000)

FORMULA ONE MOTOR RACING

SEASON	CHAMPION	CHAMPION'S TEAM	WINS (POLES)	PTS (MARGIN)	RUNNER-UP
1990	A. Senna (Bra)	McLaren Honda	6 (10)	78 (5)	A. Prost (Fra)
1991	A. Senna (Bra)	McLaren Honda	7 (8)	96 (24)	N. Mansell (UK)
1991	A. Senna (Bra)	McLaren Honda	7 (8)	96 (24)	N. Mansell (UK)
1992	N. Mansell (UK)	Williams Renault	9 (11)	108 (52)	R. Patrese (Ita)
1992	N. Mansell (UK)	Williams Renault	9 (11)	108 (52)	R. Patrese (Ita)
1993	A. Prost (Fra)	Williams Renault	7 (13)	99 (26)	A. Senna (Bra)
1993	A. Prost (Fra)	Williams Renault	7 (13)	99 (26)	A. Senna (Bra)
1994	M. Schumacher (Ger)	Benetton Ford	8 (6)	92 (1)	D. Hill (UK)
1994	M. Schumacher (Ger)	Benetton Ford	8 (6)	92 (1)	D. Hill (UK)
1995	M. Schumacher (Ger)	Benetton Renault	9 (4)	102 (33)	D. Hill (UK)
1996	D. Hill (UK)	Williams Renault	8 (7)	97 (19)	J. Villeneuve (Can)
1997	J. Villeneuve (Can)	Williams Renault	7 (10)	81 (39)	H-H. Frentzen (Ger)
1998	M. Häkkinen (Fin)	McLaren Mercedes	8 (11)	100 (14)	M. Schumacher (Ger)
1999	M. Häkkinen (Fin)	McLaren Mercedes	5 (9)	76 (2)	E. Irvine (UK)
2000	M. Schumacher (Ger)	Ferrari	9 (10)	108 (19)	M. Häkkinen (Fin)
2001	M. Schumacher (Ger)	Ferrari	9 (10)	123 (58)	D. Coulthard (UK)
2002	M. Schumacher (Ger)	Ferrari	11 (7)	144 (67)	R. Barrichello (Bra)

SEASON	CHAMPION	CHAMPION'S TEAM	WINS (POLES)	PTS (MARGIN)	RUNNER-UP
2003	M. Schumacher (Ger)	Ferrari	6 (5)	93 (2)	K. Räikkönen (Fin)
2004	M. Schumacher (Ger)	Ferrari	13 (8)	148 (34)	R. Barrichello (Bra)
2005	F. Alonso (Spa)	Renault	7 (6)	133 (21)	K. Räikkönen (Fin)
2006	F. Alonso (Spa)	Renault	7 (6)	134 (12)	M. Schumacher (Ger)
2007	K. Räikkönen (Fin)	Ferrari	6 (3)	110 (1)	L. Hamilton (UK)

Inaugural season: 1950 (seven races). Inaugural championship won by Nino Farrina (Italy) Alfa Romeo.

2008/09 Calendar: 18 races (March–November).

TOP TEN NATIONAL SURNAMES

	ENGLAND	FRANCE	GERMANY	IRELAND	ITALY
1	Smith	Martin	Müller	Murphy	Rossi
2	Jones	Bernard	Schmidt	Kelly	Russo
3	Williams	Dubois	Schneider	O'Sullivan	Ferrari
4	Taylor	Thomas	Fischer	Walsh	Esposito
5	Brown	Robert	Meyer	Smith	Bianchi
6	Davies	Richard	Weber	O'Brien	Romano
7	Evans	Petit	Schulz	Byrne	Colombo
8	Wilson	Durand	Wagner	Ryan	Ricci
9	Thomas	Leroy	Becker	O'Connor	Marino
10	Johnson	Moreau	Hoffman	O'Neill	Greco

CHRONOLOGY OF WEST COAST
HIP HOP ARTISTS

RAPPER	ORIGIN OF STAGE NAME	BIRTH NAME	ARTISTS HOME CITY	DEBUT ALBUM
Ice T (1958–)	After ex-pimp and author Iceberg Slim	Tracy Marrow	Crenshaw, CA	*Rhyme Pays* (1987)
Eazy-E (1963–95)	From the initial of his first name	Eric Lynn Wright	Compton, CA	*Eazy-Duz-It* (1988)*
Coolio (1963–)	Friends called him Coolio Iglesias because he liked playing the guitar	Artis Leon Ivey, Jr.	Compton, CA	*It Takes a Thief* (1994)**
Frost (1964–)	As a tribute to his rival, Ice T	Arturo Molina, Jr.	East LA, CA	*Hispanic Causing Panic* (1990)
Dr Dre (1965–)	From his nickname (Dre), and the nickname of his favourite basketball player – Julius 'Dr J' Erving	André Romell Young	Compton, CA	*The Chronic* (1992)*
Ice Cube (1969–)	From his cool persona and strong physique	O'Shea Jackson	South LA, CA	*AmeriKKKa's Most Wanted* (1990)*
Nate Dogg (1969–)	Mix of his name and that of his cousin (Snoop Dogg)	Nathaniel Dawayne Hale	Long Beach, CA	*The Prodigal Son* (1997)
DJ Quik (1970–)	He chose it himself, leaving the 'c' out so he wouldn't offend a rival gang	David Martin Blake	Compton, CA	*Quik Is the Name* (1991)
Warren G (1970–)	From his name	Warren Griffin III	Long Beach, CA	*Regulate... G Funk Era* (1994)
Snoop Dogg (1971–)	A nickname given by his mother because he liked the Peanuts cartoon strip	Cordozar Calvin Broadus, Jr.	Long Beach, CA	*Doggystyle* (1993)

RAPPER	ORIGIN OF STAGE NAME	BIRTH NAME	ARTISTS HOME CITY	DEBUT ALBUM
2Pac (1971–96)	Shortening of his first name	Tupac Amaru Shakur	Marin City, CA	*2Pacalypse Now* (1991)
Daz Dillinger (1973–)	From his nickname 'Daz' and the infamous bank robber John Dillinger	Delmar Arnaud	Long Beach, CA	*Retaliation, Revenge & Get Back* (1998)***
The Game (1979–)	A name given to him by family because he always seemed 'game' to do anything	Jayceon Terrell Taylor	Compton, CA	*The Documentary* (2005)

*Eazy-E, Dr Dre and Ice Cube had a prior group debut album as part of NWA with *Straight Outa Compton* (1988).

**Coolio had a prior debut album called *Aint a Damn Thing Changed* (1991) as part of WC & The Maad Circle.

***Daz Dillinger had an earlier group album debut called *Dogg Food* (1995) as one half of Dogg Pound.

FA CUP FINAL VENUES

YEARS	VENUE
1872	Kennington Oval, London
1873	Lillie Bridge, London
1874–1892	Kennington Oval, London
1893	Fallowfield, Manchester
1894	Goodison Park, Liverpool
1895–1914	Crystal Palace, London
1915	Old Trafford, Manchester
1920–1922	Stamford Bridge, London
1923–2000	Wembley Stadium, London
2001–2006	Millennium Stadium, Cardiff
2007–	Wembley Stadium, London

CONMEBOL COPA AMÉRICA

YEAR	WINNER	RUNNERS-UP	SCORE	HOST	TOP SCORER(S)
1916	Uruguay	Argentina	N/A	Argentina	Gradín (Argentina) 3
1917	Uruguay	Argentina	N/A	Uruguay	Romano (Uruguay) 4
1919	Brazil	Uruguay	1–0	Brazil	Friedenreich; Neco (Brazil) 4
1920	Uruguay	Argentina	N/A	Chile	Pérez; Romano (Uruguay) 3
1921	Argentina	Brazil	N/A	Argentina	Libonatti (Argentina) 3
1922	Brazil	Paraguay	3–0	Brazil	Francia (Argentina) 4
1923	Uruguay	Argentina	N/A	Uruguay	Aguirre (Argentina); Petrone (Uruguay) 3
1924	Uruguay	Argentina	N/A	Uruguay	Petrone (Uruguay) 4
1925	Argentina	Brazil	N/A	Argentina	Seoane (Argentina) 6
1926	Uruguay	Argentina	N/A	Chile	Arellano (Chile) 7
1927	Argentina	Uruguay	N/A	Peru	Figueroa; Petrone; Scarone (Uruguay); Carricaberry; Luna (Argentina) 3
1929	Argentina	Paraguay	N/A	Argentina	González (Paraguay) 5
1935	Uruguay	Argentina	N/A	Peru	Masantonio (Argentina) 4
1937	Argentina	Brazil	2–0	Argentina	Toro (Chile) 7
1939	Peru	Uruguay	N/A	Peru	Fernández (Peru) 7
1941	Argentina	Uruguay	N/A	Chile	Marvezzi (Argentina) 5
1942	Uruguay	Argentina	N/A	Uruguay	Masantonio; Moreno (Argentina) 7
1945	Argentina	Brazil	N/A	Chile	Méndez (Argentina); Heleno (Brazil) 6
1946	Argentina	Brazil	N/A	Argentina	Medina (Uruguay) 7
1947	Argentina	Paraguay	N/A	Ecuador	Falero (Uruguay) 7
1949	Brazil	Paraguay	7–0	Brazil	Pinto (Brazil) 9
1953	Paraguay	Brazil	3–2	Peru	Molina (Chile) 8
1955	Argentina	Chile	N/A	Chile	Micheli (Argentina) 8
1956	Uruguay	Chile	N/A	Uruguay	Hormazábal (Chile) 4
1957	Argentina	Brazil	N/A	Peru	Maschio (Argentina); Ambrois (Uruguay) 9
1959	Argentina	Brazil	N/A	Argentina	Pelé (Brazil) 8
1959	Uruguay	Argentina	N/A	Ecuador	Sanfilippo (Argentina) 6

YEAR	WINNER	RUNNERS-UP	SCORE	HOST	TOP SCORER(S)
1963	Bolivia	Paraguay	N/A	Bolivia	Raffo (Ecuador) 6
1967	Uruguay	Argentina	N/A	Uruguay	Artime (Argentina) 5
1975	Peru	Colombia	0–1 & 2–0 & 1–0	N/A	Luque (Argentina); Díaz (Columbia) 4
1979	Paraguay	Chile	3–0 & 0–1 & 0–0	N/A	Morel (Paraguay); Peredo (Chile) 4
1983	Uruguay	Brazil	2–0 & 1–1	N/A	Aguilera (Uruguay); Burruchaga (Argentina); Dinamite (Brazil) 3
1987	Uruguay	Chile	1–0	Argentina	Iguarán (Colombia) 4
1989	Brazil	Uruguay	1–0	Brazil	Bebeto (Brazil) 6
1991	Argentina	Brazil	3–2	Chile	Batistuta (Argentina) 6
1993	Argentina	Mexico	2–1	Ecuador	Dolgetta (Colombia) 4
1995	Uruguay	Brazil	1–1 (5–3 pens)	Uruguay	Batistuta (Argentina); García (Mexico) 4
1997	Brazil	Bolivia	3–1	Bolivia	Hernández (Mexico) 6
1999	Brazil	Uruguay	3–0	Paraguay	Rivaldo; Ronaldo (Brazil) 5
2001	Columbia	Mexico	1–0	Colombia	Aristizábal (Colombia) 6
2004	Brazil	Argentina	2–2 (4–2 pens)	Peru	Adriano (Brazil) 7
2007	Brazil	Argentina	3–0	Venezuela	Robinho (Brazil) 6
2011				Argentina	

Governing Body: CONMEBOL, aka CSF (Confederación Sudamericana de Fútbol). The headquarters are in Luque, Paraguay. The Copa América is the oldest surviving national team tournament in the world.

Competitors: 12 nations compete in each competition. The ten permanent participating nations are Argentina, Brazil, Bolivia, Chile, Colombia, Ecuador, Paraguay, Peru, Uruguay and Venezuela. Since 1993 two non-CONMEBOL nations have been invited to each tournament, which so far have included Costa Rica, Honduras, Japan, Mexico and the US.

Format: the South American Championship was traditionally a league-based tournament. Play-offs were originally only used to decide the winner when the top two teams finished level on points. Nowadays league stages followed by knock-out rounds are used to determine the eventual winner.

BASEBALL WORLD SERIES

YEAR	WINNER	SCORE	RUNNERS-UP	M.V.P
1990	Cincinnati Reds	4–0	Oakland Athletics	José Rijo
1991	Minnesota Twins	4–3	Atlanta Braves	Jack Morris
1992	Toronto Blue Jays	4–2	Atlanta Braves	Pat Borders
1993	Toronto Blue Jays	4–2	Philadelphia Phillies	Paul Molitor
1994	No World Series due to season-long players strike over salary capping.			
1995	Atlanta Braves	4–2	Cleveland Indians	Tom Glavine
1996	New York Yankees	4–2	Atlanta Braves	John Wetteland
1997	Florida Marlins	4–3	Cleveland Indians	Liván Hernández
1998	New York Yankees	4–0	San Diego Padres	Scott Brosius
1999	New York Yankees	4–0	Atlanta Braves	Mariano Rivera
2000	New York Yankees	4–1	New York Mets	Derek Jeter
2001	Arizona Diamondbacks	4–3	New York Yankees	Randy Johnson; Curt Schilling
2002	Anaheim Angels	4–3	San Francisco Giants	Troy Glaus
2003	Florida Marlins	4–2	New York Yankees	Josh Beckett
2004	Boston Red Sox	4–0	St. Louis Cardinals	Manny Ramírez
2005	Chicago White Sox	4–0	Houston Astros	Jermaine Dye
2006	St. Louis Cardinals	4–1	Detroit Tigers	David Eckstein
2007	Boston Red Sox	4–0	Colorado Rockies	Mike Lowell

Winners from National League: 1990, 1995, 1997, 2001, 2003, 2006.

Winners from American League: 1991–1994, 1996, 1998–2000, 2002, 2004–2005, 2007.

First Ever World Series: 1903 – Boston Americans (AL) beat Pittsburgh Pirates (NL) 5–3. Half-time show entertainment was provided by Arizona University and Michigan University bands.

Most Times Winners: 26 – New York Yankees; 10 – St Louis Cardinals.

Most Times Losers: 13 – New York Yankees; 12 – LA Dodgers, San Francisco Giants.

Most Valuable Player (MVP): The World Series MVP Award is presented to the player voted by the media, baseball officials and fans as being the outstanding player of each final. Only once has the award gone to a player from the losing team – Bobby Richardson of the New York Yankees (1960).

Most Times MVP Winner: 2 – Sandy Koufax (1963, 1965) LA Dodgers; Bob Gibson (1964, 1969) St Louis Cardinals; Reggie Jackson (1973) Oakland Athletics, (1977) New York Yankees.

Home Advantage: The games are played in a sequence of 2–3–2. The team from the league that won the last All-Star game has the advantage of playing at home in the first two and last two games of the series.

NATIONAL EMBLEMS

COUNTRY	FAUNA	FLORA
Argentina	Hornero and Puma	Flower of the Ceibo Tree
Australia	Red Kangaroo and Emu	Golden Wattle
Brazil	Rufous-Bellied Thrush	Flower of the Tabebuia Alba Flower
Canada	Beaver and Canadian Horse	Maple Leaf
China	Giant Panda	Narcissus
England	Lion	Tudor Rose
France	Gallic Rooster	Iris
Germany	Black Eagle	Cornflower
India	Peacock and Royal Bengal Tiger	Lotus
Ireland	Irish Wolfhound	Shamrock
Italy	Italian Wolf	Poppy
Japan	Pheasant	Chrysanthemum
Netherlands	Lion	Tulip
New Zealand	Kiwi	Silver Fern
Northern Ireland	Elk	Flax
Norway	Goldcrest and Lion	Heather
Poland	White Eagle	Weeping Willow
Russia	Bear	Camomile
Scotland	Lion and Golden Eagle	Thistle
Spain	Osborne's Bull	Carnation
South Africa	Springbok Antelope	King Protea
Thailand	Thai Elephant	Golden Shower Tree
US	American Bald Eagle	American Rose
Wales	Red Dragon	Daffodil

FA PREMIER LEAGUE HISTORY

SEASON	CHAMPIONS	2ND	3RD	TOP SCORER(S)
1992/1993	Manchester Utd	Aston Villa	Norwich City	Sheringham (Tottenham) 22
1993/1994	Manchester Utd	Blackburn Rovers	Newcastle Utd	Cole (Newcastle) 34
1994/1995	Blackburn Rovers	Manchester Utd	Nottingham Forest	Shearer (Blackburn) 34
1995/1996	Manchester Utd	Newcastle	Liverpool	Shearer (Blackburn) 31
1996/1997	Manchester Utd	Newcastle	Arsenal	Shearer (Newcastle) 25
1997/1998	Arsenal	Manchester Utd	Liverpool	Dublin (Coventry); Owen (Liverpool); Sutton (Blackburn) 18
1998/1999	Manchester Utd	Arsenal	Chelsea	Hasselbaink (Leeds Utd); Owen (Liverpool); Yorke (Man Utd) 18
1999/2000	Manchester Utd	Arsenal	Leeds Utd	Phillips (Sunderland) 30
2000/2001	Manchester Utd	Arsenal	Liverpool	Hasselbaink (Chelsea) 23
2001/2002	Arsenal	Liverpool	Manchester Utd	Henry (Arsenal) 24
2002/2003	Manchester Utd	Arsenal	Newcastle Utd	Van Nistelrooy (Man Utd) 25
2003/2004	Arsenal	Chelsea	Manchester Utd	Henry (Arsenal) 30
2004/2005	Chelsea	Arsenal	Manchester Utd	Henry (Arsenal) 25
2005/2006	Chelsea	Manchester Utd	Liverpool	Henry (Arsenal) 25
2006/2007	Manchester Utd	Chelsea	Liverpool	Drogba (Chelsea) 20
2007/2008	Manchester Utd	Chelsea	Arsenal	Ronaldo (Man Utd) 31

Sponsors: 1992/1993–2000/2001: Carling; 2001/2002–2003/2004: Barclaycard; 2004/2005–2008/2009: Barclays.

UK ALL-TIME BEST-SELLING ALBUMS

YEAR	TITLE	BAND/ARTIST	SALES
1981	*Greatest Hits (Volume One)*	Queen	5.4 m
1967	*Sgt Pepper's Lonely Hearts Club Band*	The Beatles	4.8 m
1995	*(What's the Story) Morning Glory?*	Oasis	4.3 m
1985	*Brothers in Arms*	Dire Straits	4.0 m
1992	*ABBA Gold: Greatest Hits*	ABBA	3.9 m
1973	*The Dark Side of the Moon*	Pink Floyd	3.8 m
1991	*Greatest Hits (Volume Two)*	Queen	3.6 m
1982	*Thriller*	Michael Jackson	3.6 m
1987	*Bad*	Michael Jackson	3.6 m
1990	*The Immaculate Collection*	Madonna	3.4 m
1991	*Stars*	Simply Red	3.4 m
1998	*Come on Over*	Shania Twain	3.3 m
1977	*Rumours*	Fleetwood Mac	3.1 m
1997	*Urban Hymns*	The Verve	3.1 m
1970	*Bridge Over Troubled Water*	Simon & Garfunkel	3.0 m
2002	*No Angel*	Dido	3.0 m

Source: www.everyhit.com

UK NEWSPAPERS

NAME	TYPICAL POLITICAL STANCE	SIZE	YEAR EST.	CURRENT OWNER
REDTOP TABLOIDS				
Morning Star	Far left	Tabloid	1930	People's Press Printing Society
Daily Mirror/Sunday Mirror	Left	Tabloid	1903/1915	Trinity Mirror Group plc
Sunday People	Left	Tabloid	1972	Trinity Mirror Group plc
Daily Sport/Sunday Sport	N/A	Tabloid	1991/1986	Sport Newspapers (David Sullivan)
Daily Star	N/A	Tabloid	1978	Northern & Shell plc (Richard Desmond)
The Sun/News of the World	Right	Tabloid	1964/1843	News International (Rupert Murdoch)
[Scotland only] *Daily Record/Sunday Mail*	Left	Tabloid	1895/1914	Trinity Mirror Group plc
[Scotland only] *The Sunday Post*	Left	Tabloid	1905	DC Thomson & Co Ltd
MIDDLE-MARKET				
Daily Express/Sunday Express	Centre right	Tabloid	1900/1918	Northern & Shell plc (Richard Desmond)
Daily Mail/Mail on Sunday	Right	Tabloid	1896	Associated Newspapers Ltd
QUALITY				
The Independent/The Independent on Sunday	Centre left	Compact/ broadsheet	1986/1990	Independent News & Media (Tony O'Reilly)
The Guardian/The Observer	Centre left	Berliner/ broadsheet	1821/1791	Guardian Media Group (The Scott Trust)
The Times/The Sunday Times	Centre right	Compact/ broadsheet	1785/1864	News International (Rupert Murdoch)
The Financial Times	Centre right	Broadsheet	1888	Pearson plc
The Daily Telegraph/ The Sunday Telegraph	Right	Broadsheet	1855/1961	Press Holdings Ltd (David & Frederick Barclay)

NAME	TYPICAL POLITICAL STANCE	SIZE	YEAR EST.	CURRENT OWNER
[Scotland only] The Herald/Sunday Herald	Centre left	Broadsheet	1783/1999	Newsquest (Gannett Company Inc.)
[Scotland only] The Scotsman/The Scotland on Sunday	Centre right	Compact/ broadsheet	1817/1988	Press Holdings Ltd (David & Frederick Barclay)

ROAD CAR CLASSIFICATIONS

CLASS	EXAMPLE MODELS
Microcar	Smart Fortwo; Microcar MC1; Bingo TE
City Car	Peugeot 106; Seat Arosa; VW Lupo
Super-Mini	Vauxhall Corsa; Ford Fiesta; VW Polo
Small Family Car	Peugeot 306; Vauxhall Astra; Skoda Octavia
Hot Hatch	Alfa Romeo 147 GTA; Honda Civic Type R; VW Golf GTI
Family Car	Honda Accord; Ford Mondeo; Vauxhall Vectra
Compact Executive	BMW 3 Series; Mercedes C-Class; Jaguar X-Type
Compact Sports Saloon	BMW M3; Subaru Impreza; Mitsubishi Lancer Evolution
Executive	BMW 5 Series; Mercedes E-Class; Jaguar S-Type
Sports Saloon	Saab 9-5 Aero; BMW M5; Audi RS6
Luxury Car	BMW 7 Series; Audi A8; Mercedes S-Class
Roadster	Porsche Boxster; Lotus Elise; BMW Z3
Grand Tourer	Mercedes CL-Class; Ferrari 599 GTB; Jaguar XK
Traditional Sports Car	Porsche 911; Audi R8; Aston Martin Vantage
Supercar	Aston Martin DB9; Ferrari Enzo; Lamborghini Gallardo
Compact MPV (Multi-Passenger Vehicle)	Toyota Corolla Verso; Fiat Multipla; VW Touran
Large MPV (Multi-Passenger Vehicle)	Citroën C8; Chrysler Grand Voyager; Mitsubishi Grandis;
Compact 4x4	Honda CR-V; Land Rover Freelander; Toyota Rav4
Large 4x4	Land Rover Discovery; BMW X5; Volvo XC90
Pick-Up	Toyota Hilux; Mitsubishi L200; Nissan Navara

GLOBAL FOOTBALL AWARD WINNERS

	BALLON D'OR	ONZE D'OR	FIFA WORLD PLAYER OF THE YEAR	WORLD SOCCER PLAYER OF THE YEAR
1990	Matthäus (Inter)	Matthäus (Inter)	N/A	Matthäus (Inter)
1991	Papin (Marseille)	Papin (Marseille)	Matthäus (Inter)	Matthäus (Inter)
1992	Van Basten (AC Milan)	Stoichkov (Barcelona)	Van Basten (AC Milan)	Van Basten (AC Milan)
1993	Baggio (Juventus)	Baggio (Juventus)	Baggio (Juventus)	Baggio (Juventus)
1994	Stoichkov (Barcelona)	Romário (Barcelona)	Romário (Barcelona)	Madini (AC Milan)
1995	Weah (AC Milan)	Weah (AC Milan)	Weah (AC Milan)	Vialli (Juventus)
1996	Sammer (Borussia Dortmund)	Cantona (Man Utd)	Ronaldo (Barcelona)	Ronaldo (Barcelona)
1997	Ronaldo (Barcelona)	Ronaldo (Barcelona)	Ronaldo (Barcelona)	Ronaldo (Barcelona)
1998	Zidane (Juventus)	Zidane (Juventus)	Zidane (Juventus)	Zidane (Juventus)
1999	Rivaldo (Barcelona)	Rivaldo (Barcelona)	Rivaldo (Barcelona)	Rivaldo (Barcelona)
2000	Figo (Real Madrid)	Zidane (Juventus)	Zidane (Juventus)	Figo (Real Madrid)
2001	Owen (Liverpool)	Zidane (Real Madrid)	Figo (Real Madrid)	Owen (Liverpool)
2002	Ronaldo (Real Madrid)	Ronaldo (Real Madrid)	Ronaldo (Real Madrid)	Ronaldo (Real Madrid)
2003	Nedvěd (Juventus)	Henry (Arsenal)	Zidane (Real Madrid)	Kahn (Bayern Munich)
2004	Shevchenko (AC Milan)	Drogba (Marseille)	Ronaldinho (Barcelona)	Ronaldinho (Barcelona)
2005	Ronaldinho (Barcelona)	Ronaldinho (Barcelona)	Ronaldinho (Barcelona)	Ronaldinho (Barcelona)
2006	Cannavaro (Real Madrid)	Henry (Arsenal)	Cannavaro (Real Madrid)	Cannavaro (Real Madrid)
2007	Kaká (Milan)	Kaká (Milan)	Kaká (Milan)	Kaká (Milan)

SPORTS ILLUSTRATED: SWIMSUIT
EDITION - COVER MODELS

YEAR	COVER MODEL(S)
1990	Judit Masco (Spa)
1991	Ashley Montana (US)
1992	Kathy Ireland (US)
1993	Vendela Kirsebom (Swe)
1994	Kathy Ireland (US); Elle Macpherson (Aus); Rachel Hunter (NZ)
1995	Daniela Pestova (Cze)
1996	Valeria Mazza (Arg); Tyra Banks (US)
1997	Tyra Banks (US)
1998	Heidi Klum (Ger)
1999	Rebecca Romijn-Stamos (US)
2000	Daniela Pestova (Cze)
2001	Elsa Benitez (Mex)
2002	Yamila Diaz (Arg)
2003	Petra Nemcová (Cze)
2004	Veronica Varekova (Cze); inset Anna Kournikova (Rus)
2005	Carolyn Murphy (US)
2006	Veronica Vareková (Cze); Elle Macpherson (Aus); Rebecca Romijn-Stamos (US); Rachel Hunter (NZ); Daniela Pestova (Cze); Elsa Benitez (Mex); Carolyn Murphy (US); Yamila Diaz (Arg); inset Heidi Klum (Ger); Maria Sharapova (Rus)
2007	Beyoncé Knowles (US); inset Bar Refaeli (Isr)
2008	Marisa Miller (Rus)

First Edition: the first annual Swimsuit Edition of the popular US Sports Illustrated magazine was published in January 1964. Babette March was the cover model. The RRP was 25 cents. Most Frequent Cover Models: Elle Macpherson (Aus) (1986, 1987, 1988, 1994, 2006); Christie Brinkley (US) (1979, 1980, 1981); Kathy Ireland (US) (1989, 1992, 1994); Cheryl Tiegs (US) (1970, 1975, 1983); Daniela Pestova (Cze) (1995, 2000, 2006).

MAGNER'S LEAGUE – RUGBY UNION

SEASON	CHAMPIONS	RUNNERS-UP
2001/2002	Leinster	Munster
2002/2003	Munster	Neath
2003/2004	Scarlets	Ulster
2004/2005	Ospreys	Munster
2005/2006	Ulster	Leinster
2006/2007	Ospreys	Cardiff Blues
2007/2008	Leinster	Cardiff Blues

2008/2009 Teams: Irish – Munster, Leinster, Connacht, and Ulster; Scottish – Edinburgh Rugby, and Glasgow Warriors; Welsh – Cardiff Blues, Llanelli Scarlets, Newport Gwent Dragons, and Ospreys.

Celtic Cup: the Celtic Cup first featured in the 2003/2004 season – Ulster beat Edinburgh in the final. In its second year Munster beat Scarlets in the final. Due to fixture congestion and confusion surrounding a possible 'Rainbow Cup' (to include sides from Italy and South Africa), the Celtic Cup ceased to exist after the 2004/2005 season.

WORLD'S LARGEST ISLANDS

	NAME	OCEAN	AREA IN KM² (MILES²)	POPULATION
1	**Greenland**	Arctic	2,175,000 (840,000)	56,000
2	**New Guinea**	Pacific	800,000 (309,000)	7,500,000
3	**Borneo**	Pacific	734,000 (283,000)	16,000,000
4	**Madagascar**	Indian	587,000 (227,000)	19,500,000
5	**Baffin Island**	Arctic	507,000 (196,000)	11,000
EU	**Great Britain (8th)**	Atlantic	217,000 (84,000)	58,800,000
UK	**Lewis and Harris**	Atlantic	2,180 (840)	20,000

Source: www.britannica.com

NATIONS WITH THE HIGHEST LEVELS OF BEER CONSUMPTION

	NATION	ANNUAL CONSUMPTION (LITRES / PINTS PER PERSON)
1	**Czech Republic**	**156.9 (276.1)**
2	Ireland	131.1 (230.7)
3	Germany	115.8 (203.7)
4	Australia	109.9 (193.3)
5	Austria	108.3 (190.5)
6	United Kingdom	99.0 (174.2)
7	Belgium	93.0 (163.6)
8	Denmark	89.9 (158.2)
9	Finland	85.0 (149.5)
10	Luxembourg	84.4 (148.5)
11	Slovakia	84.1 (147.9)
12	Spain	83.8 (147.4)
13	United States	81.6 (143.5)
14	Croatia	81.2 (142.8)
15	Netherlands	79.0 (139.0)
16	New Zealand	77.0 (135.5)
17	Hungary	75.3 (132.5)
18	Poland	69.1 (121.5)
19	Canada	68.3 (120.1)
20	Portugal	59.6 (104.8)
Source: Kirin Holdings Company Ltd (2004)		

MOTION ENGINEERING
WORLD RECORDS

RECORD	RECORD HOLDER	RECORD DETAILS	DATE
AIR			
Air Speed Record	Lockheed SR-71 Blackbird (flown by Eldon W Joersz (US))	3,530 kph (2,194 mph) at Beale Air Force Base, US.	28/7/1976
Busiest Airport	Hartsfield International, Atlanta, US	85.91 m passengers/year.	2005
Highest Capacity Passenger Aircraft	Airbus A380. A double-deck, wide-body, four-engine airliner.	Up to 853 passengers. The first commercial flight was from Singapore to Sydney.	25/10/2007
Largest Aircraft Ever Built (by length and max. takeoff weight)	Antonov An-225 (NATO codename: Cossack)	Max. gross takeoff weight of 640 t, 84 m length, and 88.4 m wingspan. Only two were ever produced. The 1947-made, Hughes H-4 Hercules, (nicknamed the 'Spruce Goose'), is the only aircraft to ever have a larger wingspan (97.54 m).	21/12/1988
Longest Non-Stop Flight	Cessna 172 (flown by Robin Timm and John Cook (US))	64 d, 22 h, 19 m, 5 s. Able to stay in flight after refuelling by dropping a rope to fuel tankers travelling on straight roads in the Mojave desert in western US.	4/12/1958–7/2/1959
Most Produced Aircraft	Cessna 172 Skyhawk	Over 43,000 produced. Four-seat, single-engine, high-wing aircraft. A Cessna 172 features in the James Bond film, GoldenEye (1995), surveying a secret satellite dish in Cuba.	1956–present
RAIL			
Conventional Rail Speed Record	SNCF Train Grande Vitesse (TGV) POS	The TGV has operated between Paris and Lyon since 1981.	3/8/2007
Magnetic Levitation Rail Speed Record	JR-Maglev MLX01	581 kph (361.01 mph). The record was set at Yamanashi test line, Japan.	2/12/2003
Longest and Heaviest Freight Train	Assembled by BHP Iron Ore	7.353 km (4.568 miles) long, and 99,732.1 tonnes. Consisted of 682 train cars, and eight diesel-electric engines.	21/6/2001

RECORD	RECORD HOLDER	RECORD DETAILS	DATE
Longest One-Train Route	Operated by Trans-Siberian railways	10,214 km (6346 miles) long (between Moscow, Russia and Pyongyang, North Korea).	Since 1917
Most Extensive Underground System	MTA New York City Transit	468 stations, 370 km (230 m) of track, and a passenger average of 5.1 m/day (1.86 bn/year).	Since 1984
ROAD			
Land Speed Record	Thrust Super Sonic (driven by Andy Green (UK))	1,233.70 kph (766 mph) at Black Rock Desert, US.	15/8/1997
Longest Car	American Dream	30.5 m (100 ft). Has 13 axles, a swimming pool (with diving board), a bar, a king-size waterbed and a helipad.	
Most Powerful Production Car	Koenigsegg CCR	4.7 litre, Supercharged V8 engine with 601 kw (806 hp) power, and 920 Nm (678 ft/lb) torque. Capable of speeds up to 395 kph (242 mph).	Since 2004
WATER			
Water Speed Record	Spirit of Australia (piloted by Ken Warby (Aus))	511.13 kph (317.60 mph). Record set at Blowering Dam, Australia.	8/10/1978
Heaviest Aircraft Carrier	Nimitz Class US Navy Carriers	104,000 t (fully loaded), 333 m long and a flight deck of 1.82 ha (4.5 acres). It is powered by four nuclear charged steam turbines, and can move at speeds of up to 55 kph (34.5 mph).	3/5/1975
Largest Cruise Ship	Royal Caribbean's Freedom of the Seas	154,407 tonnes, 338.77 m long, 38.6 m wide. Can carry 4,370 passengers and 1,360 crew. Built in Finland.	4/6/2006
Longest Ship Ever Built	Knock Nevis (previously Seawise Giant; Happy Giant; Viking Jahre)	564,763 tonnes, 458.45 m long, 65.8 m wide. With a fully loaded draft of 24.6 m it was unable to navigate any manmade canals or even the English Channel. First operated between the Middle East and the US, and then used during the Iran-Iraq conflict (where it suffered significant damage). In 2008 it was being used in a Qatari oilfield as an FSO (floating storage and offloading unit).	1981

UK CHRISTMAS NUMBER ONES

YEAR	TITLE	BAND/ARTIST
1990	'Saviour's Day'	Cliff Richard
1991	'Bohemian Rhapsody / These Are the Days of Our Lives'	Queen
1992	'I Will Always Love You'	Whitney Houston
1993	'Mr Blobby'	Mr Blobby
1994	'Stay Another Day'	East 17
1995	'Earth Song'	Michael Jackson
1996	'2 Become 1'	Spice Girls
1997	'Too Much'	Spice Girls
1998	'Goodbye'	Spice Girls
1999	'I Have a Dream / Seasons in the Sun'	Westlife
2000	'Can We Fix It?'	Bob the Builder
2001	'Somethin' Stupid'	Robbie Williams & Nicole Kidman
2002	'Sound of the Underground'	Girls Aloud
2003	'Mad World'	Michael Andrews (featuring Gary Jules)
2004	'Do They Know It's Christmas?'	Band Aid 20
2005	'That's My Goal'	Shayne Ward
2006	'A Moment Like This'	Leona Lewis
2007	'When You Believe'	Leon Jackson

UK SNOOKER CHAMPIONSHIP

YEAR	WINNER	RUNNER-UP	SCORE
1990	**Stephen Hendry (Sco)**	Steve Davis (Eng)	16–15
1991	**John Parrot (Eng)**	Jimmy White (Eng)	16–13
1992	**Jimmy White (Eng)**	John Parrott (Eng)	16–9
1993	**Ronnie O'Sullivan (Eng)**	Stephen Hendry (Sco)	10–6
1994	**Stephen Hendry (Sco)**	Ken Doherty (Ire)	10–5
1995	**Stephen Hendry (Sco)**	Peter Ebdon (Eng)	10–3
1996	**Stephen Hendry (Sco)**	John Higgins (Sco)	10–9
1997	**Ronnie O'Sullivan (Eng)**	Stephen Hendry (Sco)	10–6
1998	**John Higgins (Sco)**	Matthew Stevens (Wal)	10–6
1999	**Mark Williams (Wal)**	Matthew Stevens (Wal)	10–8
2000	**John Higgins (Sco)**	Mark Williams (Wal)	10–4
2001	**Ronnie O'Sullivan (Eng)**	Ken Doherty (Ire)	10–1
2002	**Mark Williams (Wal)**	Ken Doherty (Ire)	10–9
2003	**Matthew Stevens (Wal)**	Stephen Hendry (Sco)	10–8
2004	**Stephen Maguire (Sco)**	David Gray (Eng)	10–1
2005	**Ding Junhui (Chi)**	Steve Davis (Eng)	10–6
2006	**Peter Ebdon (Eng)**	Stephen Hendry (Sco)	10–6
2007	**Ronnie O'Sullivan (Eng)**	Stephen Maguire (Sco)	10–2

First Ever UK Championship: played at the Blackpool Tower Circus in 1977. Patsy Fagan (Ire) beat Doug Mountjoy (Wal) 12–9 in the final. The winner's purse was £2,000.

First 147: Stephen Hendry 1995

Youngest Winner: Ronnie O'Sullivan (17 y) 1993 (also youngest winner of any world-ranking event).

Most Championship Wins: Steve Davis (6) 1980–1981, 1984–1987

Ranking: the UK Championship became a ranking event and began allowing entry from all professionals (not just those holding a UK passport) in 1984. It is generally regarded as the second most prestigious event and is the only event to carry x1.5 ranking points (the World Championships carries x2 ranking points).

SPACE EXPLORATION FIRSTS

LAUNCH DATE	FIRST...	ASTRONAUT(S)	VEHICLE	AGENCY
3/10/1942	... rocket to reach space	(unmanned)	A-4(V-2)	Germany*
14/6/1949	... monkey in space	Monkey: Albert II (died on re-impact with earth)	V2	NASA
29/1/1951	... dogs in space	Dogs: Trygan and Dezik (both survived)	R-1 IIIA-1	USSR
4/10/1957	... satellite in orbit	(unmanned)	Sputnik 1	USSR
3/11/1957	... animal in orbit	Dog: Laika (died in flight)	Sputnik 2	USSR
12/9/1959	... hard landing on the moon	(unmanned)	Luna 2	USSR
7/10/1959	... first image of lunar far side	(unmanned)	Luna 3	USSR
12/4/1961	... manned space flight	Yuri Gagarin	Vostok 1	USSR
6/8/1961	... person to spend one day in space	Gherman Titov	Vostok 2	USSR
16/6/1963	... woman in space	Valentina Tereshkova	Vostok 6	USSR
12/10/1964	... multi-person craft in space	Vladimir Komarov; Konstantin Feoktistov; Boris Yegorov	Voskhod 1	USSR
18/3/1965	... spacewalk	Aleksei Leonov	Voskhod 2	USSR
31/1/1966	... first lunar soft landing	(unmanned)	Luna 9	USSR
1/3/1966	... first planetary impact (Venus)	(unmanned)	Venera 3	USSR
16/7/1969	... moon landing (20/7/1969)	Neil Armstrong; Buzz Aldrin; Michael Collins	Apollo 11	NASA
6/6/1971	... space station	Georgi Dobrovolski; Viktor Patsayev; Vladislav Volkov	Soyuz 11	USSR
20/8/1975	... Mars landing	(unmanned)	Viking 1	NASA
20/8/1977	... pictures from Neptune	(unmanned)	Voyager 2	NASA
5/9/1977	... spacecraft to reach the termination shock** (23-24/5/2005)	(unmanned)	Voyager 1	NASA

LAUNCH DATE	FIRST...	ASTRONAUT(S)	VEHICLE	AGENCY
24/12/1979	... European rocket in space	(unmanned)	Ariane I	ESA
28/1/1986	... major fatal explosion	Seven US astronauts (all died)	Challenger	NASA
18/5/1991	... Briton in space	Helen Sharman	Soyuz TM-12	RKA
3/2/1995	... Briton to spacewalk	Michael Foale	Discovery STS-63	NASA
4/12/1996	... spacecraft to explore the surface of Mars	(unmanned)	Mars Pathfinder	NASA
31/10/2001	... space tourist	Dennis Tito	Soyuz	RKA
15/10/2003	... Chinese space trip	Yang Liwei	Shenzhou V	CNSA
25/12/2004	... soft landing on Titan (one of Saturn's moons)	(unmanned)	Huygens Probe	ESA / NASA
12/1/2005	... comet impact	(unmanned)	Deep Impact	NASA

First Words Spoken From the Lunar Surface: 'That's one small step for man... one giant leap for mankind.'

On 21/7/1969 at 02:56:27 a.m. (GMT), Neil Armstrong, the commander of the Apollo 11 space mission, became the first human being to step onto the surface of the moon. Moments later, Edwin 'Buzz' Aldrin (of the same mission) became the second. The command module that transported them was called the Columbia; it was piloted by Michael Collins, however Collins never left the module.

Key: * = Developed by the Army Research Center rather than a Space Agency; CNSA = China National Space Administration; ESA = European Space Agency (Belgium, France, Germany, Greece, Italy, Netherlands, Spain, Sweden, Switzerland and the UK); NASA = National Aeronautics and Space Administration (US); RKA = Russian Federal Space Agency (Russia); USSR = The Soviet Union Space Agency. ** = The point in the heliosphere where the solar wind slows to subsonic speed. This is about 75 to 90 astronomical units (1 AU = 150 million km) from the sun.

THE JAMES BOND FILM SERIES

YEAR	TITLE	BOND ACTOR	MAIN VILLAIN	MAIN BOND GIRL	Q-BRANCH VEHICLE(S)	THEME VOCALS	WOMEN SEDUCED	KILL COUNT
1962	Dr No	SC	Dr No	Honey Ryder	Sunbeam Alpine Series II	None	3	5
1963	From Russia with Love	SC	Rosa Klebb	Tatiana Romanova	none	Matt Monro	4	17
1964	Goldfinger	SC	Auric Goldfinger	Pussy Galore	Aston Martin DB5	Shirley Bassey	2	10
1965	Thunderball	SC	Emilio Largo	Patricia Fearing	Aston Martin DB5	Tom Jones	3	22
1967	You Only Live Twice	SC	Ernst Stavro Blofeld	Kissy Suzuki	'Little Nellie'	Nancy Sinatra	3	21
1969	On Her Majesty's Secret Service	GL	Ernst Stavro Blofeld	Teresa Draco	Aston Martin DBS	Louis Armstrong	3	8
1971	Diamonds are Forever	SC	Ernst Stavro Blofeld	Plenty O'Toole	none	Shirley Bassey	1	7
1973	Live and Let Die	RM	Kananga	Solitaire	Hang Glider	Paul McCartney/ Wings	3	6
1974	The Man with the Golden Gun	RM	Francisco Scaramanga	Mary Goodnight	Seaplane	Lulu	2	1
1977	The Spy Who Loved Me	RM	Karl Stromberg	Anya Amasov	Lotus Esprit Submarine	Carly Simon	3	14
1979	Moonraker	RM	Hugo Drax	Holly Goodhead	Gondola Hovercraft	Shirley Bassey	3	14
1981	For Your Eyes Only	RM	Aris Kristatos	Melina Havelock	Lotus Esprit Turbo	Sheena Easton	2	11

YEAR	TITLE	BOND ACTOR	MAIN VILLAIN	MAIN BOND GIRL	Q-BRANCH VEHICLE(S)	THEME VOCALS	WOMEN SEDUCED	KILL COUNT
1983	Octopussy	RM	Kamal Khan	Octopussy	Acrostar Mini Jet Plane	Rita Coolidge	2	14
1985	A View to a Kill	RM	Max Zorin	Stacey Sutton	Disguised Submarine	Duran Duran	4	5
1987	The Living Daylights	TD	General Koskov	Kara Milovy	Aston Martin Volante	A-ha	2	2
1989	Licence to Kill	TD	Franz Sanchez	Pam Bouvier	none	Gladys Knight	2	12
1995	GoldenEye	PB	Alec Trevelyan	Natalya Simonova	Aston Martin DB5 / BMW Z3	Tina Turner	2	12
1997	Tomorrow Never Dies	PB	Elliot Carver	Paris Carver	BMW 750iL	Sheryl Crow	3	25
1999	The World is Not Enough	PB	Renard (Robert Carlyle)	Christmas Jones	BMW Z8 / Q Boat	Garbage	3	19
2002	Die Another Day	PB	Gustav Graves (Toby Stephens)	Giacinta 'Jinx' Johnson	Aston Martin Vanquish	Madonna	2	10
2006	Casino Royale	DC	Le Chiffre (Mads Mikkelsen)	Vesper Lynd	Aston Martin DBS	Chris Cornell	2	5
2008	Quantum of Solace	DC	Dominic Greene (Mathieu Amalric)	Camille	Aston Martin DBS	Jack White & Alicia Keys		

Key: SC = Sean Connery; GL = George Lazenby; RM = Roger Moore; TD = Timothy Dalton; PB = Pierce Brosnan; DC = Daniel Craig.

ANIMAL WORLD RECORDS

RECORD	SPECIES	RECORD DETAILS	LOCATION
Fastest Land Animal	Cheetah	Up to 112 kph (70 mph)	Afghanistan, Iran, Turkmenistan and tropical Africa
Largest Land Mammal	African Elephant	4–7 tonnes*	Sub-Saharan Africa
Largest Mammal	Blue Whale	Up to 30 m long and weighing up to 140 tonnes	Polar water in summer and in tropical seas in winter
Largest Wingspan	Wandering Albatross	Up to 3.6 m wide	Southern oceans
Loudest Animal	Blue Whale	Up to 188 dB	Polar water in summer and tropical seas in winter
Most Poisonous Land Animal	Golden Poison Frog	1 mg of poison from its skin glands is enough to kill 10–20 humans**	Central and southern America
Tallest Mammal	Giraffe	Average height of around 5.5 m	Africa

Key: * = The Asian elephant is smaller, lighter (3-5 tonnes), and has much smaller ears. The African elephant population is around ten times that of the Asian.

** = Dogs have died simply from touching objects that the frogs have walked on.

CLASSIFICATION OF CRICKET BOWLING SPEEDS

TYPE	MPH	KM/H
Fast	> 90	> 145
Fast-Medium	80–89	129–145
Medium-Fast	70–79	113–129
Medium	60–69	97–113
Medium-Slow	50–59	80–97
Slow-Medium	40–49	64–80
Slow	< 40	< 64

UEFA EUROPEAN CHAMPIONSHIPS

	WINNER	RUNNERS-UP	SCORE	HOSTS	TOP SCORER(S)
1960	USSR	Yugoslavia	2–1	France	Ivanov (USSR); Jerkovic (Yugoslavia) 2
1964	Spain	USSR	2–1	Spain	Novak (Hungary); Pereda (Spain) 2
1968	Italy	Yugoslavia	1–1 / 2–0 (replay)	Italy	Dzajic (Yugoslavia) 2
1972	W. Germany	USSR	3–0	Belgium	G. Müller (W. Germany) 4
1976	Czech Republic	W. Germany	2–2 (5–3 pens)	Yugoslavia	D. Müller (W. Germany) 4
1980	W. Germany	Belgium	2–1	Italy	Allofs (W. Germany) 3
1984	France	Spain	2–0	France	Platini (France) 9
1988	Netherlands	USSR	2–0	W. Germany	Van Basten (Netherlands) 5
1992	Denmark	Germany	2–0	Sweden	Bergkamp (Netherlands); Brolin (Sweden); Larsen (Denmark); Riedle (Germany) 3
1996	Germany	Czech Republic	2–1 (aet)	England	Shearer (England) 5
2000	France	Italy	2–1 (aet)	Belgium/ Netherlands	Kluivert (Netherlands); Milosevic (Yugoslavia) 5
2004	Greece	Portugal	1–0	Portugal	Baroš (Czech Republic) 5
2008	Spain	Germany	1–0	Austria/ Switzerland	Villa (Spain) 4
2012				Poland/ Ukraine	

Governing Body: Union of European Football Associations; founded – 1954; HQ – Nyon, Switzerland.

Official Tournament Balls (all manufactured by Adidas): Tango Italia (1980); Tango Mundial (1984); Tango Europa (1988); Etrusco Roteiro Unico (1992); Questra Europa (1996); Terrestra (2000); Silverstream (2004); Europass (2008).

FIFA WORLD CUP

YEAR	WINNER	RUNNERS-UP	SCORE	HOST(S)	TOP SCORER(S)
1930	Uruguay	Argentina	4–2	Uruguay	Stábile (Argentina) 8
1934	Italy	Czechoslovakia	2–1 (aet)	Italy	Nejedlý (C'vakia) 5
1938	Italy	Hungary	4–2	France	Da Silva (Brazil) 7
NO WORLD CUP BETWEEN 1942–1946 DUE TO WORLD WAR TWO					
1950	Uruguay	Brazil	2–1	Brazil	Ademir (Brazil) 7
1954	West Germany	Hungary	3–2	Switzerland	Kocsis (Hungary) 11
1958	Brazil	Sweden	5–2	Sweden	Fontaine (France) 13
1962	Brazil	Czechoslovakia	3–1	Chile	Albert (Hungary); Garrincha (Brazil); Ivanov (USSR); Jerković (Yugoslavia); Sánchez (Chile); Vavá (Brazil) 4
1966	England	West Germany	4–2 (aet)	England	Eusébio (Portugal) 9
1970	Brazil	Italy	4–1	Mexico	Müller (W. Germany) 10
1974	West Germany	Holland	2–1	West Germany	Lato (Poland) 7
1978	Argentina	Holland	3–1 (aet)	Argentina	Kempez (Argentina) 6
1982	Italy	West Germany	3–1	Spain	Rossi (Italy) 6
1986	Argentina	West Germany	3–2	Mexico	Lineker (England) 6
1990	West Germany	Argentina	1–0	Italy	Schillaci (Italy) 6
1994	Brazil	Italy	0–0 (3–2 pens)	US	Salenko (Russia); Stoichkov (Bulgaria) 6
1998	France	Brazil	3–0	France	Šuker (Croatia) 6
2002	Brazil	Germany	2–0	Japan/Korea	Ronaldo (Brazil) 8
2006	Italy	France	1–1 (5–3 pens)	Germany	Klose (Germany) 5
2010				South Africa	
2014				Brazil	

Governing Body: Fédération Internationale de Football Association (FIFA); founded in 1904; HQ in Zürich, Switzerland.

TEAM RECORDS

Most Tournaments: 18 – Brazil.

Most Tournaments Always Advancing From First Round: 3 – Denmark; Republic of Ireland.

Most Tournaments Never Advancing From First Round: 8 – Scotland.

Most Team Goals: 202 – Brazil. Most Cautions: 88 – Argentina (64 games).

Most Sendings Off: 10 – Argentina (64 games).

Most Matches Between Two Teams: 7 – Brazil and Sweden.

INDIVIDUAL RECORDS

Most Tournaments: 5 – Antonio Carbajal (Mexico) 1950–1966; Lothar Matthäus (Germany) 1982–1998.

Most Tournament Winners Medals: Pelé (Brazil) 1958, 1962, 1970. Most Goals: 15 – Ronaldo (Brazil) 1998–2006.

Most Goals in a Match: 5 – Oleg Salenko (for Russia vs Cameroon) 1994.

Most Goals in a Final: 3 – Geoff Hurst (for England vs West Germany) 1966.

Fastest Goal: 11 seconds – Hakan Şükür (for Turkey vs South Korea) 2002.

Most Clean Sheets: 10 – Peter Shilton (England) 1982–1990; Fabien Barthez (France) 1998–2006.

Youngest Player: 17 y 1 m 11 d – Norman Whiteside (for Northern Ireland vs Yugoslavia) 1982.

Oldest Player: 42 y 1 m 8 d – Roger Milla (for Cameroon vs Russia) 1994.

Most Cautions: 6 – Cafu (Brazil) 1994–2006.

Most Sendings Off: 2 – Rigobert Song (for Cameroon vs Brazil (1994), vs Chile (1998)); Zinedine Zidane (for France vs Saudi Arabia (1998), vs Italy (2006)).

TRACTOR MANUFACTURERS

BRAND (COLOUR(S))	YEAR FOUNDED	COUNTRY OF ORIGIN	OWNER
Case IH (red)	1842	US	CNH Global
Caterpillar (yellow)	1925	US	CAT
Claas (light green)	1913	Germany	CLAAS
Deutz-Fahr (green)	1894	Germany	SDF
Fendt (dark green)	1937	Germany	AGCO
JCB (yellow)	1945	UK	JCB
John Deere (green and yellow)	1837	US	Deere & Co
Lamborghini (silver)	1963	Italy	SDF
Landini (blue)	1925	Italy	ARGO
Massey Ferguson (red)	1847	Canada	AGCO
McCormick (red)	1834	US/UK	ARGO
New Holland (blue)	1895	US	CNH Global
SAME (red)	1942	Italy	SDF
Steyr (red and white)	1864	Austria	CNH Global
Valtra (customer choice)	1932	Finland	AGCO

Note: Above are the major global manufacturers active in the UK market; however, many more exist in foreign markets.

Ownership Key: AGCO = Allis-Gleaner Corporation (Georgia, US); ARGO = ARGO SpA (Reggio Emilia, Italy); CAT = Caterpillar Inc (Illinois, US); CLAAS = CLAAS (North Rhine-Westphalia, Germany); CNH = Case New Holland Global N.V. (Amsterdam, Netherlands); Deere & Co = Deere and Company (Illinois, US); JCB = J. C. Bamford Ltd (Staffordshire, UK); SDF = Same Deutz-Fahr (Lombardy, Italy).

HEINEKEN CUP - RUGBY UNION

SEASON	CHAMPIONS	RUNNERS-UP	SCORE	FINAL
1995/1996	Toulouse	Cardiff	21–18	Cardiff Arms Park
1996/1997	Brive	Leicester Tigers	28–9	Cardiff Arms Park
1997/1998	Bath	Brive	19–18	Stade Chaban-Delmas
1998/1999	Ulster	Colomiers	21–6	Lansdowne Road
1999/2000	Northampton Saints	Munster	9–8	Twickenham
2000/2001	Leicester Tigers	Stade Français	34–30	Parc des Princes
2001/2002	Leicester Tigers	Munster	15–9	Millennium Stadium
2002/2003	Toulouse	Perpignan	22–17	Lansdowne Road
2003/2004	London Wasps	Toulouse	27–20	Twickenham
2004/2005	Toulouse	Stade Français	18–12	Murrayfield
2005/2006	Munster	Biarritz	23–19	Millennium Stadium
2006/2007	London Wasps	Leicester Tigers	25–9	Twickenham
2007/2008	Munster	Toulouse	16–13	Millennium Stadium
2008/2009				Murrayfield

Qualification: England (top six in the Premiership); France (top six in the Top 14); Ireland (top three in the Celtic League); Italy (top two in the Super 10); Scotland (top two in the Celtic League); Wales (top three in the Celtic League). The 23rd team comes from the highest-placed non-qualifier from the league of the nation of the English, French, or Italian team who progressed furthest in the previous tournament. The 24th and final team comes from the winner of the Celtic-Italian play-off – a match between the highest placed non-qualifier from the Celtic League and the highest placed non-qualifier from the Italian League.

European Challenge Cup: The secondary European competition entrants are Celtic, English, French and Italian league teams that didn't qualify for the Heineken Cup, plus Bucureşti Rugby (a Romanian side specially formed to play in the competition), plus a single side from Portugal or Spain.

POKER HAND HIERARCHY AND PROBABILITY GUIDE

HAND	EXAMPLE HAND	COMBINATIONS	APPROXIMATE ODDS
Royal Flush	10, J, Q, K, A of hearts	4	650,000/1
Straight Flush	2, 3, 4, 5, 6 of clubs	36	72,000/1
Four of a Kind	Four 10's	624	4,100/1
Full House	Two 3's, and three 9's	3,744	700/1
Flush	10, 2, 5, 6, Q of spades	5,108	500/1
Straight	8 of clubs, 9 of spades, 10 of diamonds, J of hearts, Q of spades	10,200	250/1
Three of a Kind	Three 5's	54,912	50/1
Two Pair	Two K's, and two 4's	123,552	20/1
One Pair	Two 7's	1,098,240	1.4/1
No Pair	Any combination other than one of the nine hands above	1,302,540	1/1

The approximate odds is the likelihood of being dealt one of ten hands when drawing five cards out of any randomly shuffled 52-card pack.

STREET FIGHTER II

CHARACTER	NATIONALITY	SPECIAL ABILITIES	ACTOR IN SF: THE MOVIE (1994)
Ryu (Hoshi)	Japanese	Uppercut; Shoryuken; Hadouken	Byron Mann
Ken (Masters)	¾ Japanese; ¼ Caucasian	Uppercut; Shoryuken; Hadouken	Damian Chapa
(William F.) Guile	American	Somersault Kick; Sonic Boom; Flash Kick	Jean-Claude Van Damme
Chun-Li (Zang)	Chinese	Lightning Kick; Spinning Bird Kick	Ming-Na Wen
Blanka	Brazilian	Rolling Attack; Electric Shock	Robert Mammone
(Dr) Dhalsim	Indian	Yoga Spear; Yoga Fire	Roshan Seth
E(dmond) Honda	Japanese	Hundred Hand Slap; Sumo Smash	Peter Navy Tuiasosopo
(Victor) Zangief	Soviet Russian	Spinning Piledriver; Spinning Clothesline	Andrew Bryniarski
Balrog	American	Turn Punch; Uppercut	Grand L. Bush
Vega	Spanish	Back Flip; Tumbling Claw; Izuna Drop	Jay Tavare
(Victor) Sagat	Thai	Tiger Uppercut; Tiger Knee	Wes Studi
(General) M. Bison	unknown	Psycho Crusher; Scissor Kick; Head Stomp	Raul Julia

Playable Characters: The only playable characters in the original game (Street Fighter, released in arcades and on the C64 and ZX Spectrum), were Ryu and Ken. There were ten opposition characters but only the final opponent, Sagat, returned in the most popular and groundbreaking of the series – Street Fighter II (first released on the CPS-1 arcade board in 1991, on the Super NES in 1992, and later on 17 other platforms).

Main Characters in the 1994 Movie But Not in the Original SFII Game: Cammy (Kylie Minogue); T. Hawk (Gregg Rainwater); Dee Jay (Miguel A. Núñez Jr.); Captain Sawada (Kenya Sawada). All except Captain Sawada were included in the follow-up in the SFII series, Super Street Fighter II (1993). Only one character, Fei Long (a kung-fu expert from Hong Kong), featured in the Super SFII game but not the film.

Subsequent Series Incarnations: Street Fighter Alpha series (from 1995); Street Fighter III series (from 1997); Street Fighter IV series (arcade release 2008, Xbox 360, PS3, and PC 2009 or 2010).

EUROPEAN ALCOHOL BELTS – WHERE THE 'BIG THREE' ARE MOST POPULAR

Vodka belt	Iceland; Norway; Sweden; Finland; Poland; Lithuania; Latvia; Estonia; Belarus; Ukraine; Russia
Beer belt	Ireland; UK; north-east France; Belgium; Netherlands; Germany; Denmark; eastern Switzerland; Czech Republic; Slovakia; Austria
Wine belt	Portugal; Spain; France; western Switzerland; Italy; Hungary; Moldova; Georgia

PI (π) TRIVIA

What is Pi?	Pi is the symbol for the ratio of the circumference of a circle when divided by its diameter, thus enabling any circumference to be calculated when the diameter is known and vice versa. Pi is an 'irrational number'; this means it has an infinite number of decimal places.
Credit For Discovery	Greek mathematician Archimedes of Syracuse (287 BC–c. 212 BC) was the first to ascertain a reasonable accuracy for pi.
Reason Behind the Name	The constant is named 'π' due to it being the first letter of the Greek word περίμετρος (meaning perimeter).
Pi to 50 Decimal Places	3.14159 26535 89793 23846 26433 83279 50288 41971 69399 37510
Piphilogy	Defined as the creation and use of mnemonic techniques to recollect the number of pi.
The Cadaeic Cadenza	A 3,834 word short story by Mike Keith published in 1996 in which the number of letters in each word follows the sequence of pi.
Most Used Mnemonic For Pi	'How I want a drink, alcoholic of course, after the heavy lectures involving quantum mechanics'
World Record For Reciting Pi	100,000 digits. Set by Akira Haraguchi of Japan (born 1946) in 2006.

INTERNATIONAL SYSTEM OF UNITS (SI) BASE UNITS

UNIT	QUANTITY	CALCULATION
ampere **(A)**	electric current	If current of one amp is maintained in two infinite length parallel conductors one metre apart and of negligible cross section, it would produce in the middle a force of $2 \times 10-7$ newton per metre. In turn, one newton is equal to the force required to enable a mass of one kilogram to accelerate by one metre per second per second (m/s^2).
candela **(cd)**	luminous intensity	One candela is the luminous intensity, in a given direction, of a source that emits monochromatic radiation of frequency 540×1012 hertz and that has a radiant intensity in that direction of 1/683 watt per steradian. A household candle emits approximately 1 cd; a 100 w light bulb emits about 120 cd.
kelvin **(K)**	thermodynamic temperature	The scale starts at absolute zero, the point where no heat energy exists (which is equal to -273.15°C). The other defining point is the triple point of water (273.15 K or 0.01°C). One K has exactly the same magnitude as one degree on the Celsius scale.
kilogram **(kg)**	mass	One kg is almost exactly equal to the mass of one litre of water at the temperature of melting ice. The global constant for the kg is the International Prototype Kilogram (IPK). The IPK is a platinum and iridium alloy cylinder bar preserved in an airtight container at the International Bureau of Weights and Measures in Sèvres, France.
metre **(m)**	length	Distance travelled by light, in a vacuum, is one 300-millionth of a second. Originally (from 1791) the metre was defined as 1/10,000,000th of the distance between the equator and the North Pole along a quadrant through Paris.
mole **(mol)**	amount of substance	One mole contains 6.22×1023 (Avogadro's number) entities = number of atoms in exactly 12 grams of the carbon-12 isotope. A mole of any substance weighs its relative atomic mass in grams. E.g., one mole of iron (Fe) equals 56 g and one mole of water weighs 18 g (2 Hs (1 g/mole each) plus 1 O (16 g/mole)).
second **(s)**	time	Originally, a second was defined as 1/86,400th of the time it takes for the earth to rotate once on its axis in relation to the sun. For increased accuracy the second is nowadays defined as 9,192,631,770 cycles of the radiation which corresponds to the hyperfine energy levels of the ground state of the caesium atom.

WORLD SNOOKER CHAMPIONSHIP

YEAR	WINNER	RUNNER-UP	SCORE	HIGHEST BREAK
1990	Stephen Hendry (Sco)	Jimmy White (Eng)	18–12	John Parrott (Eng) 140
1991	John Parrott (Eng)	Jimmy White (Eng)	18–11	Jimmy White (Eng) 140
1992	Stephen Hendry (Sco)	Jimmy White (Eng)	18–14	Jimmy White (Eng) 147
1993	Stephen Hendry (Sco)	Jimmy White (Eng)	18–5	Steve Davis (Eng) 144
1994	Stephen Hendry (Sco)	Jimmy White (Eng)	18–17	Alan McManus (Sco) 144
1995	Stephen Hendry (Sco)	Nigel Bond (Eng)	18–9	Stephen Hendry (Sco) 147
1996	Stephen Hendry (Sco)	Peter Ebdon (Eng)	18–12	Tony Drago (Mal); Peter Ebdon (Eng) 144
1997	Ken Doherty (Ire)	Stephen Hendry (Sco)	18–12	Ronnie O'Sullivan (Eng) 147
1998	John Higgins (Sco)	Ken Doherty (Ire)	18–12	John Higgins (Sco); Jimmy White (Eng)143
1999	Stephen Hendry (Sco)	Mark Williams (Wal)	18–11	John Higgins (Sco) 142
2000	Mark Williams (Wal)	Matthew Stevens (Wal)	18–16	Matthew Stevens (Wal) 143
2001	Ronnie O'Sullivan (Eng)	John Higgins (Sco)	18–14	Joe Swail (Eng) 140
2002	Peter Ebdon (Eng)	Stephen Hendry (Sco)	18–17	Matthew Stevens (Wal) 145
2003	Mark Williams (Wal)	Ken Doherty (Ire)	18–16	Ronnie O'Sullivan (Eng) 147
2004	Ronnie O'Sullivan (Eng)	Graeme Dott (Sco)	18–8	Joe Perry (Eng) 145
2005	Shaun Murphy (Eng)	Matthew Stevens (Wal)	18–16	Mark Williams (Wal) 147
2006	Graeme Dott (Sco)	Peter Ebdon (Eng)	18–14	Ronnie O'Sullivan (Eng) 140
2007	John Higgins (Sco)	Stephen Macguire (Sco)	18–15	Ali Carter (Eng) 144
2008	Ronnie O'Sullivan (Eng)	Ali Carter (Eng)	18–8	Ronnie O'Sullivan (Eng); Ali Carter (Eng) 147

First Ever World Championship: 1927, won by co-organiser Joe Davis (Eng). Davis beat Tom Dennis (Eng) 20–11 in the final. Various venues were used for the first tournament and the final was held at Camkin's Hall, Birmingham. The highest break was 60 by Albert Cope. The winner's purse was £6 and 10 s (the equivalent of about £270 in 2008 money).

First 147: Cliff Thorburn (1983).

First second 147: Ronnie O'Sullivan (1997, 2003).

Longest Ever Frame: Graeme Dott vs Peter Ebdon (74 mins) 2006 Final.

Longest Odds Winners: 150–1, Joe Johnson (1986); Shaun Murphy (2005).

First (and Only) Whitewash: John Parrott 10–0 Eddie Charlton (1992).

Youngest World Champion: Stephen Hendry (21 y 3 m 16 d) 1990.

Most Championships: Joe Davis (15) 1927–1940, 1946.

Non-UK Champions: Horace Lindrum (Aus) 1952; Cliff Thorburn (Can) 1980; Ken Doherty (Ire) 1997.

GLASSWARE FOR ALCOHOL

NAME	DESCRIPTION	USE FOR
Beer Mug	Thick glass with handle – pint or ½ pint-sized.	Beer
Brandy Snifter	Stemmed with an upward tapering bowl to concentrate scents, while your hands warm the drink.	Brandy
Champagne Flute	Stemmed with a long tulip-shaped bowl.	Sparkling wine
Highball Glass	Tall and straight-sided.	Spirit and mixers
Liqueur Glass	Small with stem – good for aperitifs and digestifs.	Liqueur
Margarita Glass	Large cocktail glass with a broad rim (for holding the margarita salt).	Margaritas, other cocktails
Martini Glass	Long stemmed with a triangular bowl.	Cocktails without ice ('straight-up')
Red Wine Glass	Thin stemmed with a round bowl that's wider but less high than a white wine glass.	Red wine
Rocks Glass/Tumbler	Short with straight sides.	Spirits, cocktails
Shot Glass	Very short with straight sides – large enough for one 'shot'.	Spirits, liqueurs
White Wine Glass	Thin stemmed with a round bowl that's less wide but higher than a red wine glass.	White wine

MEN'S GRAND SLAM
TENNIS CHAMPIONS

	AUSTRALIAN OPEN	FRENCH OPEN	WIMBLEDON	US OPEN
1990	Lendl (Cze) bt Edberg (Swe)	Gómez (Spa) bt Agassi (US)	Edberg (Swe) bt Becker (Ger)	Sampras (US) bt Agassi (US)
1991	Becker (Ger) bt Lendl (Cze)	Courier (US) bt Agassi (US)	Stich (Ger) bt Becker (Ger)	Edberg (Swe) bt Courier (US)
1992	Courier (US) bt Edberg (Swe)	Courier (US) bt Korda (Cze)	Agassi (US) bt Ivanisevic (Cro)	Edberg (Swe) bt Sampras (US)
1993	Courier (US) bt Edberg (Swe)	Bruguera (Spa) bt Courier (US)	Sampras (US) bt Courier (US)	Sampras (US) bt Pioline (Fra)
1994	Sampas (US) bt Martin (US)	Bruguera (Spa) bt Berasategui (Spa)	Sampras (US) bt Ivanisevic (Cro)	Agassi (US) bt Stich (Ger)
1995	Agassi (US) bt Sampras (US)	Muster (Aus) bt Chang (US)	Sampras (US) bt Becker (Ger)	Sampras (US) bt Agassi (US)
1996	Becker (Ger) bt Chang (US)	Kafelnikov (Rus) bt Stich (Ger)	Krajicek (Net) bt Washington (US)	Sampras (US) bt Chang (US)
1997	Sampras (US) bt Moyà (Spa)	Kuerten (Bra) bt Bruguera (Spa)	Sampras (US) bt Pioline (Fra)	Rafter (Aus) bt Rusedski (UK)
1998	Korda (Cze) bt Ríos (Chile)	Moyá (Spa) bt Corretja (Spa)	Sampras (US) bt Ivanisevic (Cro)	Rafter (Aus) bt Philippoussis (Aus)
1999	Kafelnikov (Rus) bt Enqvist (Swe)	Agassi (US) bt Medvedev (Ukr)	Sampras (US) bt Agassi (US)	Agassi (US) bt Martin (US)
2000	Agassi (US) bt Kafelnikov (Rus)	Kuerten (Bra) bt Norman (Swe)	Sampras (US) bt Rafter (Aus)	Safin (Rus) bt Sampras (US)
2001	Agassi (US) bt Clement (Fra)	Kuerten (Bra) bt Corretja (Spa)	Ivanisevic (Cro) bt Rafter (Aus)	Hewitt (Aus) bt Sampras (US)
2002	Johansson (Swe) bt Safin (Rus)	Costa (Spa) bt Ferrero (Spa)	Hewitt (Aus) bt Nalbandian (Arg)	Sampras (US) bt Agassi (US)
2003	Agassi (US) bt Schüttler (Ger)	Ferrero (Spa) bt Verkerk (Net)	Federer (Swi) bt Philippoussis (Aus)	Roddick (US) bt Ferrero (Spa)
2004	Federer (Swi) bt Safin (Rus)	Gaudio (Arg) bt Coria (Arg)	Federer (Swi) bt Roddick (Aus)	Federer (Swi) bt Hewitt (Aus)
2005	Safin (Rus) bt Hewitt (Aus)	Nadal (Spa) bt Puerta (Arg)	Federer (Swi) bt Roddick (Aus)	Federer (Swi) bt Agassi (US)

	AUSTRALIAN OPEN	FRENCH OPEN	WIMBLEDON	US OPEN
2006	Federer (Swi) bt Baghdatis (Gre)	Nadal (Spa) bt Federer (Swi)	Federer (Swi) bt Nadal (Spa)	Federer (Swi) bt Roddick (US)
2007	Federer (Swi) bt Gonzalez (Chi)	Nadal (Spa) bt Federer (Swi)	Federer (Swi) bt Nadal (Spa)	Federer (Swi) bt Djokovic (Ser)
2008	Djokovic (Ser) bt Tsonga (Fra)	Nadal (Spa) bt Federer (Swi)	Nadal (Spa) bt Federer (Swi)	Federer (Swi) bt Murray (UK)
Key: bt=beat.				

NON-STANDARD CHAMPAGNE
BOTTLE SIZES

SIZE	ETYMOLOGY	VOLUME (LITRES)	SIZE	ETYMOLOGY	VOLUME (LITRES)
Piccolo	'Small' in Italian	0.1875	Balthazar	Biblical – one of the three wise men	12
Demi	'Half' in French	0.375	Nebuchadnezzar	Biblical – King of Babylon	15
Magnum	From the Latin for 'great work'	1.5	Melchior	Biblical – one of the three wise men	18
Jeroboam	Biblical – First King of Northern Kingdom	3	Solomon	Biblical – King of Israel (Son of David)	21
Rehoboam	Biblical – First King of separate Judea	4.5	Sovereign	Monarch; ruler of a country	25
Methuselah	Biblical - Patriarch of Humanity	6	Primat	From the Latin for 'prime'	27
Salmanazar	Biblical – Assyrian King	9	Melchizedek	Biblical – King of Righteousness	30

BIG BROTHER

SERIES	WINNER	RUNNER-UP
BB1 (2000)	Craig Phillips (28)	Anna Nolan (29)
CBB1 (2001)	Jack Dee (38)	Claire Sweeney (29)
BB2 (2001)	Brian Dowling (22)	Helen Adams (22)
BB3 (2002)	Kate Lawler (22)	Jonny Regan (29)
CBB2 (2002)	Mark Owen (30)	Les Dennis (49)
BB4 (2003)	Cameron Stout (32)	Ray Shah (25)
TBB1 (2003)	Paul Brennan (18)	Jade Dyer (18) / James Kelly (18)
BB5 (2004)	Nadia Almada (27)	Jason Cowan (30)
CBB3 (2005)	Mark Berry (Bez) (40)	James McKenzie (Kenzie) (19)
BB6 (2005)	Anthony Hutton (23)	Eugene Sully (27)
CBB4 (2006)	Chantelle Houghton (22)	Michael Barrymore (53)
BB7 (2006)	Pete Bennett (24)	Glyn Wise (18)
CBB5 (2007)	Shilpa Shetty (31)	Jermaine Jackson (53)
BB8 (2007)	Brian Belo (20)	Amanda & Sam Merchant (19)
BB9 (2008)	Rachel Rice (24)	Mikey Hughes (33)

Key: CBB = Celebrity Big Brother; TBB = Teen Big Brother.

UK TV Soundtrack: by Element Four (Paul Oakenfold and Andy Gray).

Production Company: Endemol (Netherlands).

Eviction Night Presenter: Davina McCall.

Daily Updates Narrator: Marcus Bentley.

THE NATO PHONETIC ALPHABET

A	Alpha	N	November
B	Bravo	O	Oscar
C	Charlie	P	Papa
D	Delta	Q	Quebec
E	Echo	R	Romeo
F	Foxtrot	S	Sierra
G	Golf	T	Tango
H	Hotel	U	Uniform
I	India	V	Victor
J	Juliet	W	Whiskey
K	Kilo	X	X-ray
L	Lima	Y	Yankee
M	Mike	Z	Zulu

The NATO alphabet was created in 1956 to minimise confusion in radio telecommunications between nations and defence units that previously used many variations.

RAF 1924–1942: Ace Beer Charlie Don Edward Freddie George Harry Ink Johnnie King London Monkey Nuts Orange Pip Queen Robert Sugar Toc Uncle Vic William X-ray Yorker Zebra.

RAF 1942–1943: Apple Beer Charlie Dog Edward Freddy George Harry In Jug/Johnny King Love Mother Nuts Orange Peter Queen Roger/Robert Sugar Tommy Uncle Vic William X-ray Yoke/Yorker Zebra.

RAF 1943–1956: Able/Affirm Baker Charlie Dog Easy Fox George How Item/Interrogatory Jig/Johnny King Love Mike Nab/Negat Oboe Peter/Prep Queen Roger Sugar Tare Uncle Victor William X-ray Yoke Zebra.

DOMESTIC FOOTBALL AWARDS

YEAR	FWA PLAYER OF THE YEAR	PFA PLAYERS' PLAYER OF THE YEAR	PFA YOUNG PLAYER OF THE YEAR	SFWA PLAYER OF THE YEAR	SPFA PLAYERS' PLAYER OF THE YEAR	SPFA YOUNG PLAYER OF THE YEAR
1990	Barnes (Liverpool)	Platt (Aston Villa)	Le Tissier (S'hampton)	McLeish (Aberdeen)	Bett (Aberdeen)	Crabbe (Aberdeen)
1991	Strachan (Leeds Utd)	Hughes (Man Utd)	Sharpe (Man Utd)	Malpas (Dundee Utd)	Elliot (Celtic)	Jess (Aberdeen)
1992	Lineker (Tottenham)	Pallister (Man Utd)	Giggs (Man Utd)	McCoist (Rangers)	McCoist (Rangers)	O'Donnell (Motherwell)
1993	Waddle (Sheffield W)	McGrath (Aston Villa)	Giggs (Man Utd)	Goram (Rangers)	Goram (Rangers)	Jess (Aberdeen)
1994	Shearer (Blackburn)	Cantona (Man Utd)	Cole (Newcastle)	Hateley (Rangers)	Hateley (Rangers)	O'Donnell (Motherwell)
1995	Klinsmann (Tottenham)	Shearer (Blackburn)	Fowler (Liverpool)	Laudrup (Rangers)	Laudrup (Rangers)	Miller (Rangers)
1996	Cantona (Man Utd)	Ferdinand (Newcastle)	Fowler (Liverpool)	Gascoigne (Rangers)	Gascoigne (Rangers)	McNamara (Celtic)
1997	Zola (Chelsea)	Shearer (Newcastle)	Beckham (Man Utd)	Laudrup (Rangers)	Di Canio (Celtic)	Winters (Dundee Utd)
1998	Bergkamp (Arsenal)	Bergkamp (Arsenal)	Owen (Liverpool)	Burley (Celtic)	MacNamara (Celtic)	Naysmith (Hearts)
1999	Ginola (Tottenham)	Ginola (Tottenham)	Anelka (Arsenal)	Larsson (Celtic)	Larsson (Celtic)	Ferguson (Rangers)
2000	Keane (Man Utd)	Keane (Man Utd)	Kewell (Leeds)	Ferguson (Rangers)	Viduka (Celtic)	Miller (Rangers)
2001	Sheringham (Man Utd)	Sheringham (Man Utd)	Gerrard (Liverpool)	Larsson (Celtic)	Larsson (Celtic)	Petrov (Celtic)
2002	Pirès (Arsenal)	Nistelrooy (Man Utd)	Bellamy (Newcastle)	Lambert (Celtic)	Amoruso (Rangers)	McNaughton (Aberdeen)
2003	Henry (Arsenal)	Henry (Arsenal)	Jenas (Newcastle)	Ferguson (Rangers)	B. Ferguson (Rangers)	McFadden (Motherwell)
2004	Lampard (Chelsea)	Henry (Arsenal)	Parker (Chelsea)	MacNamara (Celtic)	C. Sutton (Celtic)	Pearson (Celtic)

YEAR	FWA PLAYER OF THE YEAR	PFA PLAYERS' PLAYER OF THE YEAR	PFA YOUNG PLAYER OF THE YEAR	SFWA PLAYER OF THE YEAR	SPFA PLAYERS' PLAYER OF THE YEAR	SPFA YOUNG PLAYER OF THE YEAR
2005	Henry (Arsenal)	Terry (Chelsea)	Rooney (Man Utd)	Hartson (Celtic)	Hartson (Celtic); Ricksen (Rangers)	Riordan (Hibernian)
2006	Henry (Arsenal)	Gerrard (Liverpool)	Rooney (Man Utd)	Gordon (Hearts)	Maloney (Celtic)	Maloney (Celtic)
2007	Ronaldo (Man Utd)	Ronaldo (Man Utd)	Ronaldo (Man Utd)	Nakamura (Celtic)	Nakamura (Celtic)	Naismith (Kilmarnock)
2008	Ronaldo (Man Utd)	Ronaldo (Man Utd)	Fàbregas (Arsenal)	Cuellar (Rangers)	McGeady (Celtic)	McGeady (Celtic)

Football Writers Association Footballer of the Year: voted for by top football journalists. The first winner was Stanley Matthews (Blackpool) in 1948.

PFA Players' Player of the Year: voted for by members of the Professional Footballers Association. Because the players themselves vote for this award, it is usually considered the top English domestic award. The first winner was Norman Hunter (Leeds United) in 1974.

PFA Young Player of the Year: like its senior equivalent, it's voted for by members of the Professional Footballers Association. To be eligible players have to be 23 or under and playing in the English leagues. The first award was given in 1974; the winner was Kevin Beattie (Ipswich Town).

Scottish Football Writers Association Footballer of the Year: voted for by top football journalists and correspondents. The first winner was Billy McNeill (Celtic) in 1965.

Scottish PFA Players Player of the Year: this award is voted for by members of the Scottish Professional Footballers Association. The first winner was Derek Johnstone (Rangers) in 1978.

Scottish PFA Young Player of the Year: voted for by members of the Professional Footballers Association. For this award, players have to be 23 or under and playing in the Scottish leagues. The first award was won by Graeme Payne (Dundee Utd) in 1978.

ANNUAL AVN AWARDS FOR PORN INDUSTRY (BEST RELEASES)

	FILM	ALL-GIRL	ALL-SEX	CLASSIC DVD	GONZO	SEX COMEDY
2000	Seven Deadly Sins	The Four Finger Club 2	The Voyeur 12	The Devil in Miss Jones Parts III & IV	Ben Dover's The Booty Bandit	Double Feature!
2001	Watchers	Hard Love/ How to Fuck in High Heels	Buttwoman vs. Buttwoman	Chameleons Not the Sequel	Please! 12	M Caught in the Act
2002	Fade to Black	The Violation of Kate Frost	Buttwoman Iz Bella	The Opening of Misty Beethoven	Ben Dover's End Games	Cap'n Mongo's Porno Playhouse
2003	The Fashionistas	The Violation of Aurora Snow	Bring 'Um Young	Pretty Peaches 2	Shane's World 29	Kung-Fu Girls
2004	Heart of Darkness	Babes Illustrated 13	Fetish: The Dreamscape	Insatiable	Flesh Hunter 5	Space Nuts
2005	The Masseuse	The Connasseur	Stuntgirl	Deep Throat: Remastered	Gina Lynn's Darkside	Misty Beethoven: The Musical
2006	The New Devil in Miss Jones	Belladonna's Fucking Girls	Squealer	Ginger Lynn: The Movie	Slut Puppies	Camp Cuddly Pines Powertool Massacre
2007	Manhunters	Belladonna: No Warning	TIE: Blacklight Beauties / New Wave Hookers	Neon Nights	Chemistry	Joanna's Angels 2: Alt Throttle
2008	Layout	Girlvana 3	G for Gianna	Debbie Does Dallas: Collector's Edition	Brianna Love Is Buttwoman	Operation: Desert Stormy

The AVN (Adult Video News) Awards (held in January each year) are the most prestigious awards in the adult film industry.

Number of Awards Categories: 90–100 (every year new awards are added and some old ones are retired).

First Award Ceremony: February 1983. Scoundrels (directed by Cecil Howard) was the first winner of the Best Film award.

US MUSIC SALES TRENDS

	1997	2002	2007
CD Album	753.1 m	803.3 m	511.1 m
CD Single	66.7 m	4.5 m	2.6 m
Cassette Album	172.6 m	31.1 m	0.4 m
Cassette Single	42.2 m	-0.5 m*	-
LP/EP	2.7 m	1.7 m	1.3 m
Vinyl Single	7.5 m	4.4 m	0.6 m
Video	18.6 m	4.0 m	0.9 m
DVD	-	10.7 m	26.6 m
TOTAL PHYSICAL UNITS[1]	1,063.4 m	859.7 m	543.9 m
TOTAL PHYSICAL VALUE[1]	$12,236.8	$12,614.2	$7,985.8
Download Single	-	-	809.9 m
Download Album	-	-	42.5 m
Download Video	-	-	14.2 m
TOTAL DIGITAL UNITS2	-	-	868.4 m
TOTAL DIGITAL VALUE2	-	-	$1,257.5
TOTAL UNITS[1,2]	1,063.4 m	859.7 m	1,773.3 m
TOTAL VALUE[1,2]	$12,236.8	$12,614.2	$10,370.0

Key: *The negative figure indicates that more units of stock were returned to the record companies than were sold.

[1]Includes Super Audio CD (SACD) and DVD audio sales.

[2]Includes sales of singles and albums downloaded at self-service kiosks. Source: RIAA

HISTORY OF VIDEO GAMING IN THE UK

LIFESPAN	COMPANY	NAME	INPUT	POPULAR TITLE
1973–1978	Magnavox	Odyssey	Cartridge	Pong
1977–1981	Commodore	PET [series]	Cassette / 5.25" Disk	Space Invaders
1977–1984	Atari	2600 VCS	Cartridge	Pitfall!
1978–1985	Philips	VideoPac G7000	Cartridge	Gunfighter
1981–1989	IBM	PC8088	5.25" Disk	Space Invaders
1981–1983	Commodore	VIC 20	Cassette / 5.25" Disk	Alien
1981–1989	Acorn	BBC [series]	Cassette / 5.25" Disk	Adventure Quest
1981–1983	Sinclair Research	ZX81	Cassette	3D Monster Maze
1982–1988	Sinclair Research/ Amstrad	ZX Spectrum [series]	Cassette / 5.25" Disk	Dizzy in Wonderland
1982–1984	Atari	5200	Cartridge	Final Legacy
1983–1986	Commodore	C64 [series]	Cassette / 5.25" Disk / Cartridges	Buggy Boy
1984–1990	Sega	Master System	Cartridge	James Pond 2
1985–1994	Atari	ST [series]	3.5" Disk	Speedball 2: Brutal Deluxe
1985–1994	Nintendo	Nintendo Entertainment System (NES)	Cartridge	Super Mario Brothers
1986–1989	Atari	7800	Cartridge	Mario Brothers
1987–1992	Commodore	Amiga [series]	3.5" Disk	Stuntcar Racer
1988–1998	Sega	Mega Drive	Cartridge	Sonic the Hedgehog 2
1989–1993	Atari	Lynx (handheld)	Cartridge	Bubble Trouble
1989–1999	Nintendo	Game Boy (handheld)	Cartridge	Tetris
1989–1996	Sega	Game Gear (handheld)	Cartridge	Fifa Soccer 96
1989–1998	Nintendo	Super Nintendo Entertainment System	Cartridge	Super Mario World
1990–2001	SNK	Neo Geo	Cartridge	Metal Slug
1992–1996	Sega	Mega CD (add on for Mega Drive)	CD	Sonic CD

LIFESPAN	COMPANY	NAME	INPUT	POPULAR TITLE
1993–1996	Panasonic	3DO	CD	Crash n Burn
1993–1996	Atari	Jaguar	Cartridge	Rayman
1994–1999	SNK	Neo Geo CD	CD	Art of Fighting
1994–1995	Sega	32x (add on for Mega Drive)	Cartridge	Doom
1995–1998	Sega	Saturn	CD	Virtua Fighter 2
1995–2004	Sony	PlayStation	CD	Final Fantasy VII
1996–1998	Nintendo	64	Cartridge	Super Mario 64
1998–2001	Nintendo	Gameboy Colour (handheld)	Cartridge	Zelda: Oracle of Ages
1998–2001	SNK	Neo Geo Pocket Greyscale (handheld)	Cartridge	Pocket Tennis
1998–2001	SNK	Neo Geo Pocket Colour (handheld)	Cartridge	Bust-a-Move Pocket
1999–2001	Sega	Dreamcast	CD	Shenmue
2000–2007	Sony	PlayStation 2	CD	GTA: Vice City
2001–2004	Nintendo	GameBoy Advance (handheld)	Cartridge	Pokémon Ruby & Sapphire
2001–2007	Microsoft	X-Box	CD	Halo 2
2002–2007	Nintendo	GameCube	CD	Super Mario Sunshine
2003–2007	Nintendo	GameBoy Advance SP (handheld)	Cartridge	Yoshi's Island
2003–2005	Nokia	N-Gage (handheld)	Cartridge / Download	Snakes
2005–	Nintendo	DS (handheld)	Cartridge / Download	Nintendogs
2005–2006	Tiger – Telematics	Gizmondo (handheld)	SD Cards (1GB)	Richard Burns Rally
2005–	Sony	PSP (handheld)	Universal Media Disc	Daxter
2005–	Microsoft	Xbox 360	HD-DVD	Halo 3
2006–	Sony	PlayStation 3	Blu-ray Disc	Resistance: Fall of Man
2006–	Nintendo	Wii	Wii Optical Disc	Wii Sports

THE BIGGEST SHOPPING CENTRES IN THE UK

	NAME	LOCATION	RETAIL SPACE (m2)	OPENED
1	Bluewater	Greenhithe, Kent	149,574	1999
2	MetroCentre	Gateshead	148,459	1986
3	Merry Hill Centre	Brierley Hill, West Midlands	139,355	1985
4	Meadowhall	Sheffield	134,988	1990
5	Trafford Centre	Manchester	130,064	1998
6	Lakeside Shopping Centre	Thurrock, Essex	127,927	1990
7	The Centre: MK	Milton Keynes	120,774	1979
8	Whitgift Centre	Croydon, London	114,828	1970
9	Bullring	Birmingham	111,484	2003
10	Telford Shopping Centre	Telford	92,903	1973

Largest in the US: South Coast Plaza (opened 1967), Orange County, California – 250,838 m^2.

Source: Prudential (2004)

MOST VALUABLE
PROFESSIONAL SPORTS CONTRACTS
(BY ANNUAL EARNINGS)

	PROFESSIONAL	TEAM	SPORT	CONTRACT LENGTH (YEARS)	TOTAL VALUE (US$)	AVERAGE VALUE PER YEAR (US$)
1	Kimi Räikkönen	Ferrari	Formula 1	(2007–2009)	153 m	51 m
2	Fernando Alonso	McLaren	Formula 1	(2007–2010)	160 m	40 m
3	Michael Schumacher	Ferrari	Formula 1	(1996–1999)	124 m	31 m
4	Alex Rodriguez	New York Yankees	Baseball	(2008–2017)	275 m	27.5 m
5	Alex Rodriquez	Texas Rangers	Baseball	(2001–2010)	252 m	25.2 m
6	Johan Santana	New York Mets	Baseball	(2008–2013)	137.5 m	22.9 m
7	Rashard Lewis	Orland Magic	Basketball	(2007–2013)	126 m	21 m
8=	Manny Ramirez	Boston Red Sox	Baseball	(2001–2008)	160 m	20 m
8=	Shaquille O'Neal	Miami Heat	Basketball	(2005–2010)	100 m	20 m
10	Kobe Bryant	LA Lakers	Baseball	(2004–2011)	146.4 m	19.5 m
11	Miguel Cabrera	Detroit Tigers	Baseball	(2008–2015)	152.3 m	19.0 m
12=	Peyton Manning	Indianapolis Colts	US Football	(2005–2011)	132.5 m	18.9 m
12=	Derek Jeter	NY Yankees	Baseball	(2001–2010)	189 m	18.9 m
14	Jermaine O'Neal	Indiana Pacers	Basketball	(2003–2010)	126.5 m	18.1 m
15=	Kevin Garnett	Minnesota Timberwolves	Basketball	(1998–2005)	126 m	18 m
15=	Barry Zito	San Francisco Giants	Baseball	(2007–2013)	126 m	18 m
15=	Vernon Wells	Toronto Blue Jays	Baseball	(2008–2014)	126 m	18 m

ENGLISH DOMESTIC RUGBY UNION

SEASON	PREMIERSHIP CHAMPIONS	1ST IN THE PREMIERSHIP TABLE	CUP WINNERS	CUP RUNNERS-UP	SCORES
1987/1988	N/A	Leicester Tigers	Harlequins	Bristol	28–22
1988/1989	N/A	Bath	Bath	Leicester	10–6
1989/1990	N/A	Wasps FC	Bath	Gloucester	48–6
1990/1991	N/A	Bath	Harlequins	Northampton	25–13
1991/1992	N/A	Bath	Bath	Harlequins	15–12
1992/1993	N/A	Bath	Leicester	Harlequins	23–16
1993/1994	N/A	Bath	Bath	Leicester	21–9
1994/1995	N/A	Leicester Tigers	Bath	Wasps FC	36–16
1995/1996	N/A	Bath	Bath	Leicester	16–15
1996/1997	N/A	Wasps RFC	Leicester	Sale	9–3
1997/1998	N/A	Newcastle Falcons	Saracens	Wasps FC	48–18
1998/1999	N/A	Leicester Tigers	Wasps FC	Newcastle Falcons	29–19
1999/2000	N/A	Leicester Tigers	London Wasps	Northampton	31–23
2000/2001	N/A	Leicester Tigers	Newcastle Falcons	Harlequins	30–27
2001/2002	N/A	Leicester Tigers	London Irish	Northampton	38–7
2002/2003	London Wasps	Gloucester	Gloucester	Northampton	40–22
2003/2004	London Wasps	Bath	Newcastle	Sale	37–33
2004/2005	London Wasps	Leicester Tigers	Leeds	Bath	20–12
2005/2006	Sale Sharks	Sale Sharks	London Wasps	Llanelli Scarlets	26–10
2006/2007	Leicester Tigers	Gloucester	Leicester Tigers	Ospreys	41–35
2007/2008	London Wasps	Gloucester	Ospreys	Leicester Tigers	23–6

Pre-1987/1988 Organisation: up until season 1987/1988 there was no organised league system; all non-cup games were officially 'friendlies'.

2000/2001–2004/2005 Organisation: teams that finished 2nd and 3rd in the league played-off to determine which team would play the league winners in the Championship finale at Twickenham. The winner of this game was considered the Championship winner.

Post 2005/2006 Organisation: the play-off system was expanded to create two semi-finals (first v fourth, and second v third in the league). As before, a final match determined the overall winner.

LEAGUE SPONSORS

1987/1988–1996/1997: Courage

1997/1998–1999/2000: Allied Dunbar

2000/2001–2004/2005: Zurich

2005/2006–present: Guinness

Cup Format: from 2006 the main cup competition expanded to become an Anglo-Welsh cup.

First Cup Winners: Gloucester won the first domestic cup final (1972) beating Moseley 17–6. Amazingly, all of Gloucester's cup ties that season (against Bath, Bristol, London Welsh and Coventry) had been drawn away from home.

CUP SPONSORS

1972–1988: John Player

1989–1997: Pilkington

1998-2000: Tetley's Bitter

2002–2005: Powergen

2006–present: EDF Energy

TABLE OF CONSANGUINITY

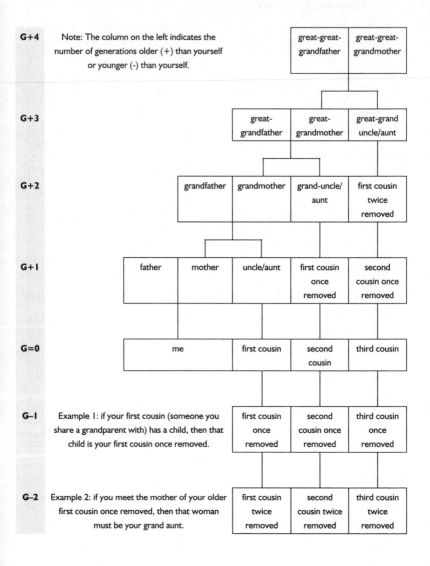

G+4 Note: The column on the left indicates the number of generations older (+) than yourself or younger (-) than yourself.			great-great-grandfather	great-great-grandmother
G+3		great-grandfather	great-grandmother	great-grand uncle/aunt
G+2	grandfather	grandmother	grand-uncle/aunt	first cousin twice removed
G+1 father	mother	uncle/aunt	first cousin once removed	second cousin once removed
G=0 me		first cousin	second cousin	third cousin
G–1 Example 1: if your first cousin (someone you share a grandparent with) has a child, then that child is your first cousin once removed.		first cousin once removed	second cousin once removed	third cousin once removed
G–2 Example 2: if you meet the mother of your older first cousin once removed, then that woman must be your grand aunt.		first cousin twice removed	second cousin twice removed	third cousin twice removed

TOP TEN MOST CAPPED HOME NATIONS FOOTBALL PLAYERS

	PLAYER	CAPS (GOALS)	PLAYER	CAPS (GOALS)
	ENGLAND		N. IRELAND	
1	Peter Shilton	125 (0)	Pat Jennings	119 (0)
2	Bobby Moore	108 (2)	Mal Donaghy	91 (0)
3	Bobby Charlton	106 (49)	Sammy McIlroy	88 (5)
4	Billy Wright	105 (3)	Keith Gillespie	79 (2)
5	David Beckham	102 (17)	Jimmy Nicholl	73 (1)
6	Bryan Robson	90 (26)	Michael Hughes	71 (5)
7	Michael Owen	89 (40)	David McCreery Maik Taylor	67 (0) 67 (0)
8	Kenny Samson	86 (1)	Nigel Worthington	66 (0)
9	Gary Neville	85 (0)	Martin O'Neill	64 (8)
10	Ray Wilkins	84 (3)	Gerry Armstrong	63 (12)
	SCOTLAND		WALES	
1	Kenny Dalglish	102 (30)	Neville Southall	92 (0)
2	Jim Leighton	91 (0)	Gary Speed	85 (7)
3	Alex McLeish	77 (0)	Dean Saunders	75 (22)
4	Paul McStay	76 (9)	Peter Nicholas Ian Rush	73 (2) 73 (28)
5	Tom Boyd	72 (1)	Mark Hughes Joey Jones	72 (16) 72 (1)
6	Christian Dailly	67 (6)	Ivor Allchurch	68 (23)
7	Willie Miller	65 (1)	Brian Flynn	66 (7)
8	Danny McGrain	62 (0)	Andy Melville	65 (3)
9	Richard Gough Ally McCoist David Weir	61 (6) 61 (19) 61 (1)	Ryan Giggs	64 (13)
10	John Collins	58 (12)	Dave Phillips	62 (0)

Stats correct up to end of June 2008.

CAF AFRICAN CUP OF NATIONS

YEAR	WINNER	RUNNERS-UP	SCORE	HOST(S)	TOP SCORER(S)
1957	Egypt	Ethiopia	4–0	Sudan	El-Attar (Egypt) 5
1959	Egypt	Sudan	2–1	Egypt	Al-Gohari (Egypt) 3
1962	Ethiopia	Egypt	4–2 (aet)	Ethiopia	Badawi (Egypt); Worku (Ethiopia) 5
1963	Ghana	Sudan	3–0	Ghana	El Shazly (Egypt) 6
1965	Ghana	Tunisia	3–2 (aet)	Tunisia	Acheampong (Ghana); Osei Kofi (Ghana); Mangle (Ivory Coast) 3
1968	DR Congo	Ghana	1–0	Ethiopia	Pokou (Ivory Coast) 6
1970	Sudan	Ghana	1–0	Sudan	Pokou (Ivory Coast) 8
1972	Congo	Mali	3–2	Cameroon	Keita (Mali) 5
1974	Zaire	Zambia	2–2 (2–0 replay)	Egypt	Ndaye (Zaire) 9
1976	Morocco	Guinea	No Final	Ethiopia	N'jo Léa' (Guinea) 4
1978	Ghana	Uganda	2–0	Ghana	Omondi (Uganda); Ofriye (Ghana); Odegbami (Nigeria) 3
1980	Nigeria	Algeria	3–0	Nigeria	Abyad Labied (Morocco); Odegbami (Nigeria) 3
1982	Ghana	Libya	1–1 (7–6 pens)	Libya	Alhassan (Ghana) 4
1984	Cameroon	Nigeria	3–1	Ivory Coast	Abou Zeid (Egypt) 4
1986	Egypt	Cameroon	0–0 (5–4 pens)	Egypt	Milla (Cameroon) 4
1988	Cameroon	Nigeria	1–0	Morocco	Abdelhamid (Egypt); Belloumi (Algeria); Milla (Cameroon); Traore (Ivory Coast) 2
1990	Algeria	Nigeria	1–0	Algeria	Menad (Algeria) 4
1992	Ivory Coast	Ghana	0–0 (11–10 pens)	Senegal	Yekini (Nigeria) 4
1994	Nigeria	Zambia	2–1	Tunisia	Yekini (Nigeria) 5
1996	South Africa	Tunisia	2–0	South Africa	Williams (South Africa); Bwalya (Zambia) 5

YEAR	WINNER	RUNNERS-UP	SCORE	HOST(S)	TOP SCORER(S)
1998	Egypt	South Africa	2–0	Burkino Faso	Hassan (Egypt); McCarthy (South Africa) 7
2000	Cameroon	Nigeria	2–2 (4–3 pens)	Ghana / Nigeria	Bartlett (South Africa) 5
2002	Cameroon	Senegal	0–0 (3–2 pens)	Mali	Mboma (Cameroon); Olembé (Cameroon); Aghahowa (Nigeria) 3
2004	Tunisia	Morocco	2–1	Tunisia	Mboma (Cameroon); Kanouté (Mali); Okocha (Nigeria); Mokhtari (Morocco); Dos Santos (Tunisia) 4
2006	Egypt	Ivory Coast	0–0 (4–2 pens)	Egypt	Eto'o (Cameroon) 5
2008	Egypt	Cameroon	1–0	Ghana	Eto'o (Cameroon) 5
2010				Angola	

Governing Body: Confédération Africaine de Football (CAF); founded – 1957; HQ – Cairo, Egypt.

Competitors: the 53 CAF member nations play qualifying rounds to reduce the final tournament size to 16 teams.

Most Titles: Egypt (5); Cameroon, Ghana (4); Congo DR, Nigeria (2); Algeria, Congo, Cote d'Ivoire, Ethiopia, Morocco, South Africa, Sudan, Tunisia (1).

PREMATURE ROCK 'N' ROLL DEATHS

DATE	NAME	BAND	CAUSE	AGE
1/1/1953	Hank Williams	-	Accidental overdose	29
25/12/1954	Johnny Ace	-	Suicide	25
3/2/1959	Buddy Holly	The Crickets	Plane crash	22
13/5/1959	Richie Valens	-	Plane crash	17
10/4/1962	Stuart Sutcliffe	The Beatles	Brain haemorrhage	21
27/8/1967	Brian Epstein	The Beatles (manager of)	Accidental overdose	32
10/12/1967	Otis Redding	-	Plane crash	26
3/7/1969	Brian Jones	The Rolling Stones	Death by misadventure (drowned in swimming pool)	27
18/9/70	Jimi Hendrix	-	Inconclusive (choked on vomit after drinking wine and taking sleeping pills)	27
4/10/1970	Janis Joplin	Big Brother and the Holding Company	Overdose	27
3/7/1971	Jim Morrison	The Doors	Inconclusive (drowned in bath – probable heroin overdose)	27
14/7/1973	Clarence White	The Byrds	Manslaughter	29
17/8/1973	Paul Williams	The Temptations	Suicide	34
29/7/1974	Cass Elliot	The Mamas & Papas	Heart failure	32
25/11/1974	Nick Drake	-	Overdose	26
22/2/1976	Florence Ballard	The Supremes	Coronary thrombosis	32
4/12/1976	Tommy Bolin	Deep Purple	Overdose	25
16/8/1977	Elvis Presley	-	Overdose	42
16/9/1977	Marc Bolan	T.Rex	Car crash	29
7/9/1978	Keith Moon	The Who	Suicide	32
2/2/1979	Sid Vicious	The Sex Pistols	Heroin overdose	21

DATE	NAME	BAND	CAUSE	AGE
27/9/1979	Jimmy McCulloch	Wings	Heroin overdose	26
19/2/1980	Bon Scott	AC/DC	Alcohol poisoning	33
18/5/1980	Ian Curtis	Joy Division	Suicide	23
25/9/1980	John Bonham	Led Zeppelin	Asphyxiation	32
8/12/1980	John Lennon	The Beatles	Murdered	40
15/2/1981	Mike Bloomfield	-	Heroin overdose	37
11/5/1981	Bob Marley	The Wailers	Tumour	36
16/6/1982	James Honeyman-Scott	The Pretenders	Cocaine-induced heart failure	25
4/2/1983	Karen Carpenter	The Carpenters	Heart problems due to anorexia	32
14/4/1983	Pete Farndon	The Pretenders	Overdose	30
28/12/1983	Dennis Wilson	The Beach Boys	Drowning	39
1/4/1984	Marvin Gaye	-	Manslaughter	44
4/1/1986	Phil Lynott	Thin Lizzy	Accidental overdose	36
27/9/1986	Cliff Burton	Metallica	Traffic accident whilst touring	24
25/6/1988	Hillel Slovak	Red Hot Chilli Peppers	Overdose	26
26/7/1990	Brent Mydland	Grateful Dead	Overdose	37
8/1/1991	Steve Clark	Def Leppard	Accidental overdose	30
24/11/1991	Freddie Mercury	Queen	Complications of AIDS	45
5/4/1994	Kurt Cobain	Nirvana	Suicide	27
16/4/1994	Kristen Pfaff	Janitor Joe; Hoel; Palm	Overdose (heroin)	27
12/7/1996	Jonathon Melvoin	Smashing Pumpkins	Overdose (heroin)	34
22/11/1997	Michael Hutchence	INXS	Suicide* (hanging)	37
2/2/1999	David McComb	The Triffids	Heart failure (partly due to heroin and alcohol abuse)	36

DATE	NAME	BAND	CAUSE	AGE
18/12/2000	**Kirsty MacColl**	The Pogues	Speedboat accident	41
7/1/2002	**Jon Lee**	Feeder	Suicide	33
5/4/2002	**Layne Staley**	Alice in Chains	Overdose	34

* = Although the coroner officially concluded that the death was a suicide, his family suggest that factors including the absence of a suicide note lead them to believe that the death was more likely to be accidental – possibly a result of autoerotic asphyxiation.

COCA-COLA VS. PEPSI IN THE UK

VARIETY	THE COCA-COLA COMPANY	PEPSICO
Cola	Coca-Cola	Pepsi
Diet Cola	Diet Coke	Diet Pepsi
Sugar-free Cola	Coca-Cola Zero	Pepsi Max
Cherry Flavoured Cola	Cherry Coke	Wild Cherry Pepsi
Lemonade	Sprite	7up
Still Orange Juice	Minute Maid	Tropicana
Fizzy Orange	Fanta	-
Sports Drink	Powerade	Gatorade
Water	-	Aquafina

The Coca-Cola Company. Founded: 1892. HQ: Atlanta, Georgia, US.

PepsiCo. Founded: 1902. HQ: Purchase, New York, US.

ICC CRICKET WORLD CUP

YEAR	HOST(S)	FINAL VENUE (CAPACITY)	WINNER	RUNNERS-UP	RESULT
1975	England	Lord's, London (30,000)	West Indies 291 for 8 (60 overs)	Australia 274 all out (58.4 overs)	West Indies won by 17 runs
1979	England	Lord's, London (30,000)	West Indies 286 for 9 (60 overs)	England 191 all out (50 overs)	West Indies won by 92 runs
1983	England	Lord's, London (30,000)	India 183 all out (54.4 overs)	West Indies 140 all out (52 overs)	India won by 43 runs
1987	India/ Pakistan	Eden Gardens, Calcutta (90,000)	Australia 253 for 5 (50 overs)	England 246 for 8 (50 overs)	Australia won by 7 runs
1992	Australia/ New Zealand	MCG, Melbourne (96,000)	Pakistan 249 for 6 (50 overs)	England 227 all out (49.2 overs)	Pakistan won by 22 runs
1996	India/ Pakistan/ Sri Lanka	Gaddafi Stadium, Lahore (25,000)	Sri Lanka 245 for 3 (46.2 overs)	Australia 241 for 7 (50 overs)	Sri Lanka won by 7 wickets
1999	England	Lord's, London (30,000)	Australia 133 for 2 (20.1 overs)	Pakistan 132 all out (39 overs)	Australia won by 8 wickets
2003	South Africa	Wanderers, Johannesburg (27,000)	Australia 359 for 2 (50 overs)	India 234 all out (39.2 overs)	Australia won by 125 runs
2007	West Indies	Kensington Oval, Bridgetown (28,000)	Australia 281 for 4 (38 overs)	Sri Lanka 215 for 8 (36 overs)	Australia won by 53 runs
2011	India/ Pakistan/ Sri Lanka/ Bangladesh	Wankhede Stadium, Mumbai (40,000)			

Governing Body: International Cricket Council; founded – 1909; HQ – Dubai, UAE. Highest Team Score: 413/5 – India vs Bermuda (2007). Lowest Team Score: 36 – Canada vs Sri Lanka (2003). Most Indivdual Runs: 1796 – Sachin Tendulkar (India) 1992–2007. Most Individual Runs in a Game: 188 – Gary Kirsten (for SA v UAE) 1996. Most Individual Wickets: 71 – Glenn McGrath (Australia) 1996–2007. Most Individual Catches: 24 – Ricky Ponting (Aus) 1996–2007.

MTV EUROPE MUSIC AWARDS

	LOCATION	BEST MALE	BEST FEMALE	BEST GROUP	BEST SONG	BEST ALBUM
1994	Brandenburger Tor, Berlin	Bryan Adams	Mariah Carey	Take That	'7 Seconds' (Youssou N'Dour & Nina Cherry)	n/a
1995	Le Zenith, Paris	Michael Jackson	Björk	U2	'Zombie' (The Cranberries)	n/a
1996	Alexandra Palace, London	George Michael	Alanis Morissette	Oasis	'Wonderwall' (Oasis)	n/a
1997	Ahoy Rotterdam, Rotterdam	Jon Bon Jovi	Janet Jackson	Spice Girls	'MMMBop' (Hanson)	n/a
1998	Fila Forum, Milan	Robbie Williams	Madonna	Spice Girls	'Torn' (Natalie Imbruglia)	Ray of Light (Madonna)
1999	Point Depot, Dublin	Will Smith	Britney Spears	Backstreet Boys	'Baby, One More Time' (Britney Spears)	By Request (Boyzone)
2000	Stockholm Globe Arena, Stockholm	Ricky Martin	Madonna	Backstreet Boys	'Rock DJ' (Robbie Williams)	The Marshall Mathers LP (Eminem)
2001	Festhalle Frankfurt, Frankfurt	Robbie Williams	Jennifer Lopez	Limp Bizkit	'Clint Eastwood' (Gorillaz)	Chocolate Starfish (Limp Bizkit)
2002	Palau Sant Jordi, Barcelona	Eminem	Jennifer Lopez	Linkin Park	'Get the Party Started' (Pink)	The Eminem Show (Eminem)
2003	Ocean Terminal, Edinburgh	Justin Timberlake	Christina Aguilera	Coldplay	'Crazy in Love' (Beyoncé ft Jay-Z)	Justified (Justin Timberlake)
2004	Tor di Valle, Rome	Usher	Britney Spears	Outkast	'Hey Ya!' (Outkast)	Confessions (Usher)

	LOCATION	BEST MALE	BEST FEMALE	BEST GROUP	BEST SONG	BEST ALBUM
2005	Pavilhão Atlântico, Lisbon	Robbie Williams	Shakira	Gorillaz	'Speed of Sound' (Coldplay)	American Idiot (Green Day)
2006	Bella Center, Copenhagen	Justin Timberlake	Christina Aguilera	Depeche Mode	'Crazy' (Gnarls Barkley)	Stadium Arcadium (Red Hot Chilli Peppers)
2007	Olympiahalle, Munich	Avril Lavigne**	Linkin Park	Bedwetters***	Loose (Nelly Furtado)	

Key: ** = Male and female solo awards were merged in 2007. *** = Award changed to 'New Sounds of Europe' in 2007.

Ceremony Date: end of October/beginning of November. Most Awards: Eminem (9, including one as part of D12); Britney Spears, Justin Timberlake, Muse, The Prodigy (5); Backstreet Boys, Coldplay, Linkin Park, Madonna, Red Hot Chilli Peppers, Robbie Williams (4).

GRAND SLAM TENNIS TOURNAMENTS

GRAND SLAM	DATE	SINCE	VENUE	SURFACE
Australian Open	Mid January	1905	Melbourne Park, Melbourne. Final: Rod Laver Arena (15,000)	Hard (Plexicushion – Blue)
French Open	Mid May	1891	Roland Garros, Paris. Final: Court Philippe Chatrier (15,000)	Clay (Red)
Wimbledon	Late June	1877	Wimbledon, London. Final: Centre Court (15,000)	Grass
US Open	Late August	1881	Flushing Meadows, New York. Final: Arthur Ashe Stadium (22,500)	Hard (DecoTurf – Blue)

In 1968 the French Open became the first to be opened up to professionals, followed by Wimbledon and the US Open that year and the Australian Open in 1969.

FERMENTED AND
DISTILLED ALCOHOLS

KEY INGREDIENT	NAME	MAIN PRODUCTION AREA(S)	TYPICAL % ABV	EXAMPLE BRANDS
GRAIN				
Barley	Beer (ale) (F)	Worldwide	3–6%	John Smith's
Barley	Irish whiskey (D)	Ireland	40–50%	Jameson
Barley	Scotch whiskey (D)	Scotland	40–50%	The Famous Grouse
Maize	Bourbon whiskey (D)	Kentucky, US	37.5%	Jim Beam
Maize	Tennessee whiskey (D)	Tennessee, US	40%	Jack Daniel's
Rye	Rye beer (F)	Scandinavia, US	5%	Founders Red's Rye
Rye	Rye bread drink (Kvass) (F)	Eastern European	0–4%	Kbac
Sorghum	Sorghum beer (bil-bil) (F)	Africa	1–8%	Chibuku
Sorghum	Baijiu (D)	China	40–60%	Kweichow Moutai
Wheat	Wheat beer (weißbier / witbier) (F)	Germany / Belgium	4–5%	Hoegaarden Witbier
FRUIT				
Apple	Cider (F)	Worldwide	3–9%	Magner's
Apple	Apple brandy (D)	US / Calvados, France	40%	Laird's Applejack
Apricot	Brandy (barack) (D)	Hungary	30–40%	Kecskemeti Barack
Apricot	Apricot brandy (palinka / slivovitz) (D)	Hungary, Romania / Slavic nations	40%	Zwack Nemes
Grape	Red and white wine (F)	Europe, Australia, South Africa, South America, US	10–14%	Jacob's Creek

KEY INGREDIENT	NAME	MAIN PRODUCTION AREA(S)	TYPICAL % ABV	EXAMPLE BRANDS
Grape	Brandy (Armagnac / Cognac (D)	Armagnac, France / Cognac, France	40%	Martell Cognac
Juniper berry	Gin (D)	Netherlands, England	35–40%	Gordon's
VEGETABLE				
Agave	Pulque (F)	Central America	2–8%	Del Razo
Agave	Mezcal (D)	Oaxaca, Mexico	40–50%	Scorpion Silver
Agave	Tequila (D)	Tequila, Mexico	38–40%	Sierra Silver
Potato	Aquavit / brennivin (D)	Scandinavia / Iceland	40%	Linie
Potato	Snaps (D)	Denmark, Sweden	35%	The First
Potato	Vodka (D)	Russia, Eastern Europe	35–50%	Smirnoff
Sugarcane	Batavia arrack (D)	Indonesia	35%	Batavia Arrack Van Oosten
Sugarcane	Cachaça (aquadente / guaro / seco) (D)	Brazil / Costa Rica / Panama	38–48%	Cachaça Brazil
Sugarcane	Rum (light / golden / dark) (D)	Caribbean; Guyana	30–40%	Bacardi Superior
OTHER				
Angostura bark	Bark distillate (D)	Trinidad & Tobago	45%	Angostura Bitters
Anise	Absinthe (D)	Central Europe	45–75%	Un Emile
Anise	Arak (D)	Middle East	45–80%	Arak Rayan
Coconut	Arrack (D)	South East Asia	40–45%	Lambanog
Honey	Honey wine (mead) (F)	Germany; UK	15%	Barenmet
Honey	Vodka (krupnik) (D)	Lithuania Poland	40–50%	Sobieski Krupnik

KEY INGREDIENT	NAME	MAIN PRODUCTION AREA(S)	TYPICAL % ABV	EXAMPLE BRANDS
Milk	Kumis (F)	North Central Asia	0.7–2.5%	Kymbic
Milk	Blaand (F)	Scandinavia, Scotland	10–15%	Fallachan

Key: (D) = distilled; (F) = fermented. * = Although in English it's usually referred to as 'rice wine', sake is technically a rice beer since it is brewed with multiple fermentations. True wine is made with a single fermentation of the plant juices (except sparkling wine, which is fermented twice).

Whisky v Whiskey: In Canada, Japan, Scotland, and Wales, whisky is spelled without the 'e'. Whiskey from Ireland and the US is spelled with the 'e'. Whisky originated in Ireland but nowadays Scotland has many more distilleries. The 'e' was added by Irish and American distillers in 1870 to differentiate their whiskey from the growing amount of (at the time) lower quality Scottish brands.

AGE WORLD RECORDS

RECORD	NAME	NATION	LIFESPAN	AGE AT DEATH
Oldest Ever Woman	Jeanne Louise Calment	France	21/2/1875– 4/8/1997	122 y 164 d
Oldest Ever Man	Shigechiyo Izumi	Japan	29/6/1865– 21/2/1986	120 y 237 d
Oldest Living Woman	Edna Parker	US	20/4/1893– present	n/a
Oldest Living Man	Tomoji Tanabe	Japan	18/9/1895– present	n/a
Oldest Ever British Woman	Charlotte Hughes	England	1/8/1887– 17/3/1993	115 y 228 d
Oldest Ever British Man	John Evans	Wales	19/8/1877– 10/6/1990	112 y 295 d
Oldest Living British Woman	Florrie Baldwin	England	31/3/1896– present	n/a
Oldest Living British Man	Henry Allingham	England	6/6/1896– present	n/a

ALL-TIME TOP GROSSING STEVEN SPIELBERG FILMS

FILM	YEAR	BUDGET ($)	WORLD BOX OFFICE ($)
Jurassic Park	1993	63 m	920 m
E.T.	1982	11 m	757 m
Jurassic Park: The Lost World	1997	73 m	614.4 m
War of the Worlds	2005	128 m	591.4 m
Indiana Jones and the Last Crusade	1989	39 m	494.8 m
Saving Private Ryan	1998	70 m	479.3 m
Jaws	1975	12 m	471 m
Indiana Jones and the Raiders of the Lost Ark	1981	20 m	384 m
Minority Report	2002	102 m	342 m
Catch Me if You Can	2002	52 m	336.3 m
Indiana Jones and the Temple of Doom	1984	28 m	333.1 m
Schindler's List	1993	25 m	321.2 m
Hook	1991	70 m	300.9 m
Close Encounters of the Third Kind	1977	20 m	300 m

LIQUEURS

KEY INGREDIENT	NAME	MAIN PRODUCTION AREA(S)	TYPICAL % ABV	EXAMPLE BRANDS
Almond	Amaretto	Italy	40%	Disaronno Originale
Anise	Ouzo	Greece	40%	No. 12
Anise	Pastis	France	40–45%	Pastis Anilou
Anise	Pernod	France	40%	Pernod
Anise	Sambuca	Italy	38%	Sambuca Oro Borghetti
Anise	Sassolino	Modena, Italy	40%	Sassolino Stampa
Artichoke	Amaro (carciofo)	Italy	17%	Cynar
Cashew	Fenny	Goa, India	42%	Big Boss
Cinnamon	Tentura	Patras, Greece	25%	Vantana Tentura Especial
Cinnamon	Goldschläger	Switzerland	43.5%	Goldschläger
Cocoa bean	Crème de Cacao	France, Netherlands	20–25%	Godiva Liqueur
Coconut	Coconut rum	Barbados	21%	Malibu
Corsican mint	Crème de Menthe	France	20–25%	Gabriel Boudier
Cream	Whiskey liqueur	Ireland	17%	Baileys
Grapes	Amaro (vermouth)	Italy	40–60%	Martini Extra Dry
Grapes	Fortified wine (Madeira / Marsala / Port / Sherry)	Madeira, Portugal / Sicily, Italy / Douro Valley, Portugal / Jerez, Spain	16–20%	Croft Orginal
Hazelnut	Frangelico	Canale, Italy	24%	Frangelico
Honey	Bärenjäger	Germany	30–45%	Barenjager
Lemon zest	Limoncello	Southern Italy	30%	Villa Massa
Orange peel	Triple sec	Saumur, France	30–40%	Cointreau
Pomegranate	Grenadine	France, UK	0–4%	Monin Grenadine

KEY INGREDIENT	NAME	MAIN PRODUCTION AREA(S)	TYPICAL % ABV	EXAMPLE BRANDS
Sloe berries	Patxaran / Sloe Gin	Spain / UK	25–30%	Plymouth Sloe Gin
Truffles	Amaro (tartufo)	Umbria, Italy	30%	Antica Vale Amaro Al Tartufo
Vanilla	Galliano	Tuscany, Italy	30%	Galliano

'BIG FOUR' INDIAN SNAKES

SNAKE	BINOMIAL NAME (GENUS, SPECIES)	AVERAGE LENGTH	EFFECTS OF BEING BITTEN
Common Krait	*Bungarus caeruleus*	100 cm	Little or no pain. Severe abdominal cramps, followed by progressive muscle paralysis. Causes more fatalities per bite than any of the other 'big four'.
Indian Cobra	*Naja naja*	100 cm	Muscle paralysis, possibly leading to respiratory failure or cardiac arrest.
Russell's Viper	*Daboia russelii*	120 cm	Severe pain, swelling and blistering and bleeding gums. Can cause death within 15 mins. Responsible for over 6,000 deaths per year in Asia.
Saw-Scaled Viper	*Echis carinatus*	55 cm	Pain, blistering around the bite area, internal bleeding, nosebleeds and oliguria (decreased production of urine).

KONAMI'S FOOTBALL TITLES

EDITION	UK COVER	COMMENTARY	PLATFORM(S)	UK RELEASE
International Superstar Soccer 64	CGI of a player wearing a white strip about to kick a ball toward viewpoint	Tony Gubba	N64	1/6/1997
International Superstar Soccer 98	Black and white photo of Fabrizio Ravanelli and Paul Ince staring at each other	Tony Gubba	N64; Game Boy Colour	22/9/1998
ISS Pro Evolution	CGI of red textured background and a player wearing white heading a ball towards viewpoint	Martin Williams and Terry Butcher	PlayStation	26/5/2000
International Superstar Soccer 2000	Two players wearing white celebrating a goal	Chris James and Terry Butcher	N64	29/9/2000
International Superstar Soccer	CGI of a player in an England strip being challenged for the ball by a player in a France strip	John Champion	PlayStation; (Game Boy Advance)	24/11/2000; (23/11/2001)
ISS Pro Evolution 2	CGI of a player running toward viewpoint, wearing all blue, with a green textured background	Chris James and Terry Butcher	PlayStation	23/3/2001
Pro Evolution Soccer 1	CGI of a player in grey running toward viewpoint and a grey textured background	Chris James and Terry Butcher	PS2; (PlayStation)	23/11/2001; (15/2/2002)
Pro Evolution Soccer 2	CGI upper body of a player wearing an England strip	Trevor Brooking and Peter Brackley	PlayStation; (PS2)	15/2/2002; (25/10/2002)
International Superstar Soccer 2	Close-up shot of an Umbro ball being kicked by an Umbro boot	Jon Champion and Mark Lawrenson	GameCube; (Xbox); ((PS2))	3/5/2002; (10/5/2002); ((17/5/2002))

EDITION	UK COVER	COMMENTARY	PLATFORM(S)	UK RELEASE
International Superstar Soccer 3	Close-up action shot of a player about to kick the ball away from the outstretched hands of a goalkeeper	Jon Champion and Mark Lawrenson	PS2; (GameCube); ((PC))	28/3/2003; (4/7/2003); ((23/8/2005))
Pro Evolution Soccer 3	Pierluigi Collina	Trevor Brooking and Peter Brackley	PS2; (PC)	17/10/2003; (21/11/2003)
Pro Evolution Soccer 4	Thierry Henry, Pierluigi Collina and Francesco Totti	Trevor Brooking and Peter Brackley	PS2; Xbox; (PC)	26/11/2004; (2/12/2004)
Pro Evolution Soccer 5	John Terry & Thierry Henry	Trevor Brooking and Peter Brackley	PC; PS2; PSP; Xbox	21/10/2005
Pro Evolution Soccer 6	Adriano and John Terry	Trevor Brooking and Peter Brackley	PC; PS2; PSP; Xbox 360; (Nintendo DS; PSP)	27/10/2006; (9/2/2007)
Pro Evolution Soccer 2008	Michael Owen and Cristiano Ronaldo	Jon Champion and Mark Lawrenson	PC; PS2; PS3; Xbox 360; (PSP); ((Nintendo Wii))	26/10/2007; (1/3/2008); ((28/3/2008))
Pro Evolution Soccer 2009	Lionel Messi	(unconfirmed)	(unconfirmed)	17/10/2008

Previous Konami Football Games: Konami Hyper Soccer (NES) 1991; International Superstar Soccer (SNES) 1994; International Superstar Soccer Deluxe (SNES, PlayStation, Sega Mega Drive) 1995.

UK/US MUSIC RECORD SALES CERTIFICATIONS

	SILVER	GOLD	PLATINUM	MULTI-PLATINUM	DIAMOND
Singles in the UK	>200,000	>400,000	>600,000	>1.2 m	n/a
Singles in the US	n/a	>500,000	>1 m	> 2 m	>10 m
Albums in the UK	>60,000	>100,000	>300,000	>600,000	n/a
Albums in the US	n/a	>500,000	>1 m	>2 m	>10 m

As defined by the BPI (British Phonographic Industry), and the RIAA (Recording Industry Association of America).

MTV MOVIE AWARDS

YEAR	BEST MOVIE	BEST MALE PERFORMANCE	BEST FEMALE PERFORMANCE
1992	Terminator 2: Judgement Day	Arnold Schwarzenegger (Terminator 2: Judgement Day)	Linda Hamilton (Terminator 2: Judgement Day)
1993	A Few Good Men	Denzel Washington (Malcolm X)	Sharon Stone (Basic Instinct)
1994	Menace II Society	Tom Hanks (Philadelphia)	Janet Jackson (Poetic Justice)
1995	Pulp Fiction	Brad Pitt (Interview with the Vampire)	Sandra Bullock (Speed)
1996	Se7en	Jim Carrey (Ace Ventura: Pet Detective)	Alicia Silverstone (Clueless)
1997	Scream	Tom Cruise (Jerry Maguire)	Claire Danes (Romeo + Juliet)
1998	Titanic	Leonardo Di Caprio (Titanic)	Neve Campbell (Scream 2)
1999	There's Something About Mary	Jim Carrey (The Truman Show)	Cameron Diaz (There's Something About Mary)
2000	The Matrix	Keanu Reeves (The Matrix)	Sarah Michelle Gellar (Cruel Intentions)
2001	Gladiator	Tom Cruise (Mission: Impossible II)	Julia Roberts (Erin Brockovich)
2002	The Lord of the Rings: The Fellowship of the Ring	Will Smith (Ali)	Nicole Kidman (Moulin Rouge)
2003	The Lord of the Rings: The Two Towers	Eminem (8 Mile)	Kirsten Dunst (Spider-Man)
2004	The Lord of the Rings: The Return of the King	Johnny Depp (Pirates of the Caribbean: The Curse of the Black Pearl)	Uma Thurman (Kill Bill Vol. 1)
2005	Napoleon Dynamite	Leonardo Di Caprio (The Aviator)	Lindsay Lohan (Mean Girls)
2006	Wedding Crashers	Jake Gyllenhaal (Brokeback Mountain)*	Hayden Christensen (Star Wars Episode III: Revenge of the Sith)

YEAR	BEST MOVIE	BEST MALE PERFORMANCE	BEST FEMALE PERFORMANCE
2007	*Pirates of the Caribbean: Dead Man's Chest*	Johnny Depp (*Pirates of the Caribbean: Dead Man's Chest*)*	Jack Nicholson (*The Departed*)
2008	*Transformers*	Will Smith (*I Am Legend*)	Ellen Page (*Juno*)

*The 2006 and 2007 'Best Male Performance' and 'Best Female Performance' awards were merged.

Voting: nominees are chosen by a special panel at the award production company (Tenth Planet Productions); winners are decided by the general public. Currently voting is done through the MTV website. Production: up until 2007 the show was taped, cut into the correct sequence and broadcast several days later. Since 2007 the ceremony has moved towards the more traditional live broadcast model. The ceremony is held in June each year.

MULTI-EVENT ATHLETICS

NO. OF EVENTS	CONTEST	SPECIFICS (DISTANCES/TARGETS CAN VARY BETWEEN COMPETITIONS)	COUNTRIES WITH MOST OLYMPIC GOLDS
2	**Biathlon**	Cross-country skiing; .22 calibre rifle shooting	Russia/Soviet Union (16); Germany (14); Norway (9)
3	**Duathlon**	Running; Cycling	n/a
3	**Triathlon**	Swimming; Cycling; Running	Australia (1); Austria (1); Canada (1); Germany (1); New Zealand (1); Switzerland (1)
5	**Modern Pentathlon**	Swimming; Horse riding and jumping; Cross-country running; Fencing; Pistol shooting	Sweden (9); Hungary (5); Russia (3); Germany (2); Poland (2)
7	**Heptathlon***	Javelin; Hurdles; High jump; Long jump; Shot put; Sprint; 800 metres	US (2); Australia (1); Sweden (1); Syria (1); UK (1); Ukraine (1)
10	**Decathlon****	Long jump; High jump; Pole vault; Shot put; Discus; Javelin; 110 metre hurdles; 100 metres; 400 metres; 1,500 metres	US (12); Czechoslovakia/Czech Rep (2); East Germany/Germany (2); UK (2)

Key: * = Female event; ** = Male event.

APPROXIMATE
SUNRISE/SUNSET TIMES

1ST OF MONTH	LONDON (51N 0W/E)			EDINBURGH (56N 3W)		
	RISE	SET	TOTAL SUNLIGHT	RISE	SET	TOTAL SUNLIGHT
JANUARY	08:05	16:00	7 h 55 m	08:45	15:50	8 h 5 m
FEBRUARY	07:40	16:50	9 h 10 m	08:10	16:50	8 h 40 m
MARCH	06:45	17:40	10 h 55 m	07:05	17:50	10 h 45 m
APRIL	06:35	19:35	13 h	06:45	19:50	13 h 5 m
MAY	05:35	20:25	14 h 50 m	05:30	20:55	15 h 25 m
JUNE	04:50	21:10	16 h 20 m	04:35	21:50	16 h 15 m
JULY	04:50	21:20	16 h 30 m	04:35	22:00	17 h 25 m
AUGUST	05:25	20:50	15 h 25 m	05:20	21:20	16 h
SEPTEMBER	06:15	19:45	13 h 30 m	06:20	20:05	13 h 45 m
OCTOBER	07:00	18:40	11 h 40 m	07:20	18:50	11 h 30 m
NOVEMBER	06:55	16:35	9 h 40 m	07:20	16:35	9 h 15 m
DECEMBER	07:45	15:55	8 h 10 m	08:20	15:45	7 h 25 m

FACTS:

1. No matter where you are on earth, there will be a total of 182.5 days of daylight, and 182.5 days of night during the course of a 365-day cycle.

2. In the extremes of latitude in the north and the south, winter days are extremely short and summer days extremely long.

3. Winter/summer months in the southern/northern hemisphere are June, July and August.

4. Winter/summer months in the northern/southern hemisphere are December, January and February.

5. On any given day in the northern hemisphere, the number of daylight hours is exactly equal to the number of night hours at the same latitude in the southern hemisphere, and vice versa.

6. On the equator there are twelve hours of daylight each day, all year round. The sun rises between 6 and 7 a.m. and sets between 6 and 7 p.m. every day of the year.

7. Northern hemisphere summer solstice (around June 21 each year) – on this day there will 24 hours of daylight in the northern polar circle, and 24 hours of darkness in the southern polar circle.

8. Southern hemisphere summer solstice (around September 21 each year) – On this day there will be 24 hours of daylight in the southern polar circle, and 24 hours of darkness in the northern polar circle.

TOP 12 LARGEST UK NIGHTCLUBS

CLUB	LOCATION	CAPACITY	OPENED	REVERED PAST PARTIES/ CLUB NIGHTS
The Fridge	Brixton, London	1,500	1985	Pendragon; Love Muscle; Escape From Samsara
The Arches	Glasgow	2,000	1991	Colours; Inside Out; Octopussy
Ministry of Sound	Southwark, London	1,200	1991	Milkshake; Saturday Sessions; Smoove
Nation	Liverpool	3,000	1992	Cream; Godskitchen; Yo-Yo
Turnmills	Clerkenwell, London	1,000	1992	Gallery; Trade
The End	Bloomsbury, London	1,200	1995	Underwater; Discotec; Milk 'n' 2 Sugars
Fabric	Smithfield, London	1,600	1999	DTPM; Night of Tru Playaz; Tyrant
Scala	King's Cross, London	1,100	1999	Popstarz
AIR	Birmingham	1,500	2000	Godskitchen; Helter Skelter Rave; Polysexual
Kelly's	Portrush, NI	1,200	2000	Lush!
Gatecrasher One	Sheffield	1,500	2003	Gatecrasher; Hed Kandy; Slummin
Digital	Newcastle	1,400	2004	Supafly; Wax:On; Shindig

Smallest Nightclub in the UK: Miniscule of Sound, London. Opened in 1998 and, including the DJ, has a capacity of just 14.

World's Biggest Nightclub: Privilege Nightclub, San Rafael, Ibiza. The club is home to the famous Manumission club nights and can hold up to 10,000 people. The main room is the size of an aircraft hangar; it has a 25 m high ceiling and includes a large party swimming pool.

SPORTING DEATHS PER 100,000 US PARTICIPANTS

Horse Racing	128
Sky Diving	123
Hang Gliding	56
Mountaineering	51
Scuba Diving	11
Motorcycle Racing	7
College Football	3
Professional Boxing	1

From the 1984 study by R. J. McCunney and P. K. Russo entitled 'Brain Injuries In Boxing'. The study aimed to show that boxing was a safer sport than perceived. Taking actual death totals into account, this was proved to be true. But sceptics maintained that even if the risk of death was lower the risk of chronic brain injury was still unacceptably high.

'BIG FOUR' MAJOR RECORD LABELS

RECORD LABEL	WORLD MARKET SHARE (2006)	BRIT AWARD WINNERS (2008)	PARENT COMPANY
Universal Music Group	32%	Take That; Mika; Kanye West	Vivendi (Fra)
Sony BMG	27%	Mark Ronson; Adele	Sony Corp (50%) (Jap); Bertelsmann AG (50%) (Ger)
Warner Music Group	18%	Arctic Monkeys	Warner Music Group Corp (US)
EMI	10%	Kylie Minogue; Foo Fighters	EMI Group (UK)

ALL-TIME GRAND SLAM TENNIS RECORDS

	AUSTRALIAN OPEN	FRENCH OPEN	WIMBLEDON	US OPEN
FIRST MEN'S SINGLES CHAMPIONS[1]	Rodney Heath (1905)	René Lacoste (1904)	Spencer Gore (1877)	Richard Sears (1881)
FIRST LADIES' SINGLES CHAMPIONS[1]	Margaret Molesworth (1922)	Suzanne Lenglen (1925)	Maud Watson (1884)	Ellen Hansell (1887)
LAST NATIVE MALE WINNERS	Mark Edmondson (1976)	Yannick Noah (1983)	Fred Perry (1936)	Andy Roddick (2003)
LAST NATIVE FEMALE WINNERS	Christine O'Neill (1978)	Mary Pierce (2000)	Virginia Wade (1977)	Serena Williams (2002)
MOST TIMES MEN'S SINGLES CHAMPIONS[2]	Andre Agassi (US) 4	Björn Borg (Swe) 6	Pete Sampras (US) 7	Jimmy Connors (US); Pete Sampras (US) 5
MOST TIMES LADIES' SINGLES CHAMPIONS[2]	M. Smith Court (Aus); Monica Seles (Yug); Steffi Graf (Ger) 4	Chris Evert (US) 7	Martina Navrátilová (Cze) 9	Chris Evert (US) 7
MEN'S SINGLES WINNERS PRIZES[3]	Norman Brookes Challenge Cup + AU$1.22m	Coupe des Mousquetaires + €940,000	The Gentlemen's Singles Trophy + £700,000	The US Open Men's Singles Trophy + US$1.4m
LADIES' SINGLES WINNERS TROPHIES & PRIZE MONEYS[3]	Daphne Akhurst Memorial Cup + AU$1.22m	Coupe Suzanne Lenglen + €940,000	Venus Rosewater Dish + £700,000	The US Open Ladies Singles Trophy + US$1.4m

Key: [1] = All winners of the first-ever championships were native to the host nation.

[2] = Most times champions are only for the modern 'open' era (post 1967).

[3] = Prize values are for the 2007 tournaments.

GLOSSARY OF JAPANESE SEX INDUSTRY TERMS

Ashikoki	Footjob - using the feet to perform a sexual action on the recipient's penis.
Bukkake	Ejaculation onto the face or body of a sexual partner. Often performed in groups.
Cosplay	Sexual role-play using costumes.
Futanari	Anime portraying female-looking characters that have male genitals.
Fuzoku	Sexual culture.
Gokkun	A genre of pornography in which women swallow semen.
Gravure idol	Glamour model.
H (ecchi)	A prefix for something with a pornographic element – e.g. H anime, H computer game. The letter H is an abbreviation for the word 'hentai', meaning perversion.
Hadaka	Japanese word for 'nude'.
Image club	A brothel that offers a 'menu' of women in various different uniforms/costumes.
No-pan kissa	A cafe where the waitresses wear short skirts and no underwear.
Nyotaimori	Eating sashimi or sushi off a woman's body.
Omorashi	A fetish for the sensation of having a full bladder or being attracted to someone else who has.
Panchira	Seeing up women's skirts.
Pink salon	A brothel specialising in oral sex in booths.
Seme	Literally 'top'. Having the more dominant role during sex. Opposite of 'uke'.
Shibari	Bondage.
Soapland	A brothel where men can bathe with female sex workers.
Sumata	Non-penetrative male-female 'dry' sex.
Tamakeri	A fetish involving being kicked in the testicles.
Tekoki	Handjob.
Telekura	Telephone dating services that often act as a front for arranging meetings with prostitutes.
Uke	Literally 'bottom'. Having the less dominant role during sex. Opposite of 'seme'.

Wakamezake	Drinking alcohol from the trianglular 'basin' between a woman's closed thighs and body.
Yuri	Lesbian comics or anime.
Zenra	Genre of pornography in which women perform everyday tasks completely nude.

THE FIVE MAJOR GLOBAL BEER FIRMS

BREWERY	HQ	TURNOVER	EMPLOYEES	VOLUME (hl)	MAIN BRANDS SOLD IN THE UK
InBev	Leuven, Belgium	£11.4 bn	86,000	271 m	Stella Artois (Bel); Brahma (Bra); Beck's (Ger); Leffe (Bel); Hoegaarden (Bel); Staropramen (Cze)
SABMiller	London, UK	£9.3 bn	67,000	216 m	Miller (US); Peroni (Ita); Nastro Azzurro (Ita); Castle (SA)
Anheuser-Busch	St Louis, US	£9.5 bn	31,000	161 m	Budweiser (US); Busch (US); Michelob (US)
Heineken	Amsterdam, Netherlands	£9.9 bn	54,000	119.8 m	Heineken (Net); Amstel (Net); Murphy's (Ire)
Carlsberg Group	Copenhagen, Denmark	£5.5 bn	31,000	115.2 m	Carlsberg (Den); Special Brew (UK); Tetley (UK); Chang (Tha); Holsten (Ger); Skol (Bra)

All figures relate to 2007. 1 hectolitre = 176 UK pints. Countries in brackets denote nation of origination.

FIVE/SIX NATIONS RUGBY UNION CHAMPIONSHIPS ALL-TIME TABLE

NATION	HOME STADIUM	CAPACITY	CHAMPIONSHIP WINS	TRIPLE CROWNS	GRAND SLAMS	OTHERS
England	Twickenham, London	82,000	25 (10)	23	12	62 (14) CC; 14 MT
Wales	Millennium Stadium, Cardiff	72,500	24 (11)	20	10	-
France	Stade de France, Paris	80,000	16 (7)	N/A	8	2 GG
Scotland	Murrayfield, Edinburgh	67,500	14 (8)	10	3	39 (14) CC; 11 (1) MQ
Ireland	Lansdowne Road, Dublin	49,250	10 (8)	9	1	8 (1) MQ; 7 MT
Italy	Stadio Flaminio, Rome	25,000	0	N/A	0	0 GG

Figures relate to matches up to the end of the 2008 Championship, and detail outright wins, additional shared wins are in brackets.

Key: Championship Win = Trophy for finishing top of the Championship table; Triple Crown = Inter British Isles trophy, collected by any team who beats all three of the other British Isles teams in a Championship season; Grand Slam = no trophy. Term used for when a team wins all of their Championship matches; CC = Calcutta Cup. Trophy awarded (since 1879) to the winner of the match between Scotland and England; CQ = Centenary Quaich. A Celtic drinking vessel trophy awarded (since 1989) to the winner of the annual Ireland-Scotland match; GG = Giuseppe Garibaldi Trophy. Trophy awarded (since 2007) to the winner of the annual match between France and Italy; MT = Millennium Trophy. Trophy awarded (since 2000) to the winner of the match between Ireland and England; Wooden Spoon = no actual object exists, but the team that finishes bottom of the Championship table is jokingly said to have 'won the wooden spoon'.

History: the Championship began as the 'Home Championship' in 1883 (England, Ireland, Scotland, Wales). It became the 'Five Nations Championship' in 1910 when France joined (France was expelled in 1930 after being accused of professionalism, but readmitted in 1939). When Italy joined in 2000, the tournament became the 'Six Nations Championship'.

UK SPORTS STADIA

	STADIUM	UEFA STATUS	CITY	TEAM	CAPACITY ^
1	Wembley	5*	London	England (Football)	90,000 (2)
2	Twickenham	n/a	London	England (Rugby)	82,000 (7)
3	Old Trafford	5*	Manchester	Manchester United FC	76,000 (14)
4	Millennium Stadium	5*	Cardiff	Wales (Rugby/Football)	72,500 (15)
5	Murrayfield	n/a	Edinburgh	Scotland (Rugby)	67,500 (21)
6	Parkhead	none	Glasgow	Celtic FC	60,800 (26)
7	Emirates	none	London	Arsenal FC	60,400 (27)
8	St James' Park	none	Newcastle	Newcastle United FC	52,300 (42)
9	Hampden Park	5*	Glasgow	Scotland (Football)	52,000 (45)
10	Ibrox	5*	Glasgow	Rangers FC	50,400 (50)
11	Stadium of Light	none	Sunderland	Sunderland FC	49,000 (60)
12	City of Manchester Stadium	4*	Manchester	Manchester City FC	47,700 (61)
13	Anfield	4*	Liverpool	Liverpool FC	45,400 (67)
14	Villa Park	4*	Birmingham	Aston Villa FC	42,500 (72)
15	Stamford Bridge	none	London	Chelsea FC	42,100 (75)

Position in overall Europe-wide capacity rankings (2007) in brackets.

Stadium Etymology: the word 'stadium' derives from the Latin form of a Greek word that was originally used to describe a measure of length. In ancient Greek games arenas, oval running tracks were one 'stadium' long. One 'stadium' was equal to 600 Greek feet (about 185 metres).

UEFA Status: At the beginning of the 2008/2009 football season, there were 27 5-Star, and 14 4-Star stadia on UEFA's Elite Stadium List. Only 5-Star stadia may bid to host finals of the Champions League, UEFA Cup, and European Championships; 4-Star stadia may bid to host the final of the UEFA Cup. Amongst other factors, to be on the list, stadia must have: (a) a pitch of 105m x 68m (entirely fence free), (b) sufficient space around the pitch for at least 18 TV cameras, (c) sufficient room behind the goals for at least 150 photographers, (d) first-rate dressing rooms for both teams of equal size and furnishings, (e) parking space for 400 buses, and secure parking for at least 150 VIP's, (f) a minimum of 1,500 VIP seats, (g) at least 40 covered TV and radio commentary positions, (h) a pressroom with at least 100 seats, (i) floodlights with minimum luminosity of 1,400 lux, along with an instantaneous back-up power system in case of power failure, and (j) 5-Star stadia must have a minimum capacity of 50,000, and 4-Star stadia must have a minimum capacity of 30,000.

EUROPEAN FOOTBALL LEAGUE
TOP GOALSCORERS

	CHAMPIONS LEAGUE	ENGLAND	FRANCE	GERMANY
2000/2001	Raúl (Real Madrid) 7	Hasselbaink (Chelsea) 23	Anderson (Lyon) 22	Barbarez (Hamburg); Sand (Schalke) 22
2001/2002	Van Nistelrooy (Man Utd) 10	Henry (Arsenal) 24	Cissé (Auxerre) 26; Pauleta (Bordeaux) 22	Amoroso (Dortmund); Max (1860 Munich) 18
2002/2003	Van Nistelrooy (Man Utd) 12	Van Nistelrooy (Man Utd) 25	Nonda (Monaco) 26	Christiansen (Bochum); Elber (B Munich) 21
2003/2004	Morientes (Monaco) 9	Henry (Arsenal) 30	Cissé (Auxerre) 26	Ailton (W Bremen) 28
2004/2005	Van Nistelrooy (Man Utd) 7	Henry (Arsenal) 25	Frei (Rennes) 20	Mintal (Nurnberg) 24
2005/2006	Shevchenko (Milan) 9	Henry (Arsenal) 27	Pauleta (PSG) 21	Klose (W Bremen) 25
2006/2007	Kaká (Milan) 10	Drogba (Chelsea) 20	Pauleta (PSG) 15	Gekas (Bochum) 20
2007/2008	Ronaldo (Man Utd) 8	Ronaldo (Man Utd) 31	Benzema (Lyon) 20	Toni (Bayern Munich) 24

	ITALY	N'LANDS	SCOTLAND	SPAIN
2000/2001	Crespo (Lazio) 26	Kežman (PSV) 24	Larsson (Celtic) 35	Raúl (Real Madrid) 24
2001/2002	Hübner (Piacenza); Trezeguet (Juventus) 24	Van Hooijdonk (Feyenoord) 24	Larsson (Celtic) 29	Tristán (Deportivo) 20
2002/2003	Vieri (Inter) 24	Kežman (PSV) 35	Larsson (Celtic) 28	Makaay (Deportivo) 29
2003/2004	Shevchenko (Milan) 24	Kežman (PSV) 31	Larsson (Celtic) 30	Ronaldo (Real Madrid) 24
2004/2005	Lucarelli (Livorno); Gilardino (Parma) 24	Kuyt (Feyenoord) 29	Hartson (Celtic) 25	Forlan (Villarreal) 25
2005/2006	Toni (Fiorentina) 31	Huntelaar (Heerenveen / Ajax) 33	Hartson (Celtic) 18	Eto'o (Barcelona) 26
2006/2007	Totti (Roma) 26	Alves (Heerenveen) 34	Boyd (Rangers) 20	Van Nistelrooy (Real Madrid) 25
2007/2008	Del Piero (Juventus) 21	Huntelaar (Ajax) 33	McDonald (Celtic) 25	Güiza (Real Mallorca) 27

MOST PREVALENT FOOTBALL
LEAGUE CUP WINNERS

	CLUB	LAST WIN	WINS	RUNNERS-UP
1	Liverpool	2003	7	2
2	Aston Villa	1996	5	2
3	Nottingham Forest	1990	4	2
4=	Chelsea	2007	4	2
4=	Tottenham Hotspur	2008	4	2
6	Leicester City	2000	3	2
7	Manchester United	2006	2	4
8=	Arsenal	1993	2	4
8=	Norwich City	1985	2	2
8=	Manchester City	1976	2	1
8=	Wolverhampton Wanderers	1980	2	0

Inception: 1960/1961. Sponsors: 1961/1962 to 1985/1986 – Milk Marketing Board; 1986/1987 to 1989-1990 – Littlewoods; 1990/1991 to 1991/1992 – Rumbelows; 1992/1993 to 1997/1998 – Coca-Cola; 1998/1999 to 2002/2003 – Worthington; 2003/2004 to present – Carling. Most Finals Without Winning: Bolton Wanderers, Everton, West Ham (2).

BEAUFORT WIND SCALE AND SAFFIR-SIMPSON HURRICANE SCALE

SCALE	DESCRIPTION	WIND SPEED (mph)	VISUAL SIGNS ON LAND
0	Calm	<1	Smoke drifts vertically.
1	Light Air	1–3	Smoke drifts with air but no breeze is felt.
2	Light Breeze	4–7	Leaves rustle.
3	Gentle Breeze	8–12	Leaves and small twigs move constantly.
4	Moderate Breeze	13–18	Small branches move; dust swirls.
5	Fresh Breeze	19–24	Small trees sway.
6	Strong Breeze	25–31	Large branches in motion; leaves fly through the air.
7	Near Gale	32–38	Large trees in motion; walking is more difficult.
8	Gale	39–46	Twigs break off trees; walking is significantly more difficult.
9	Strong Gale	47–54	Slates blow off roofs.
10	Storm	55–63	Trees uprooted; considerable structural damage.
11	Violent storm	64–73	Moderate to severe structural damage.
12 +	Hurricane (cat. 1)	74–95	Unanchored caravans tip over.
	Hurricane (cat. 2)	96–110	Considerable damage to anything poorly constructed.
	Hurricane (cat. 3)	111–130	Gable end roofs peel off.
	Hurricane (cat. 4)	131–155	Most house roofs are blown off completely.
	Hurricane (cat. 5)	>155	Widespread levelling of structures, starting with the smallest, and those with the weakest foundations.

The Beaufort Wind Scale was devised in 1805 by Irish hydrographer Francis Beaufort.

The Saffir-Simpson Hurricane Scale is used for most western hemisphere +74 mph sustained wind speed storms, and was devised in 1971 by US civil engineer Herbert Saffir and US meteorologist Bob Simpson.

CAR MARQUES SOLD IN THE UK

MARQUE	NAME DERIVED FROM:	EST'D	ORIGIN	TYPE	OWNER
Alfa Romeo	Anonima Lombarda Fabbrica Automobili (Lombard Automobile Factory) and 1916 owner Nicola Romeo.	1907	Italy	3	Fiat
Aston Martin	Aston Clinton hill climb race and co-founder, Lionel Martin.	1913	UK	5	Ford
Audi	Latin equivalent of founder's name, August Horch (horch means 'listen' in German).	1899	Germany	3	VW
Bentley	Founder, Walter Owen Bentley.	1919	UK	4	VW
BMW	Bayerische Motoren Werke (Bavarian Motor Works).	1916	Germany	4	BMW
Bugatti	Founder, Ettore Bugatti.	1898	France	5	VW
Cadillac	Seventeenth-century French explorer Antoine Laumet de La Mothe, sieur de Cadillac, founder of Detroit in 1701.	1902	US	4	GM
Chevrolet	Co-founder, Louis Chevrolet.	1911	US	2	GM
Chrysler	Founder, Walter Percy Chrysler.	1925	US	3	D-C
Citroën	Founder, André-Gustave Citroën.	1919	France	2	PSA
Dacia	Dacia was the name of an ancient country in Eastern Europe (roughly equivalent to Romania).	1968	Romania	1	Renault
Daewoo	Daewoo is Korean for 'Great Universe'.	1967	S Korea	1	GM
Daihatsu	Daihatsu is formed from the first Chinese character for the southern Japanese city of Osaka, and the first character for the word 'engine manufacturer'.	1907	Japan	1	Toyota
Ferrari	Founder, Enzo Ferrari.	1929	Italy	5	Fiat
Fiat	Fabbrica Italiana Automobili Torino (Italian Car Factory of Turin).	1899	Italy	2	Fiat
Ford	Founder, Henry Ford.	1903	US	2	Ford
Honda	Founder, Honda Soichiro.	1946	Japan	2	Honda
Hummer	Shortening of 'high mobility multipurpose wheeled vehicle'.	1979	US	6	GM

MARQUE	NAME DERIVED FROM:	EST'D	ORIGIN	TYPE	OWNER
Hyundai	Hyundai means 'modernity' in Korean.	1947	S. Korea	2	Hyundai
Jaguar	Due to the negative (but unlinked) connotions with the initials of Swallow Sidecar Company, the company rebranded to Jaguar after WW2.	1922	UK	4	Ford
Jeep	Originally solely used in the military, the brand derives from its original use - GP (general purpose) army vehicle.	1940	US	6	D-C
Kia	Kia translates to 'Arising from Asia' in Korean.	1944	S. Korea	2	Hyundai
Lamborghini	Founder, Ferruccio Lamborghini.	1963	Italy	5	VW
Lancia	Founder, Vincenzo Lancia.	1906	Italy	3	Fiat
Land Rover	Rover means 'roamer' and the Land Rover was the 1947 all-terrain model of the Rover company.	1947	UK	6	Ford
Lexus	Luxury EXport to the US.	1989	US	4	Toyota
Maserati	Founding brothers Alfieri, Bindo, Carlo, Ettore, Ernesto and Mario Maserati.	1914	Italy	5	Fiat
Mazda	Anglicisation of the founder's name, Jujiro Matsuda.	1920	Japan	2	Mazda
Mercedes-Benz	Benz & Cie, founded by Karl Benz, merged with Daimler Motoren Gesellschaft (DMG), founded by Gottlieb Daimler.	1926	Germany	4	D-C
Mini	So-called because of it's compact size.	1959	UK	3	BMW
Mitsubishi	'Mitsu' means 'three' and 'bishi' means 'water chestnut' (diamond shape) in Japanese.	1917	Japan	3	Mitsubishi
Nissan	Through the abbreviation of its parent company name 'Nippon Sangyo'. Its sister brand, Datsun, was discontinued in 1986.	1925	Japan	2	Nissan
Peugeot	Founder, Armand Peugeot.	1889	France	2	PSA
Porsche	Founder, Ferdinand Porsche.	1931	Germany	5	Porsche

MARQUE	NAME DERIVED FROM:	EST'D	ORIGIN	TYPE	OWNER
Renault	Founding brothers Fernand, Louis and Marcel Renault.	1898	France	2	Renault
Rolls-Royce	Co-founders, Henry Royce, and C.S. Rolls.	1904	UK	4	BMW
Saab	Svenska Aeroplan AB (Swedish Aeroplane Limited Company); AB stands for the Swedish term for 'limited company', aktibolaget.	1937	Sweden	3	GM
SEAT	Sociedad Española de Automóviles de Turismo (Spanish Corporation of Touring Cars).	1950	Spain	2	VW
Skoda	Named after the Bohemian founder of Skoda Works, Emil Skoda.	1905	Czech Rep	2	VW
Smart	The original project was supported by the Swatch company; the name is an acronym – Swatch Mercedes ART.	1994	Germany	0	D-C
Suzuki	Founder, Michio Suzuki.	1909	Japan	2	Suzuki
Toyota	From base company, Toyota Loom Works (founder, Sakichi Toyoda).	1933	Japan	2	Toyota
Vauxhall	Named after the location of the founding company's factory, Vauxhall Iron Works's, Vauxhall, London.	1903	UK	2	GM
Volkswagen	Means 'people's car' in German.	1937	Germany	2	VW
Volvo	Volvo is Latin for 'I roll/turn'.	1927	Sweden	4	Ford

Key: 0 = Micro Car; 1 = Entry Level; 2 = Popular Market; 3 = Semi-luxury; 4 = Luxury; 5 = Performance; 6 = 4x4.

BMW = Bayerische Motoren Werke (Bavarian Motor Works); D-C = Daimler-Chrysler; GM = General Motors; PSA = Peugeot Société Anonyme Peugeot Citroën; VW = Volkswagen (People's Car).

FIFA WORLD CUP PLAYER OF THE TOURNAMENT AWARD WINNERS

	GOLDEN BALL	SILVER BALL	BRONZE BALL
1982 Spain	Paolo Rossi (Italy)	Falcão (Brazil)	Karl-Heinz Rummenigge (Germany)
1986 Mexico	Diego Maradona (Argentina)	Harald Schumacher (Germany)	Preben Elkjær (Denmark)
1990 Italy	Salvatore Schillaci (Italy)	Lothar Matthäus (Germany)	Diego Maradona (Argentina)
1994 US	Romário (Brazil)	Roberto Baggio (Italy)	Hristo Stoichkov (Bulgaria)
1998 France	Ronaldo (Brazil)	Davor Šuker (Croatia)	Lilian Thuram (France)
2002 Japan/Korea	Oliver Kahn (Germany)	Ronaldo (Brazil)	Hong Myung-Bo (South Korea)
2006 Germany	Zinedine Zidane (France)	Fabio Cannavaro (Italy)	Andrea Pirlo (Italy)

Voting: A shortlist is drawn up by the FIFA technical committee and voting is made by selected media representatives.

TOBACCO PRODUCTION

	NATION	ANNUAL TONNAGE
1	China	2,750,000
2	Brazil	905,000
3	India	550,000
4	US	338,000
5	Argentina	164,000
6	Indonesia	141,000
7	Turkey	140,000
8	Greece	126,000
9	Italy	120,000
10	Pakistan	113,000

Figures relate to unmanufactured tobaccos produced in 2006.

Source: Food and Agricultural Organisation of the United Nations

IRB RUGBY WORLD CUP

YEAR	HOST(S)	WINNER	CAPTAIN	COACH	SCORE	RUNNERS-UP
1987	New Zealand and Australia	New Zealand	David Kirk	Brian Lochore	29–9	France
1991	England (also Ire, Fra)	Australia	Nick Farr-Jones	Bob Dwyer	12–6	England
1995	South Africa	South Africa	Francois Pienaar	Kitch Christie	15–12	New Zealand
1999	Wales (also Eng, Ire, Sco, Fra)	Australia	John Eales	Rod Macqueen	35–12	France
2003	Australia	England	Martin Johnson	Clive Woodward	20–17	Australia
2007	France (also Sco, Wal)	South Africa	John Smit	Jake White	15–6	England

Governing Body: International Rugby Board; formed – 1886; headquarters – Dublin, Ireland.

Most Points in a Match: 145–17 – New Zealand vs Japan (4/6/1995).

Most Individual Points: 243 – Jonny Wilkinson (Eng) 1999, 2003, 2007.

Most Individual Tries: 15 – Jonah Lomu (NZ) 1995, 1999.

Most Individual Conversions: 39 – Gavin Hastings (Sco) 1987, 1991, 1995.

Most Individual Penalties: 53 – Jonny Wilkinson (Eng) 1999, 2003, 2007.

Most Individual Drop Goals: 13 – Jonny Wilkinson (Eng) 1999, 2003, 2007.

Most Appearances: 22 – Jason Leonard (Eng) 1991, 1995, 1999, 2003.

MEN'S MAGAZINES

MAGAZINE	FACT	LAUNCH	OWNER
Playboy	First cover model – Marilyn Monroe	1953	Playboy Enterprises
Penthouse	First UK adult magazine to show pubic hair – April 1970	1965	Penthouse Media Group
Mayfair	Banned in Ireland 1968–2003	1966	Paul Raymond
Arena	Self-stated target market – 'black-collar' workers	1986	EMAP
FHM	28 different national editions	1987	EMAP
GQ	Originally launched in the US in 1957 as 'Apparel Arts'	1989	Condé Nast
Esquire	First cover model – Brigitte Bardot	1991	NMC (Hearst Corp)
Loaded	First cover model – Gary Oldman	1994	IPC
Maxim	First cover model – Lisa Snowdon	1995	Dennis Publishing
Men's Health	An annual competition allows one reader to become a cover model	1995	Rodale
Stuff	First cover model – Gabrielle Richens	1996	Haymarket
Bizarre	First cover model – Teri Hatcher	1997	Dennis Publishing
Men's Fitness	Original UK tagline – 'Get Fit or Feel Sh*t'	1999	Dennis Publishing
Boys Toys	Tagline – 'Because You Only Live Once'	1999	Freestyle
Nuts	First cover model – Kelly Brook	2004	IPC
Zoo	First cover model – Nell McAndrew	2004	EMAP

MAJOR GOLF CHAMPIONSHIPS

YEAR	MASTERS (APRIL)	US OPEN (JUNE)	THE OPEN (JULY)	US PGA (AUGUST)
1990	Nick Faldo (Eng)	Hale Irwin	Nick Faldo (Eng)	Wayne Grady (Aus)
1991	Ian Woosnam (Wal)	Payne Stewart	Ian Baker-Finch (Aus)	John Daly
1992	Fred Couples	Tom Kite	Nick Faldo (Eng)	Nick Price (Zim)
1993	Bernhard Langer (Ger)	Lee Janzen	Greg Norman (Aus)	Paul Azinger
1994	José María Olazábal (Spa)	Ernie Els (SA)	Nick Price (Zim)	Nick Price (Zim)
1995	Ben Crenshaw	Corey Pavin	John Daly	Steve Elkington (Aus)
1996	Nick Faldo (Eng)	Steve Jones	Tom Lehman	Mark Brooks
1997	Tiger Woods	Ernie Els (SA)	Justin Leonard	Davis Love III
1998	Mark O'Meara	Lee Janzen	Mark O'Meara	Vijay Singh (Fij)
1999	José María Olazábal (Spa)	Payne Stewart	Paul Lawrie (Sco)	Tiger Woods
2000	Vijay Singh (Fij)	Tiger Woods	Tiger Woods	Tiger Woods
2001	Tiger Woods	Retief Goosen	David Duval	David Toms
2002	Tiger Woods	Tiger Woods	Ernie Els (SA)	Rich Beem
2003	Mike Weir (Can)	Jim Furyk	Ben Curtis	Shaun Micheel
2004	Phil Mickelson	Retief Goosen (SA)	Todd Hamilton	Vijay Singh (Fij)
2005	Tiger Woods	Michael Campbell (NZ)	Tiger Woods	Phil Mickelson
2006	Phil Mickelson	Geoff Ogilvy (Aus)	Tiger Woods	Tiger Woods
2007	Zach Johnson	Ángel Cabrera (Arg)	Pádraig Harrington (Ire)	Tiger Woods
2008	Trevor Immelman (SA)	Tiger Woods	Pádraig Harrington (Ire)	Pádraig Harrington (Ire)

Nationality: US (unless stated).

Masters Venue: Augusta National Golf Club, Augusta, Georgia, US.

Masters First Winner: Horton Smith (US) 1934.

Masters Youngest Winner: Tiger Woods (1997) 21 years 3 months 14 days.

Masters Oldest Winner: Jack Nicklaus (1986) 46 years 2 months 23 days.

US Open Venue: the tournament venue alternates between courses all over the US.

US Open First Winner: Horace Rawlins (England) 1895. The tournament was held at Newport, Rhode Island.

US Open Youngest Winner: John McDermott (1911) 19 years, 10 months, 14 days.

US Open Oldest Winner: Hale Irwin (1990) 45 years, 0 months 15 days.

The Open Venue: the tournament venue alternates between a current rota of nine links courses (five in Scotland, four in England). Years ending 0 or 5 – Old Course St Andrews, Fife; years ending 1, 3, 6, or 8 – England; years ending 2, 4, 7, 9 – Scotland. The English courses are – Royal St George's, Kent; Royal Birkdale, Merseyside; Royal Lytham & St Annes, Lancashire; and Royal Liverpool, Merseyside. The Scottish courses (apart from St Andrews) are – Carnoustie, Angus; Muirfield, East Lothian; Royal Troon, South Ayrshire; Turnberyy, South Ayrshire.

The Open First Winner: Willie Park Snr (Scotland) 1860. The tournament was held at Prestwick Golf Club, South Ayrshire.

The Open Youngest Winner: Young Tom Morris (1868) 17 years, 5 months, 8 days.

The Open Oldest Winner: Old Tom Morris (1867) 46 years 3 months 7 days.

US PGA Venue: the tournament venue alternates between courses all over the US.

US PGA First Winner: Jim Barnes (US) 1916: the original tournament was held at Siwanoy Country Club, Bronxville, New York.

US PGA Youngest Winner: Gene Sarazen (1922) 20 years, 5 months, 22 days.

US PGA Oldest Winner: Julius Boros (1968) 48 years, 4 months 18 days.

AMERICAN FOOTBALL SUPER BOWL

YEAR	WINNER	SCORE	RUNNERS-UP	FINAL VENUE	MVP
1990	San Francisco 49ers	55–10	Denver Broncos	Louisiana Superdome, New Orleans	Joe Montana
1991	New York Giants	20–19	Buffalo Bills	Tampa Stadium, Tampa	Ottis Anderson
1992	Washington Redskins	37–24	Buffalo Bills	Metrodome, Minneapolis	Mark Rypien
1993	Dallas Cowboys	52–17	Buffalo Bills	Rose Bowl, Pasadena	Troy Aikman
1994	Dallas Cowboys	30–13	Buffalo Bills	Georgia Dome, Atlanta	Emmitt Smith
1995	San Francisco 49ers	49–26	San Diego Chargers	Joe Robbie Stadium, Miami	Steve Young
1996	Dallas Cowboys	27–17	Pittsburgh Steelers	Sun Devil Stadium, Tempe	Larry Brown
1997	Green Bay Packers	35–21	New England Patriots	Louisiana Superdome, New Orleans	Desmond Howard
1998	Denver Broncos	31–24	Green Bay Packers	Qualcomm Stadium, San Diego	Terrell Davis
1999	Denver Broncos	34–19	Atlanta Falcons	Pro Player Stadium, Miami	John Elway
2000	St. Louis Rams	23–16	Tennessee Titans	Georgia Dome, Atlanta	Kurt Warner
2001	Baltimore Ravens	34–7	New York Giants	Raymond James Stadium, Atlanta	Ray Lewis
2002	New England Patriots	20–17	St. Louis Rams	Louisiana Superdome, New Orleans	Tom Brady
2003	Tampa Bay Buccaneers	48–21	Oakland Raiders	Qualcomm Stadium, San Diego	Dexter Jackson
2004	New England Patriots	32–29	Carolina Panthers	Reliant Stadium, Houston	Tom Brady
2005	New England Patriots	24–21	Philadelphia Eagles	Alltel Stadium, Jacksonville	Deion Branch

YEAR	WINNER	SCORE	RUNNERS UP	FINAL VENUE	MVP
2006	Pittsburgh Steelers	21–10	Seattle Seahawks	Ford Field, Detroit	Hines Ward
2007	Indianapolis Colts	29–17	Chicago Bears	Dolphin Stadium, Miami	Peyton Manning
2008	New York Giants	17–14	New England Patriots	University of Phoenix Stadium, Phoenix	Eli Manning

Winners from National Football Conference: 1990–1997; 2000; 2003; 2008.

Winners from American Football Conference: 1998–1999; 2001–2002; 2004–2007.

Super Bowl I: 1967, Green Bay Packers (NFL) beat Kansas City Chiefs (AFL) 35–10 at Los Angeles Memorial Coliseum, LA. Half-time show entertainment was provided by Arizona University and Michigan University bands.

Most Times Winners: five - Pittsburgh Steelers (AFL/C); Dallas Cowboys (NFL/C); San Francisco 49ers (NFL/C).

Most Times Losers: four – Denver Broncos (AFC/L); Buffalo Bills (AFC/L); Minnesota Vikings (NFC/L).

Most Valuable Player (MVP): The Pete Rozelle Trophy is awarded to the player voted by the media panel (80 per cent weight) and fans (20 per cent) as being the outstanding player of each final. Only once has the award gone to a player from the losing team – Chuck Howley of the Dallas Cowboys in Super Bowl V (1971).

Most Times MVP Winner: Three – Joe Montana (1982, 1985, 1990) San Francisco 49ers.

Most MVP Wins by Position: Quarterbacks (20); Running Backs (7); Wide Receivers (5).

The Title: the title of the play-off game between the champions of the American and National leagues came from AFL founder Lamar Hunt. Hunt's half-joking inspiration was the football shaped 'Super Ball' toy his daughter had been playing with. The name became a popular nickname for the 'AFL-NFL World Championship Game' and was made the official title in 1969.

TOP TEN WINE PRODUCERS

	WINE PRODUCTION		PERCENTAGE OF WORLD EXPORT MARKET	
	NATION	**ANNUAL LITRES (MILLION)**	**NATION**	**PERCENTAGE OF VALUE**
1	France	5.349 m	France	34.01
2	Italy	4.712 m	Italy	18.03
3	Spain	3.644 m	Australia	10.24
4	US	2.232 m	Spain	9.18
5	Argentina	1.540 m	Chile	4.13
6	Australia	1.410 m	Germany	3.25
7	China	1.400 m	Portugal	3.17
8	South Africa	1.013 m	US	3.00
9	Chile	977 m	South Africa	2.90
10	Germany	892 m	New Zealand	1.61

Production figures relate to 2006; export market figures relate to 2005.

Source: Food and Agricultural Organisation of the United Nations

INTERNATIONAL RUGBY BOARD (IRB) AWARDS

YEAR	PLAYER	TEAM	COACH	SEVENS TEAM
2001	Keith Wood (Ire)	Australia	Rod Macqueen (Aus)	no award
2002	Fabien Galthié (Fra)	France	Bernard Laporte (Fra)	New Zealand
2003	Jonny Wilkinson (Eng)	England	Clive Woodward (Eng)	New Zealand
2004	Schalk Burger (SA)	South Africa	Jake White (SA)	New Zealand
2005	Daniel Carter (NZ)	New Zealand	Graham Henry (NZ)	Fiji
2006	Richie McCaw (NZ)	New Zealand	Graham Henry (NZ)	Fiji
2007	Bryan Habana (SA)	South Africa	Jake White (SA)	New Zealand

Current Judges: Jonathan Davies (Wal) 32 caps; Fabien Galthié (Fra) 64 caps; Will Greenwood (Eng) 55 caps; Gavin Hastings (Sco) 61 caps; Michael Jones (NZ) 55 caps; Dan Lyle (US); Federico Méndez (Arg) 74 caps; Francois Pienaar (SA) 29 caps; and Keith Wood (Ire) 58 caps.

ALL-TIME TOP FIVE FOOTBALL TRANSFER FEES (BY POSITION)

NAME	TEAM	FEE
GOALKEEPERS		
Buffon (Ita)	Parma > Juventus	£32.6 m (2001)
Toldo (Ita)	Fiorentina > Inter	£18 m (2001)
Peruzzi (Ita)	Inter > Lazio	£11.2 m (2000)
Gordon (Sco)	Hearts > Sunderland	£9 m (2007)
Barthez (Fra)	Monaco > Man Utd	£7.8 m (2000)
DEFENDERS		
Ferdinand (Eng)	Leeds Utd > Man Utd	£29.1 m (2002)
Thuram (Fra)	Parma > Juventus	£22 m (2001)
Pepe (Bra)	Porto > Real Madrid	£20.3 m (2007)
Carvalho (Por)	Porto > Chelsea	£19.85 m (2004)
Nesta (Ita)	Lazio > Milan	£19.12 m (2002)
MIDFIELDERS		
Zidane (Fra)	Juventus > Real Madrid	£45.62 m (2001)
Figo (Por)	Barcelona > Real Madrid	£37 m (2000)
Mendieta (Spa)	Valencia > Lazio	£29 m (2001)
Veron (Arg)	Lazio > Man Utd	£28.1 m (2001)
Rui Costa (Por)	Fiorentina > Milan	£28 m (2001)
FORWARDS*		
Crespo (Arg)	Parma > Lazio	£35.5 m (2001)
Robinho (Bra)	Real Madrid > Man City	£32.5 m (2008)
Vieri (Ita)	Lazio > Inter	£32 m (1999)
Berbatov (Bul)	Tottenham > Man Utd	£30.75 m (2008)
Ronaldo (Bra)	Inter > Real Madrid	£28.49 m (2002)

*Media outlets speculated that the fee in Andrei Shevchenko's 2006 transfer from AC Milan to Chelsea may have been between £30-32 m. However, the official transfer fee was never disclosed and so shouldn't be included in official lists.

UK BANK NOTES

NOTE	COLOUR (SIZE)	FRONT DESIGN	REVERSE DESIGN
ENGLISH (BANK OF ENGLAND)			
£5	Turquoise (135 mm x 70 mm)	Queen Elizabeth II	Elizabeth Fry (1780–1845). Fry was a philanthropist and social reformer. She is illustrated reading to prisoners at Newgate Prison.
£10	Orange (142 mm x75 mm)	Queen Elizabeth II	Charles Darwin (1809–1882). Also features the *HMS Beagle*, on which Darwin was employed as a naturalist when he was a young man.
£20 (old)	Purple (149 mm x 80 mm)	Queen Elizabeth II	Sir Edward Elgar (1857–1934). The first full performance of his Enigma Variation took place in Worcester Cathedral in 1899. The cathedral is included to the left on the back of the note.
£20 (new)	Purple (149 mm x 80 mm)	Queen Elizabeth II	Adam Smith (1723–1790). Smith's research helped set the foundation for modern capitalist economic policies. Released in 2007, this is the first English bank note to feature a Scottish person.
£50	Red (56 mm x 85 mm)	Queen Elizabeth II	Sir John Houblon (1632–1712). Houblon was the first governor of the Bank of England, and the note was issued in 1994, 300 years after it was founded. Included is a picture of Houblon's house on Threadneedle Street, on the site of the bank's present HQ.

The Bank of England was founded in 1694.

Northern Irish Notes: Bank of Ireland (founded 1783): £5, 10, 20, 50, 100; First Trust Bank (founded 1991): £10, 20, 50, 100; Northern Bank (founded 1824): £5, 10, 20, 50, 100; Ulster Bank (founded 1836): £5, 10, 20, 50, 100.

Scottish Notes: Bank of Scotland (founded 1695): £5, 10, 20, 50, 100; Clydesdale Bank (founded 1838): £5, 10, 20, 50, 100; Royal Bank of Scotland (founded 1727): £1, 5, 10, 20, 50, 100.

Number of UK Notes in Circulation in 2006: £5 (210.2 m); £10 (559.1 m); £20 (1134.5 m); £50 (130.2 m).

Number of New Notes Issued in 2006: £5 (63 m); £10 (229 m); £20 (341 m); £50 (7 m).

THE BIGGEST NATIONAL
FOOTBALL RIVALRIES

TEAMS	NAME	COUNTRY
Boca Juniors (1905) v River Plate (1901)	El Superclasico	Argentina
Flamengo (1895) v Vasco da Gama (1898)	Classico Dos Milhoes	Brazil
CSKA Sofia (1948) v Levski Sofia (1914)	Eternal Derby	Bulgaria
Brondby IF (1964) v FC Kopenhavn (1992)	New Firm	Denmark
Olympique Marseille (1899) v Paris Saint Germain (1970)	P-M Derby	France
BVB Borussia Dortmund (1909) v FC Shalke 04 (1904)	Revierderby	Germany
Olympiakos Piraeus (1925) v Panathinaikos Athens (1908)	Derby of Eternal Enemies	Greece
AC Milan (1899) v FC Internazionale (1908)	Derby Della Madonnina	Italy
Jubilo Iwata (1970) v Kashima Antlers (1947)	National Derby of Japan	Japan
Club América (1916) v Guadalajara (1906)	Super Clasico	Mexico
Ajax Amsterdam (1900) v Feyenoord Rotterdam (1908)	National Derby (De Klassieker)	Netherlands
Cracovia Kraków (1906) v Wisła Kraków (1906)	Holy War (święta Wojna)	Poland
Benfica (1904) v FC Porto (1893)	O' Classico	Portugal
Anyang LG Cheetahs (1983) v Suwon Samsung Bluewings (1996)	Ji Ji Dae Derby	S. Korea
Kaizer Chiefs (1970) v Orlando Pirates (1937)	Soweto Derby	South Africa
Barcelona (1899) v Real Madrid (1902)	El Derbi Español	Spain
FC Zürich (1896) v Grasshopper-Club Zürich (1886)	Zurich Derby	Switzerland
Fenerbahçe (1905) v Galatasaray (1907)	Istanbul Derby	Turkey
Nacional (1899) v Peñarol (1891)	Superclásico	Uruguay

FOOTBALL SONGS THAT CHARTED
IN THE UK TOP TEN

SONG	YEAR	TEAM (EVENT)	NON-TEAM SQUAD ARTIST(S)	UK CHART PLACING
'Back Home'	1970	England (World Cup)	-	1
'Blue is the Colour'	1972	Chelsea (League Cup Final)	-	5
'Leeds United'	1972*	Leeds Utd (FA Cup Final)	-	10
'Ally's Tartan Army'	1978	Scotland (World Cup)	Andy Cameron	6
'Ole Ola' (Mulher Brasileira)	1978	Scotland (World Cup)	Rod Stewart	4
'Ossie's Dream (Spurs are on Their Way to Wembley)'	1981*	Tottenham (FA Cup Final)	-	5
'We Have a Dream'	1982	Scotland (World Cup)	-	5
'This Time (We'll Get It Right)/(England) We'll Fly the Flag'	1982	England (World Cup)	-	2
'We All Follow Man United'	1985*	Man Utd (FA Cup Final)	-	10
'You'll Never Walk Alone'	1985	(Bradford City stadium fire disaster fund)	The crowd (led by Gerry Marsden)	1
'The Anfield Rap'	1988	Liverpool (FA Cup Final)	-	3
'Ferry 'Cross the Mersey'	1989	(Hillsborough stadium disaster fund)	The Christians, Holly Johnson, Paul McCartney, Gerry Marsden and Stock, Aitken & Waterman	1
'World in Motion'	1990	England (World Cup)	New Order	1
'Fog on the Tyne'	1990	n/a	Paul Gascoigne and Lindisfarne	2

SONG	YEAR	TEAM (EVENT)	NON-TEAM SQUAD ARTIST(S)	UK CHART PLACING
'Come on You Reds'	1994*	Man Utd (FA Cup Final)	Status Quo	1
'We're Gonna Do It Again'	1995	Man Utd (FA Cup Final)	Stryker	6
'England's Irie'	1996	England (Euro C'ships)	Black Grape featuring Joe Strummer and Keith Allen	6
'Three Lions'	1996	England (Euro C'ships)	Lightning Seeds and Baddiel and Skinner	1
'Move Move Move (The Red Tribe)'	1996*	Man Utd (FA Cup Final)	-	6
'Pass and Move (It's the Liverpool Groove)'	1996	Liverpool (FA Cup Final)	Boot Room Boyz	4
'Vindaloo'	1998	England (World Cup)	Fat Les	2
'Three Lions '98'	1998	England (World Cup)	Lightning Seeds and Baddiel and Skinner	1
'(How Does It Feel To Be) On Top of the World'	1998	England (World Cup)	England Utd (Ian McCulloch, Simone Fowler, Tommy Scott and Mel C)	9
'Hot Stuff'	1998*	Arsenal (FA Cup Final)	-	9
'Jerusalem'	2000	England (Euro C'ships)	Fat Les	10
'Sven Sven Sven'	2001	(Tribute to England manager Sven-Goran Eriksson)	Bell & Spurling	7
'We're on the Ball'	2002	England (World Cup)	Ant and Dec	3
'Altogether Now'	2004	England (Euro C'ships)	The Farm	5
'World at Your Feet'	2006	England (World Cup)	Embrace	3

Key: * = the team won the competition.

TOP TEN HOME NATIONS GOALSCORERS

PLAYER	GOALS (CAPS)	PLAYER	GOALS (CAPS)	PLAYER	GOALS (CAPS)	PLAYER	GOALS (CAPS)
ENGLAND		**N. IRELAND**		**SCOTLAND**		**WALES**	
Bobby Charlton	49 (106)	David Healy	34 (64)	Dennis Law	30 (55)	Ian Rush	28 (73)
Gary Lineker	48 (80)	Billy Gillespie	13 (25)	Kenny Dalglish	30 (102)	Trevor Ford	23 (38)
Jimmy Greaves	44 (57)	Colin Clarke	13 (38)	Hughie Gallacher	24 (20)	Ivor Allchurch	23 (68)
Michael Owen	40 (89)	Joe Bambrick	12 (11)	Lawrie Reilly	22 (38)	Dean Saunders	22 (75)
Nat Lofthouse	30 (33)	Gerry Armstrong	12 (63)	Ally McCoist	19 (61)	Cliff Jones	16 (59)
Alan Shearer	30 (63)	Jimmy Quinn	12 (46)	Robert Hamilton	15 (11)	Mark Hughes	16 (72)
Tom Finney	30 (76)	Iain Dowie	12 (59)	Mo Johnston	14 (38)	John Charles	15 (38)
V. Woodward	29 (23)	Johnny Crossan	10 (24)	Robert Smith McColl	13 (13)	Craig Bellamy	15 (47)
Steve Bloomer	28 (23)	Peter McParland	10 (34)	James McFadden	13 (37)	John Hartson	14 (51)
David Platt	27 (62)	Jimmy McIllroy	10 (55)	Andrew Wilson	12 (12)	Robert Earnshaw	13 (39)

Stats correct up to end of June 2008.

WORLD'S HIGHEST WATERFALLS

	NAME	LOCATION	HEIGHT M (FT)
1	**Angel Falls**	Venezuela	979 (3,212)
2	**Tugela**	South Africa	948 (3,110)
3	**Utigard**	Norway	818 (2,684)
EU	**Krimmler**	Austria	380 (1,247)
UK	**Eas a' Chual Aluinn**	Near Glen Coul, Scottish Highlands	200 (656)
US	**Yosemite Falls**	Sierra Nevada mountains, California	739 (2,425)

TOP TEN MOST USED UK PLAYGROUND INSULTS

	PUT-DOWN	PERCENTAGE OF UK TEACHERS WHO SAID THEY HEARD THE INSULT REGULARLY
1	Gay	83%
2	Bitch	59%
3	Slag	45%
4	Poof	29%
5	Batty boy	29%
6	Slut	26%
7	Queer	26%
8	Lezzie	24.8%
9	Homo	22%
10	Faggot	11%

Source: Association of Teachers and Lecturers (ATL) survey (2008)

RUGBY UNION - 5/6 NATIONS CHAMPIONSHIP TABLES

	CHAMPIONS	RUNNERS-UP	THIRD	FOURTH	FIFTH	SIXTH
1990	Scotland – 8	England – 6	France – 4	Ireland – 2	Wales – 0	
1991	England – 8	France – 6	Scotland – 4	Wales – 1	Ireland – 1	
1992	England – 8	France – 4	Scotland – 4	Wales – 4	Ireland – 0	
1993	France – 6	England – 6	Scotland – 6	Ireland – 6	Wales – 2	
1994	Wales – 6	England – 6	France – 4	Ireland – 3	Scotland – 1	
1995	England – 8	Scotland – 6	France – 4	Ireland – 2	Wales – 0	
1996	England – 6	Scotland – 6	France – 4	Wales – 2	Ireland – 2	
1997	France – 8	England – 6	Wales – 2	Scotland – 2	Ireland – 2	
1998	France – 8	England – 6	Wales – 4	Scotland – 2	Ireland – 0	
1999	Scotland – 6	England – 6	Wales – 4	France – 2	Ireland – 2	
2000	England – 8	France – 6	Ireland – 6	Wales – 6	Scotland – 2	Italy – 2
2001	England – 8	Ireland – 8	Scotland – 5	Wales – 5	France – 4	Italy – 0
2002	France – 10	England – 8	Ireland – 6	Scotland – 4	Wales – 2	Italy – 0
2003	England – 10	Ireland – 8	France – 6	Scotland – 4	Italy – 2	Wales – 0
2004	France – 10	Ireland – 8	England – 6	Wales – 4	Italy – 2	Scotland – 0
2005	Wales – 10	France – 8	Ireland – 6	England – 4	Scotland – 2	Italy – 0
2006	France – 8	Ireland – 8	Scotland – 6	England – 4	Wales – 3	Italy – 1
2007	France – 8	Ireland – 8	England – 6	Italy – 4	Wales – 2	Scotland – 2
2008	Wales – 10	England – 6	France – 6	Ireland – 4	Scotland – 2	Italy –2

'BIG FOUR' GLOBAL SEARCH ENGINES

SEARCH ENGINE	REVENUE	MILLIONS OF SEARCHES	SEARCH ENGINE MARKET SHARE (IN RELATION TO TOP 10 TOTAL) (%)
Baidu	$0.228 bn	8,428	13.76%
Google	$16.6 bn	28,454	46.47%
Live Search	$51.1 bn (Microsoft)	7,880	12.87%
Yahoo!	$7.0 bn	10,505	17.16%
Stats from 2007.			

FIFA SOCCER PROMOTION

EDITION	UK COVER	TAGLINE	TITLE SONG/ ARTIST
FIFA International Soccer	David Platt (Eng) in action vs Poland; Pat Bonner (ROI) punching the ball vs Netherlands	FIFA International Soccer has it all... Experience sheer brilliance	-
FIFA Soccer 95	Erik Thorstvedt (Tottenham) making a save	The best console football can get	-
FIFA Soccer 96	Ronald De Boer (Net) chasing Jason McAteer (ROI); George Hagi (Brescia) being tackled	Next generation soccer	-
FIFA 97	David Ginola (Newcastle Utd)	Emotion captured	-
FIFA 98: Road to the World Cup	David Beckham (England)	Your only goal – qualify	'Song 2' Blur
FIFA 99	Dennis Bergkamp (Arsenal)	All The Clubs, Leagues and Cups	'The Rockefeller Skank' Fatboy Slim
FIFA 2000	Sol Campbell (England)	-	'It's Only Us' Robbie Williams
FIFA 2001	Paul Scholes (England)	-	'Bodyrock' Moby
FIFA Football 2002	Thierry Henry (Arsenal)	-	'19-2000'Gorillaz
FIFA Football 2003	Roberto Carlos (Brazil); Ryan Giggs (Man Utd); Edgar Davids (Juventus)	Be the twelfth man	'To Get Down' Timo Maas
FIFA Football 2004	Alessandro Del Piero (Juventus); Thierry Henry (Arsenal); Ronaldinho (Brazil)	-	'Red Morning Light' Kings of Leon
FIFA Football 2005	Patrick Viera (Arsenal); Fernando Morientes (Real Madrid); Andrei Shevchenko (AC Milan)	A great player needs a great first touch	-
FIFA 06	Wayne Rooney (Man Utd); Ronaldinho (Barcelona)	You play, they obey	'Helicopter' Bloc Party
FIFA 07	Wayne Rooney (Man Utd); Ronaldinho (Barcelona)	This is the season	-
FIFA 08	Wayne Rooney (Man Utd); Ronaldinho (Barcelona)	Can you FIFA 08?/ Got what it takes?	-

SOAP STARS IN THE
UK SINGLES CHART

ACTOR/ ACTRESS	CHARACTER	SOAP	CHART DEBUT	DEBUT SINGLE	DEBUT SINGLE CHART HIGH
Anita Dobson	Angie Watts (1985–1988)	EastEnders	1986	'Anyone Can Fall in Love'	4
Letitia Dean & Paul Medford	Sharon Watts (1985–1992, 2001–2006) & Kelvin Carpenter (1985–1987)	EastEnders	1986	'Something Outa Nothing'	12
Nick Berry	Simon Wicks (1985–1990)	EastEnders	1986	'Every Loser Wins'	1
Jason Donovan	Scott Robinson (1986–1988)	Neighbours	1988	'Nothing Can Divide Us'	5
Kylie Minogue	Charlene Mitchell (1986–1989)	Neighbours	1988	'I Should Be So Lucky'	1
Stefan Dennis	Paul Daniels (1985–1993, 2004–present)	Neighbours	1989	'Don't It Make You Feel Good'	16
Craig McLachlan	Henry Ramsay (1986–1989)	Neighbours	1990	'Mona'	2
Sophie Lawrence	Diane Butcher (1988–1991, 1997)	EastEnders	1991	'Love's Unkind'	21
Dannii Minogue	Emma Jackson (1989–1991)	Home & Away	1991	'Love and Kisses'	8
Bill Tarmey	Jack Duckworth (1979–present)	Coronation Street	1993	'One Voice'	16
Michelle Gayle	Hattie Tavernier (1990–1993)	EastEnders	1993	'Looking Up'	11
Ant & Dec	PJ and Duncan (1990–1993)	Byker Grove	1994	'Let's Get Ready to Rumble'	9
Sean Maguire	Aidan Brosnan (1993)	EastEnders	1994	'Someone to Love'	14

ACTOR/ ACTRESS	CHARACTER	SOAP	CHART DEBUT	DEBUT SINGLE	DEBUT SINGLE CHART HIGH
Gillian and Gayle Blakeney	Caroline and Christina Alessi (1991–1993)	Neighbours	1994	'Wanna Be Your Lover'	65
Natalie Imbruglia	Beth Brennan (1991–1994)	Neighbours	1997	'Torn'	2
Matthew Marsden	Chris Collins (1997–1998)	Coronation Street	1998	'The Heart's Lone Desire'	13
Tracy Shaw	Maxine Peacock (1995–2003)	Coronation Street	1998	'Happenin' All Over Again'	46
Adam Rickett	Nick Tilsley (1997–2002)	Coronation Street	1999	'I Breathe Again'	5
Martine McCutcheon	Tiffany Mitchell (1995–1998)	EastEnders	1999	'Perfect Moment'	1
Kevin Kennedy	Curly Watts (1983–2003)	Coronation Street	2000	'Bulldog Nation'	n/a
Sid Owen	Ricky Butcher (1988–2000, 2002–2004)	EastEnders	2000	'Good Thing Going'	14
Claire Sweeney	Lindsey Corkhill (1995–2001)	Brookside	2002	'When You Believe'	n/a
Holly Valance	Flick Scully (1999–2003)	Neighbours	2002	'Kiss Kiss'	1
Jennifer Ellison	Emily O'Leary (Nee Shadwick) (1998–2003)	Brookside	2003	'Baby I Don't Care'	6
Shane Richie	Alfie Moon (2002–2005)	EastEnders	2003	'I'm Your Man'	2
Delta Goodrem	Nina Tucker (2002–2004)	Neighbours	2003	'Born To Try'	3

ACADEMY AWARDS (FILMS)

	BEST PICTURE	DIRECTION	ORIGINAL SCREENPLAY	ADAPTED SCREENPLAY
1990 (63rd)	*Dances with Wolves*	Kevin Costner (*Dances with Wolves*)	B. Joel Ruben (*Ghost*)	M. Blake (*Dances with Wolves*)
1991 (64th)	*The Silence of the Lambs*	Jonathan Demme (*The Silence of the Lambs*)	C. Khouli (*Thelma & Louise*)	T. Tally (*The Silence of the Lambs*)
1992 (65th)	*Unforgiven*	Clint Eastwood (*Unforgiven*)	N. Jordan (*The Crying Game*)	R. Prawer Jhabvala (*Howard's End*)
1993 (66th)	*Schindler's List*	Steven Spielberg (*Schindler's List*)	J. Campion (*The Piano*)	S. Zaillian (*Schindler's List*)
1994 (67th)	*Forrest Gump*	Robert Zemeckis (*Forrest Gump*)	Q. Tarantino & R. Avary (*Pulp Fiction*)	E. Roth (*Forrest Gump*)
1995 (68th)	*Braveheart*	Mel Gibson (*Braveheart*)	C. McQuarrie (*The Usual Suspects*)	E. Thompson (*Sense and Sensibility*)
1996 (69th)	*The English Patient*	Anthony Minghella (*The English Patient*)	E. Coen & J. Coen (*Fargo*)	B. Bob Thornton (*Sling Blade*)
1997 (70th)	*Titanic*	James Cameron (*Titanic*)	M. Damon & B. Affleck (*Good Will Hunting*)	B. Helgeland and C. Hanson (*L.A. Confidential*)
1998 (71st)	*Shakespeare in Love*	Steven Spielberg (*Saving Private Ryan*)	M. Norman & T. Stoppard (*Shakespeare in Love*)	B. Condon (*Gods and Monsters*)
1999 (72nd)	*American Beauty*	Sam Mendes (*American Beauty*)	A. Ball (*American Beauty*)	J. Irving (*The Cider House Rules*)
2000 (73rd)	*Gladiator*	Steven Soderbergh (*Traffic*)	C. Crowe (*Almost Famous*)	S. Gaghan (*Traffic*)
2001 (74th)	*A Beautiful Mind*	Ron Howard (*A Beautiful Mind*)	J. Fellowes (*Gosford Park*)	A. Goldsman (*A Beautiful Mind*)
2002 (75th)	*Chicago*	Roman Polanski (*The Pianist*)	P. Almodóvar (*Talk to Her*)	R. Harwood (*The Pianist*)
2003 (76th)	*The Lord of the Rings: The Return of the King*	Peter Jackson (*The Lord of the Rings: The Return of the King*)	S. Coppola (*Lost in Translation*)	F. Walsh, P. Boyens & P. Jackson (*The Lord of the Rings: The Return of the King*)

	BEST PICTURE	DIRECTION	ORIGINAL SCREENPLAY	ADAPTED SCREENPLAY
2004 (77th)	Million Dollar Baby	Clint Eastwood (Million Dollar Baby)	C. Kaufman, M. Gondry, P. Bismuth (Eternal Sunshine of the Spotless Mind)	A. Payne & J. Taylor (Sideways)
2005 (78th)	Crash	Ang Lee (Brokeback Mountain)	P. Haggis & B. Moresco (Crash)	L. McMurtry & D. Ossana (Brokeback Mountain)
2006 (79th)	The Departed	Martin Scorsese (The Departed)	M. Arndt (Little Miss Sunshine)	W. Monahan (The Departed)
2007 (80th)	No Country For Old Men	Joel and Ethan Coen (No Country For Old Men)	D. Cody (Juno)	J. and E. Coen (No Country for Old Men)

Awards are made in spring for films that premiered in the previous year.

OVERALL RECORDS

Only Films to Have Won All of the 'Big Five' Awards (Best Picture, Best Director, Best Actor, Best Actress, Best Writing): It Happened One Night (1934); One Flew Over the Cuckoo's Nest (1975); The Silence of the Lambs (1991).

BEST PICTURE WINNER 'FIRSTS'

Western: Cimarron (1931). Foreign Film: Hamlet (1948). Comedy: It Happened One Night (1934). All Colour Film: Gone with the Wind (1939). (And Only) Thriller: Rebecca (1940). (And Only) X-Rated Film: Midnight Cowboy (1969). Sequel: The Godfather Pt 2 (1974). Sports: Rocky (1976). (And Only) Fantasy Film: The Lord of the Rings: The Return of the King (2003). Longest Winner: Gone with the Wind (1939) 3 h 54 m. Shortest Winner: Marty (1955) 1 h 31 m.

BEST DIRECTOR WINNER RECORDS

Youngest: Norman Taurog (32 years) Skippy (1931). Oldest Director: Clint Eastwood (74 years) Million Dollar Baby (2004). Most Awards: John Ford (four).

ACADEMY AWARDS (ACTORS)

YEAR	ACTOR IN A LEADING ROLE	ACTRESS IN A LEADING ROLE	ACTOR IN A SUPPORTING ROLE	ACTRESS IN A SUPPORTING ROLE
1990 (63rd)	Jeremy Irons (Reversal of Fortune)	Kathy Bates (Misery)	Joe Pesci (Goodfellas)	Whoopi Goldberg (Ghost)
1991 (64th)	Anthony Hopkins (The Silence of the Lambs)	Jodie Foster (The Silence of the Lambs)	Jack Palance (City Slickers)	Mercedes Ruehl (The Fisher King)
1992 (65th)	Al Pacino (Scent of a Woman)	Emma Thompson (Howard's End)	Gene Hackman (Unforgiven)	Marisa Tomei (My Cousin Vinny)
1993 (66th)	Tom Hanks (Philadelphia)	Holly Hunter (The Piano)	Tommy Lee Jones (The Fugitive)	Anna Paquin (The Piano)
1994 (67th)	Tom Hanks (Forrest Gump)	Jessica Lange (Blue Sky)	Martin Landau (Ed Wood)	Dianne Wiest (Bullets Over Broadway)
1995 (68th)	Nicolas Cage (Leaving Las Vegas)	Susan Sarandon (Dead Man Walking)	Kevin Spacey (The Usual Suspects)	Mira Sorvino (Mighty Aphrodite)
1996 (69th)	Geoffrey Rush (Shine)	Frances McDormand (Fargo)	Cuba Gooding Jr. (Jerry Maguire)	Juliette Binoche (The English Patient)
1997 (70th)	Jack Nicholson (As Good as it Gets)	Helen Hunt (As Good as it Gets)	Robin Williams (Good Will Hunting)	Kim Basinger (L.A. Confidential)
1998 (71st)	Roberto Benigni (Life is Beautiful)	Gwyneth Paltrow (Shakespeare in Love)	James Coburn (Affliction)	Judi Dench (Shakespeare in Love)
1999 (72nd)	Kevin Spacey (American Beauty)	Hilary Swank (Boys Don't Cry)	Michael Caine (The Cider House Rules)	Angelina Jolie (Girl, Interrupted)
2000 (73rd)	Russell Crowe (Gladiator)	Julia Roberts (Erin Brockovich)	Benicio Del Toro (Traffic)	Marcia Gay Harden (Pollock)

YEAR	ACTOR IN A LEADING ROLE	ACTRESS IN A LEADING ROLE	ACTOR IN A SUPPORTING ROLE	ACTRESS IN A SUPPORTING ROLE
2001 (74th)	Denzel Washington (*Training Day*)	Halle Berry (*Monster's Ball*)	Jim Broadbent (*Iris*)	Jennifer Connelly (*A Beautiful Mind*)
2002 (75th)	Adrien Brody (*The Pianist*)	Nicole Kidman (*The Hours*)	Chris Cooper (*Adaptation*)	Catherine Zeta-Jones (*Chicago*)
2003 (76th)	Sean Penn (*Mystic River*)	Charlize Theron (*Monster*)	Tim Robbins (*Mystic River*)	Renée Zellweger (*Cold Mountain*)
2004 (77th)	Jamie Foxx (*Ray*)	Hilary Swank (*Million Dollar Baby*)	Morgan Freeman (*Million Dollar Baby*)	Cate Blanchett (*The Aviator*)
2005 (78th)	Philip Seymour Hoffman (*Capote*)	Reese Witherspoon (*Walk the Line*)	George Clooney (*Syriana*)	Rachel Weisz (*The Constant Gardener*)
2006 (79th)	Forest Whitaker (*The Last King of Scotland*)	Hellen Mirren (*The Queen*)	Alan Arkin (*Little Miss Sunshine*)	Jennifer Hudson (*Dreamgirls*)
2007 (80th)	Daniel Day-Lewis (*There Will Be Blood*)	Marion Cotillard (*La Vie en Rose*)	Javier Bardem (*No Country For Old Men*)	Tilda Swinton (*Michael Clayton*)

BEST ACTOR RECORDS

Most Awards: Spencer Tracy, Freric March, Gary Cooper, Dustin Hoffman, Tom Hanks, Jack Nicholson, Daniel Day-Lewis (2 each). Oldest Winner: Henry Fonda (76 years) *On Golden Pond* (1981). Youngest Winner: Adrian Brody (29 years) *The Pianist* (2002).

BEST ACTRESS RECORDS

Most Awards: Katharine Hepburn (4). Youngest Winner: Marlee Matlin (21 years) *Children of a Lesser God* (1986). Oldest Winner: Jessica Tandy (80 years) *Driving Miss Daisy* (1989).

BEST SUPPORTING ACTOR RECORDS

Most Awards: Walter Brennan (3). Youngest Winner: Timothy Hutton (20 years) *Ordinary People* (1980). George Burns (80 years) *The Sunshine Boys* (1975).

BEST SUPPORTING ACTRESS RECORDS

Most Awards: Shelley Winters; Dianne Wiest (2). Youngest Winner: Tatum O'Neal (10 years) *Paper Moon* (1973). Oldest Winner: Peggy Ashcroft (77 years) *A Passage To India* (1984).

BEER GLOSSARY

TERM	MEANING	EXAMPLE BRANDS
ABV	Measure of the percentage of alcohol in beer compared to volume. This varies in beer from non-alcoholic (0%), to low (1–3%), to medium (4–6%), to high (7–9%), and highest (10–12%).	
Ale	More traditional, though less widely drunk of two main varieties of beer. Originally (though not nowadays) ale was made without hops.	
Altbier	German pale ale, which literally means 'old beer'. A rivalry exists in the traditional western heartlands between altbier from Düsseldorf and Kölsch from Cologne.	Diebels Alt
Barley Wine	A bottled, very strong variety of ale (around 8–12% abv).	Golden Pride
Berliner Weiße	A low-alcohol (around 2.8%) wheat beer, served with its sediment. The name means 'Berlin wheat beer' and it is brewed exclusively in Berlin.	Berliner Kindl
Bitter	Traditional English ale with a sharp taste. Made with a higher dosage of hops than lager.	Tetley's
Bock	Strong (typically 6.3–7.4%), usually dark-coloured German lager. Originated in Einbeck in central Germany. Doppelbock is a stronger (6–10%) variation; there is also the even stronger eisbock (9–14%).	Einbecker Bock
Bottle Conditioning	The process of adding leftover sugar and yeast to the beer at the bottling stage (to induce a second fermentation).	
Brown ale	Ale made with dark malt. Tastes strong and malty.	Newcastle Brown
Fermentation	The process of making a product, typically alcohol (such as beer), or pharmaceuticals. The action of the zymase enzyme in yeast breaks down simple sugars into ethanol (an alcohol) and CO_2.	
Fermenting Wort	The liquid to which yeast and hops are added during the brewing process. Wort is made up of sugar, crushed malted grain and water.	
Gueuze	A beer made by blending old (two to three year-old) and young (one year-old) lambic to make a new variety. Sometimes colloquially called Brussels Champagne.	Olde Gueuze Boon
Hops	The dried female flowers of the hop plant – what gives beer its bitter flavour.	
India Pale Ale (IPA)	Made with a very heavy dosage of hops, giving it a higher alcohol content. Originally created specifically for the purpose of withstanding the long sea journey between Britain and the Indian Empire.	Deuchers IPA

TERM	MEANING	EXAMPLE BRANDS
Kölsch	Much like altbier but brewed at slightly lower temperatures and using lighter malt.	Dom Kölsch
Lager	More modern and widely drunk of the two main varieties of beer. The name stems from the German word for 'storehouse'.	Miller
Lambic	Belgian wheat beer made using wild (rather than conditioned) yeast. Has European Protected Regional Indication and may only be brewed in the Pajottenland region of Belgium.	3 Fonteinen
Malt	Grains that have begun to ferment after being soaked in water (used predominantly in brewing).	
Mild Ale	Dark-coloured. Light-tasting. Lower alcohol content.	Brains Dark
Osiris	Mythical legend states that it was Osiris (Egyptian God of agriculture, the underworld and the dead) who orchestrated the first acts of beer making.	
Pils/Pilsner	A dry, hoppy-tasting, golden-coloured lager. Named after the city of Pilsen in the Czech Republic where it was first brewed.	Holsten Pils
Porter	Dark (due to longer roasting of the malt). Sweeter tasting and less bitter than stout.	Fuller's London Porter
Real Ale/Cask Ale	British non-carbonated ales that are fermented twice, the second time in the cask.	Abbot Ale
Scotch Ale	Malty-tasting ale made with a much lower dose of hops.	Belhaven's Wee Heavy
Stout	Dark (due to longer roasting of malt). Commonly drier, more bitter tasting and of medium to high alcohol content.	Guinness
Trappist Beer	Strong, bottle-conditioned ale that is produced by Trappist monks in monasteries mainly in Belgium, but also in Holland and Germany.	Chimay
White/Wheat Beer	Beer made of a combination of wheat and barley. Usually pale in colour, frothy and light in texture, and with a more fruity flavour.	Hoegaarden
Yeast	A single-celled fungus that reproduces by budding. Grown in a substrate base of sugars, nitrogen sources, minerals and water.	

TEAM SPORTS

SPORT	PLAYING AREA	GAME DURATION	SCORING POINTS	PLAYERS
American Football	109.7 m x 48.8 m (360 ft x 160 ft). Goal lines are 100 yards apart.	Four quarters. 15 minutes/quarter. Clock stops when ball is out of play.	Touchdown: 6; extra point (conversion): 1; 2 conversion: 2; field goal: 3; safety: 3	11
Australian Rules Football	Oval. 135–185 m long x 110–155 m wide.	Four quarters. 20 minutes/quarter. Clock stops when ball is out of play.	Goal: 6; behind: 1	18
Baseball	>99 m from the home plate to fences in the left and right field, and >121 m to the centre fence.	Continues until the last batter is 'out'.	Running safely 'home' around all 4 bases: 1 run	9
Basketball	28 m x 15 m (international rules); 29 m x 15 m (NBA rules).	Four quarters. Ten minutes/quarter (international rules). 12 minutes/quarter (NBA rules).	Scoring from inside the 'D': 2; scoring from outside the 'D': 3	5
Cricket	Oval or circular. Around 137-150 m in diameter.	Test matches are usually played over three or more days.	Running safely between wickets: 1 run	11
Field Hockey	91.4 m × 55 m (100 yds × 60 yds)	Two halves. 35 minutes/half.	Single goals	11
Football	100–110 m x 64–75 m	Two halves. 45 minutes/half.	Single goals	11
Gaelic Football	130–145 m x 80–90 m	Two halves. 30 minutes/half. Senior inter-county matches, 35 minutes/half.	Goal: 3; point: 1	15
Hurling	137 m x 82 m	Two halves. 30 minutes/half. Senior inter-county matches, 35 minutes/half.	Goal: 3; point: 1	15

SPORT	PLAYING AREA	GAME DURATION	SCORING POINTS	PLAYERS
Ice Hockey	International: 60 m x 30 m with corner radius of 8.5 m and 4 m behind goal areas. NHL: 61m x 26m.	Three periods. 20 minutes/period. Clock stops when ball is out of play.	Single goals	6
Rugby League	100 m x 68 m plus scoring areas of 6–11 m.	Two halves. 40m/half.	Try: 4; conversion kick: 2; penalty kick: 2; drop-goal: 1	13
Rugby Union	100 m x 70 m plus in-goal areas of 10–22 m.	Two halves. 40 minutes/half.	Try: 5; conversion kick: 2; penalty kick: 3; drop-goal: 3	15
Shinty	<155 m x <73 m	Two halves. 45 minutes/half.	Single goals	12

ITC 'PROTECTED' LIVE SPORT

The Epsom Derby	FA Cup Final
FIFA World Cup	The Grand National
Olympic Games	Rugby League Challenge Cup Final
Rugby Union World Cup Final	Scottish Cup Final (in Scotland)
UEFA Euro Championships	Wimbledon

Note: The International Television Commission has given special protective status to the above UK sports events. The ruling means that these 'Category A' events must be shown live on free-to-view terrestrial TV in the UK. Category B event rights can be bought by subscription TV companies but highlights must be allowed to be shown on terrestrial TV. Category B events include: home England cricket tests, Six Nations rugby, Commonwealth Games, IAAF World Championships, Cricket World Cup, Ryder Cup, and British Open Golf.

RICHEST PEOPLE

	UK (SUNDAY TIMES – 2007)			WORLD (FORBES – 2008)		
	NAME	**INDUSTRY**	**FORTUNE (£BN)**	**NAME**	**INDUSTRY**	**FORTUNE ($BN)**
1	**Lakshmi Mittal & family**	**Steel**	**27.7**	**Warren Buffett**	**Investments**	**62**
2	Roman Abramovich	Oil	11.7	Carlos Slim Helu	Communications	60
3	The Duke of Westminster	Property	7.0	William Gates III	Software	58
4	Sri & Gopi Hinduja	Finance	6.2	Lakshmi Mittal	Manufacturing	45
5	Alisher Usmanov	Steel	5.73	Mukesh Ambani	Manufacturing	43
6	Emesto and Kirsty Berarelli	Pharmaceuticals	5.65	Anil Ambani	Diversified	42
7	Hans Rausing and family	Packaging	5.4	Ingvar Kamprad	Retail	31
8	John Fredriksen	Shipping	4.65	KP Singh	Property	30
9	Sir Phillip and Lady Green	Retailing	4.33	Oleg Deripaska	Diversified	28
10	David and Simon Reuben	Property	4.3	Karl Albrecht	Retail	27

ALL-TIME OLYMPIC GAMES
MEDALS TABLES

	SUMMER OLYMPICS		WINTER OLYMPICS	
RANK	NATION	G/S/B (TOTAL)	NATION	G/S/B (TOTAL)
1	US	930/730/638 (2,298)	Germany[2]	118/116/94 (328)
2	Soviet Union	395/319/296 (1,010)	Norway	98/98/84 (280)
3	Germany[1]	400/413/447 (1,260)	USA	78/80/58 (216)
4	Great Britain	207/255/253 (715)	Soviet Union	78/57/59 (194)
5	France	191/212/233 (636)	Austria	51/64/70 (185)
6	Italy	190/158/174 (522)	Sweden	43/31/44 (118)
7	China	163/117/106 (386)	Finland	41/58/52 (151)
8	Hungary	159/140/159 (458)	Canada	38/38/43 (119)
9	Sweden	142/160/173 (475)	Switzerland	38/37/43 (118)
10	Australia	131/137/164 (432)	Italy	36/31/34 (101)
11	Japan	123/112/125 (360)	Russia	33/24/19 (76)
12	Russia	108/97/110 (315)	Netherlands	25/30/23 (78)
13	Finland	101/83/115 (299)	France	25/24/34 (83)
14	Romania	86/89/116 (291)	South Korea	17/8/6 (31)
15	Netherlands	71/79/96 (246)	Japan	9/10/13 (32)
16	South Korea	68/74/73 (215)	Unified Team[3]	9/6/8 (23)
17	Cuba	67/64/63 (194)	Great Britain	8/3/10 (21)
18	Poland	59/74/118 (251)	China	4/16/13 (33)
19	Canada	58/94/108 (260)	Croatia	4/3/0 (7)
20	Norway	54/48/43 (145)	Estonia	4/1/1 (6)

Key: G = Gold medals won; S = Silver medals won; B = Bronze medals won.

[1] – This figure includes German performances as Germany (163/163/203 (529)), West Germany (56/67/81 (204)), East Germany (153/129/127 (409)), and the United Team of Germany (28/54/36 (118)).

[2] – This figure includes German performances as Germany (60/59/41 (160)), West Germany (11/15/13 (39)), East Germany (39/36/35 (110)), and the United Team of Germany (8/6/5 (19)).

[3] – The name of the Soviet Union team, without the Baltic States or Georgia, at the 1992 Summer Games and the 1992 Winter Games.

All figures include all games up to the end of the 2008 Beijing Games.

'BIG FOUR' WORLD BOXING BODIES

BODY	BELT COLOUR	FIRST HEAVYWEIGHT CHAMPION	UK HEAVYWEIGHT CHAMPIONS
International Boxing Federation	Red	1983 – Larry Holmes (US)	Lennox Lewis (13/11/1999–22/4/2001; 17/11/2001–5/9/2002)
World Boxing Association	Black	1921 – Jack Dempsey (US)	Lennox Lewis (13/11/1999–29/4/2000)
World Boxing Council	Green	1963 – Sonny Liston (US)	Lennox Lewis (14/12/1992–24/9/1994; 7/2/1997–22/4/2001; 17/11/2001–6/2/2004); Frank Bruno (2/9/1995–16/3/1996)
World Boxing Organization	Brown	1988 – Francesco Damiani (Italy)	none

US ALL-TIME BEST-SELLING SINGLES

YEAR	TITLE	BAND/ARTIST	SALES
1997	'Candle in the Wind 1997'	Elton John	10 m +
1956	'Hound Dog/Don't Be Cruel'	Elvis Presley	4 m +
1968	'Hey Jude'	The Beatles	
1980	'Another One Bites the Dust'	Queen	
1982	'Eye of the Tiger'	Survivor	
1985	'We are the World'	USA for Africa	
1992	'I Will Always Love You'	Whitney Houston	
1993	'Whoomp! (There It Is)'	Tag Team	
1995	'Macarena'	Los Del Rio	
1956	'Love Me Tender/Any Way You Want Me'	Elvis Presley	3 m +
1995	'Gangsta's Paradise'	Coolio	
1997	'How Do I Live'	LeAnn Rimes	
1997	'I'll Be Missing You'	Puff Daddy & Faith Evans	

SENDINGS OFF IN INTERNATIONAL RUGBY UNION

COUNTRY	TOTAL FOR	FIRST	LAST	TOTAL AGAINST
France	9	J-P Garuet v Ireland (1984)	J-J Crenca v New Zealand (1999)	9
South Africa	7	JT Small v Australia (1993)	PC Montgomery v Wales (2005)	3
Tonga	6	F Mahoni v France (1995)	HT Pole v Samoa (2007)	0
Wales	6	GAD Wheel v Ireland (1977)	GR Jenkins v South Africa (1995)	6
Fiji	6	J Sovau v Australia (1976)	M Vunibaka v Canada (1999)	0
Samoa	5	MG Keenan v Argentina (1991)	A Tuilagi v England 2005	3
England	4	MA Burton v Australia (1975)	LW Moody v Samoa (2005)	12
Canada	4	ME Cardinal v France (1994)	DR Baugh v Namibia (1999)	3
Italy	3	M Giovanelli v Scotland (1999)	A Troncon v Ireland (2001)	0
Argentina	3	FE Mendez v England (1990)	R Travaglini v France (1997)	2
Namibia	2	A Stoop v Wales (1990)	J Nieuwenhuis v France (2007)	1
Scotland	2	NJ Hines v US (2002)	S Murray v Wales (2006)	3
New Zealand	2	CJ Brownlie v England (1925)	CE Meads v Scotland (1967)	7
Romania	1	C Cojocariu v France (1991)	C Cojocariu v France (1991)	0
Australia	1	D Codey v Wales (1987)	D Codey v Wales (1987)	5
Ireland	1	WP Duggan v Wales (1977)	WP Duggan v Wales (1977)	4

Includes all matches involving the nine major nations up to May 2008 plus all World Cup finals matches up to the end of the 2007 World Cup.

CALENDAR OF MAJOR
BRITISH HORSE RACES

MONTH	RACE	FIRST RUN	COURSE	DISTANCE	ENTRY	TYPE
March	Queen Mother Champion Chase	1959	Cheltenham	2 m	5 yo +	NH (12)
March	Cheltenham Gold Cup	1924	Cheltenham	3 m 2½ f	5 yo +	NH (22)
April	Grand National	1836	Aintree	4½ m	6 yo +	NH (30)
April	Scottish Grand National	1867	Ayr	4 m 1 f	5 yo +	NH (27)
April	Betfred Gold Cup	1957	Sandown	3 m 5½ f	5 yo +	NH (24)
May	Two Thousand Guineas*	1809	Newmarket	1 m	3 yo	F
May	One Thousand Guineas*	1814	Newmarket	1 m	3 yo fi	F
June	Northumberland Plate	1833	Newcastle	2 m 19 y	3 yo +	F
June	Epsom Oaks*	1779	Epsom	1 m 4 f 10 y	3 yo fi	F
June	Epsom Derby*	1780	Epsom	1 m 4 f 10 y	3 yo	F
June	Gold Cup	1807	Ascot	2 m 4 f	4 yo +	F
July	Eclipse Stakes	1886	Sandown	1 m 2 f 7 y	3 yo +	F
July	King George VI and Queen Elizabeth Diamond Stakes	1951	Ascot	1 m 4 f	3 yo +	F
July	July Cup	1876	Newmarket	6 f	3 yo +	F
July/August	Nassau Stakes	1840	Goodwood	1 m 1 f 192 y	3 yo + fi/ma	F
August	International Stakes	1972	York	1 m 2½ f	3 yo +	F
September	St Leger Stakes*	1776	Doncaster	1 m 6 f 132 y	3yo	F
September	Haydock Sprint Cup	1966	Haydock	6 f	3 yo +	F
September	Queen Elizabeth II Stakes	1955	Ascot	1 m	3 yo +	F
September	Ayr Gold Cup	1804	Ayr	6 f	3 yo +	F
October	Dewhurst Stakes	1875	Newmarket	7 f	2 yo	F

MONTH	RACE	FIRST RUN	COURSE	DISTANCE	ENTRY	TYPE
October	Champion Stakes	1877	Newmarket	1 m 2½ f	3 yo +	F
October	Racing Post Trophy	1961	Doncaster	1 m	2 yo	F
November	Hennessy Gold Cup	1957	Newbury	3 m 2½ f	5 yo +	NH (21)
November	Paddy Power Gold Cup	1960	Cheltenham	2 m 4½ f	5 yo +	NH (15)
December	Tingle Creek Trophy	1957	Sandown	2 m	5 yo +	NH (13)
December	Welsh National	1949	Chepstow	3 m 5½ f	5 yo +	NH (22)
December	King George VI Chase	1937	Kempton	3 m	4 yo +	NH (18)

Key: * = one of the five Classics; fi = fillies; ma = mares; yo = years old; F = flat; NH = National Hunt; (x) = number of fences. Furlong Length: 1 furlong = 201 m = 1/8 mile = 660 ft.

TOP TEN UK BILLBOARD POSTERS OF THE TWENTIETH CENTURY

ORGANISATION	CAMPAIGN	YEAR
The Conservative Party	Labour Isn't Working	1978
The Government	Lord Kitchener Wants You	1914
Benson & Hedges	Pyramids	1977
Guinness	For Strength	1934
The Economist	Management Trainee	1989
Health Education Council	Pregnant Mum	1969
Araldite	Sticks	1982
The Ministry of War	Careless Talk Costs Lives	1940
Benetton	Baby	1991
Wonderbra	Hello Boys	1994

Source: *Campaign* (advertising trade magazine) 1999

WOMEN'S ATHLETICS
WORLD RECORDS

EVENT	RECORD	NAME (NATIONALITY)	VENUE	DATE
100 m	10.49 s	Florence Griffith-Joyner (USA)	Indianapolis, US	16/07/1988
200 m	21.34 s	Florence Griffith-Joyner (USA)	Seoul, S Korea	29/09/1988
400 m	47.60 s	Marita Koch (GDR)	Canberra, Australia	06/10/1985
800 m	1:53.28	Jarmila Kratochvílová (TCH)	Munich, Germany	26/07/1983
1,000 m	2:28.98	Svetlana Masterkova (RUS)	Brussels, Belgium	23/08/1996
1,500 m	3:50.46	Yunxia Qu (CHN)	Beijing, China	11/09/1993
1 Mile	4:12.56	Svetlana Masterkova (RUS)	Zürich,Switzerland	14/08/1996
2,000 m	5:25.36	Sonia O'Sullivan (IRL)	Edinburgh	08/07/1994
3,000 m	8:06.11	Junxia Wang (CHN)	Beijing, China	13/09/1993
5,000 m	14:11.15	Tirunesh Dibaba (ETH)	Oslo, Norway	06/06/2008
10,000 m	29:31.78	Junxia Wang (CHN)	Beijing, China	08/09/1993
Marathon	2:15:25	Paula Radcliffe (GBR)	London	13/04/2003
100 m Hurdles	12.21 s	Yordanka Donkova (BUL)	Stara Zagora, Bulgaria	20/08/1988
400 m Hurdles	52.34 s	Yuliya Pechenkina (RUS)	Tula, Russia	08/08/2003
3,000 m Steeplechase	8:58.81	Gulnara Samitova-Galkina (RUS)	Beijing, China	17/08/2008
4x100 m Relay	41.37 s	Gladisch-Möller Silke, Rieger-Günther Sabine, Auerswald-Lange Ingrid, Göhr Marlies (GDR)	Canberra, Australia	06/10/1985
4x400 m Relay	3:15.17	Ledovskaya Tatyana, Nazarova Olga V., Kulchunova-Pinigina Mariya, Vladykina-Bryzgina Olga (USSR)	Seoul, S. Korea	01/10/1988

EVENT	RECORD	NAME (NATIONALITY)	VENUE	DATE
Discus	76.80 m	Gabriele Reinsch (GDR)	Neubrandenburg, Germany	09/07/1988
Hammer	77.80 m	Tatyana Lysenko (RUS)	Tallinn, Estonia	15/08/2006
High Jump	2.09 m	Stefka Kostadinova (BUL)	Rome, Italy	30/08/1987
Javelin	71.70 m	Osleidys Menéndez (CUB)	Helsinki, Finland	14/08/2005
Long Jump	7.52 m	Galina Chistyakova (URS)	Leningrad, Russia	11/06/1988
Pole Vault	5.05 m	Yelena Isinbaeva (RUS)	Beijing, China	18/08/2008
Shot Put	22.63 m	Natalya Lisovskaya (URS)	Moscow, Russia	07/06/1987
Triple Jump	15.50 m	Inessa Kravets (UKR)	Gothenburg, Sweden	10/08/1995
Heptathlon	7,291 pts	Jackie Joyner-Kersee (USA)	Seoul, S Korea	24/09/1988

Records accurate up to the end of the 2008 Olympics

TOP TEN MOVIE WEAPONS

1	**Lightsabre**	*Star Wars* **(1977)**
2	.44 Magnum	*Dirty Harry* (1971)
3	Bullwhip	*Indiana Jones* (1981)
4	Samurai sword	*Kill Bill* (2003)
5	Chainsaw	*Texas Chainsaw Massacre* (1974)
6	Golden gun	*The Man with the Golden Gun* (1974)
7	Bow and arrow	*Robin Hood* (1991)
8	Machine gun	*Scarface* (1983)
9	The Death Star	*Star Wars* (1977)
10	Bowler hat	*Goldfinger* (1964)

Source: Twentieth Century Fox survey of 2,000 film enthusiasts (2008)

THE WORLD'S BUSIEST AIRPORTS (BY ANNUAL PASSENGER NUMBERS)

	AIRPORT	IATA CODE	TOTAL PASSENGERS
1	Hartsfield-Jackson, Atlanta (US)	ATL	89,379,287
2	O'Hare, Chicago (US)	ORD	76,159,324
3	London Heathrow (UK)	LHR	68,068,554
4	Tokyo (Japan)	HND	66,671,435
5	Los Angeles (US)	LAX	61,895,548
6	Charles de Gaulle, Paris (France)	CDG	59,919,383
7	Dallas Fort Worth (US)	DFW	59,784,876
8	Frankfurt (Germany)	FRA	54,161,856
9	Beijing Capital (China)	PEK	53,736,923
10	Madrid Barajas (Spain)	MAD	52,122,214

Top Three By International Passengers: 1. London Heathrow (61.35 m); 2. Paris Charles De Gaulle (51.89 m); 3. Amsterdam Schiphol (45.94 m).

Top Three By Cargo: 1. Memphis, TN, US (3.69 m t); 2. Hong Kong (3.61 m t); 3. Anchorage, AK, US (2.69 m t).

Top Three By International Freight: 1. Hong Kong (3.58 m t); 2. Seoul, South Korea (2.31 m t); 3. Tokyo, Japan (2.24 m t).

Top ten figures relate to 2007; all others relate to 2006.

Source: Airports Council International

COMICBOOK SUPERHEROES

SUPERHERO	ALTER EGO	SUPERPOWER(S)	DEBUT
Zorro	Don Diego Vega	Sword-fighting; unarmed combat	1919
The Shadow	Lamont Cranston	Master of disguise	1930
Superman	Clarke Kent	Flight; speed; strength; x-ray vision	1938
Batman	Bruce Wayne	Flight; gadgetry	1939
Captain Marvel	Billy Batson	Flight; strength; wisdom	1940
Flash	Jay Garrick	Speed	1940
Captain America	Steve Rogers	Enhanced human physiology	1941
Wonder Woman	Diana Prince	Combat; flight; speed; strength	1941
Radioactive Man*	Claude Kane III	Flight; nuclear eyes; strength	1952
Marvelman	Micky Moran	Flight; forcefield creation; speed; strength	1954
Supergirl	Linda Lee	Flight; speed; strength; x-ray vision	1958
Incredible Hulk	Bruce Banner	Strength	1962
Spider-man	Peter Parker	Psychic sense; speed; webbing ability	1962
Black Panther	T'Challa	Acute senses; combat; gymnastics	1966
Bananaman	Eric Twinge	Flight; invulnerability; strength	1980
He-Man	Prince Adam	Stamina; strength; sword skills	1983
Zenith	Robert MacDowell	Durability; flight; strength	1987

* = A parody of a superhero portrayed within The Simpsons cartoon.

BRIT AWARDS

YEAR	SINGLE	ALBUM	FEMALE SOLO ARTIST	MALE SOLO ARTIST	GROUP
1990	Phil Collins 'Another Day in Paradise'	Fine Young Cannibals – The Raw and the Cooked	Annie Lennox	Phil Collins	Fine Young Cannibals
1991	Depeche Mode 'Enjoy the Silence'	George Michael – Listen Without Prejudice	Lisa Stansfield	Elton John	The Cure
1992	Queen 'Those Are the Days of our Lives'	Seal – Seal (1991)	Lisa Stansfield	Seal	KLF / Simply Red
1993	Take That 'Could It Be Magic'	Annie Lennox – Diva	Annie Lennox	Mick Hucknall	Simply Red
1994	Take That 'Pray'	Stereo MC's – Connected	Dina Carroll	Sting	Stereo MCs
1995	Blur 'Parklife'	Blur – Parklife	Eddi Reader	Paul Weller	Blur
1996	Take That 'Back For Good'	Oasis – (What's the Story) Morning Glory?	Annie Lennox	Paul Weller	Oasis
1997	Spice Girls 'Wannabe'	Manic Street Preachers – Everything Must Go	Gabrielle	George Michael	Manic Street Preachers
1998	All Saints 'Never Ever'	The Verve – Urban Hymns	Shola Ama	Finley Quaye	The Verve
1999	Robbie Williams 'Angels'	Manic Street Preachers – This is My Truth Tell Me Yours	Des'ree	Robbie Williams	Manic Street Preachers
2000	Robbie Williams 'She's the One'	Travis – The Man Who	Beth Orton	Tom Jones	Travis
2001	Robbie Williams 'Rock DJ'	Coldplay – Parachutes	Sonique	Robbie Williams	Coldplay

YEAR	SINGLE	ALBUM	FEMALE SOLO ARTIST	MALE SOLO ARTIST	GROUP
2002	S Club 7 'Don't Stop Movin''	Dido – No Angel	Dido	Robbie Williams	Travis
2003	Liberty X 'Just a Little'	Coldplay – A Rush of Blood to the Head	Ms Dynamite	Robbie Williams	Coldplay
2004	Dido 'White Flag'	The Darkness – Permission To Land	Dido	Daniel Bedingfield	The Darkness
2005	Will Young 'Your Game'	Keane – Hopes & Fears	Joss Stone	The Streets	Franz Ferdinand
2006	Coldplay 'Speed of Sound'	Coldplay – X&Y	KT Tunstall	James Blunt	Kaiser Chiefs
2007	Take That 'Patience'	Arctic Monkeys – Whatever People Say I Am, That's What I'm Not	Amy Winehouse	James Morrison	Arctic Monkeys
2008	Take That 'Shine'	Arctic Monkeys – Favourite Worst Nightmare	Kate Nash	Mark Ronson	Arctic Monkeys

ENGLISH LEAGUE FOOTBALL SALARIES

	GOALKEEPER	DEFENDER	MIDFIELDER	FORWARD	OVERALL
PREMIER LEAGUE	£533,000	£653,000	£754,000	£806,000	£676,000
CHAMPIONSHIP	£179,500	£167,000	£185,950	£292,900	£195,750
LEAGUE 1	£53,500	£61,000	£79,000	£75,000	£67,850
LEAGUE 2	£45,900	£44,400	£46,800	£67,900	£49,600

Figures relate to basic salary in 2006. Actual earnings may be as much as 100 per cent higher if bonuses are taken into consideration.

Source: Survey by The Independent (2006)

UK BEST-SELLING RECORDS
OF THE YEAR

YEAR	TITLE	BAND/ARTIST	SALES THAT YEAR
1980	'Don't Stand So Close To Me'	Police	0.8m
1981	'Don't You Want Me'	Human League	1.4m
1982	'Come on Eileen'	Dexy's Midnight Runners	1.2m
1983	'Karma Chameleon'	Culture Club	1.4m
1984	'Do They Know It's Christmas?'	Band Aid	3.5m
1985	'Power of Love'	Jennifer Rush	1.3m
1986	'Don't Leave Me This Way'	Communards	0.75m
1987	'Never Gonna Give You Up'	Rick Astley	0.78m
1988	'Mistletoe and Wine'	Cliff Richard	0.75m
1989	'Ride on Time'	Blackbox	0.97m
1990	'Unchained Melody'	Righteous Brothers	0.84m
1991	'(Everything I Do) I Do It For You'	Bryan Adams	1.5m
1992	'I Will Always Love You'	Whitney Houston	1.35m
1993	'I'd Do Anything For Love (But I Won't Do That)'	Meat Loaf	0.76m
1994	'Love Is All Around'	Wet Wet Wet	1.78m
1995	'Unchained Melody'	Robson and Jerome	1.84m
1996	'Killing Me Softly'	The Fugees	1.35m
1997	'Candle in the Wind' 1997/'Something About The Way You Look Tonight'	Elton John	4.77m
1998	'Believe'	Cher	1.5m
1999	'(Hit Me) Baby One More Time'	Britney Spears	1.45m
2000	'Can We Fix It?'	Bob the Builder	0.85m
2001	'It Wasn't Me'	Shaggy feat. RikRok	1.15m
2002	'Anything is Possible/Evergreen'	Will Young	1.78m
2003	'Where is the Love?'	Black-Eyed Peas	0.63m
2004	'Do They Know It's Christmas?'	Band Aid 20	1.07m
2005	'Is This the Way to Amarillo?'	Tony Christie feat. Peter Kay	1.1m
2006	'Crazy'	Gnarls Barkley	0.87m
2007	'Bleeding Love'	Leona Lewis	0.79m

Source: Official Chart Company

INTERNATIONAL RUGBY UNION
PLAYER RECORDS

	CAPS	TRIES	PENALTIES	CONVERSIONS	POINTS
Argentina	L. Arbizu; R. Martin (86)	J. M. N. Plossek (29)	G. Quesada (103)	H. Porta (84)	H. Porta (593)
Australia	G. Gregan (139)	D. Campese (64)	M. Lynagh (177)	M. Lynagh (140)	M. Lynagh (911)
England	J. Leonard (114)	R. Underwood (49)	J. Wilkinson (209)	J. Wilkinson (144)	J. Wilkinson (1090)
France	F. Pelous (118)	S. Blanco (38)	T. Lecroix (89)	C. Lamaison (59)	C. Lamaison (380)
Ireland	M. O'Kelly (91)	B. O'Driscoll (31)	R. O'Gara (156)	R. O'Gara (128)	R. O'Gara (827)
Italy	A. Troncon (101)	M. Cuttita (25)	D. Dominguez (209)	D. Dominguez (127)	D. Dominguez (983)
New Zealand	S. Fitzpatrick (92)	C. Howlett (49)	A. Mehrtens (188)	A. Mehrtens (169)	A. Mehrtens (967)
Scotland	S. Murray (87)	T. Stanger; I. Smith (24)	G. Hastings (140)	G. Hastings (86)	G. Hastings (667)
South Africa	P. Montgomery (94)	J. Van der Westhuizen (38)	P. Montgomery (145)	P. Montgomery (150)	P. Montgomery (873)
Wales	G. Thomas (100)	S. Williams (41)	N. Jenkins (235)	N. Jenkins (130)	N. Jenkins (1049)
British & Irish Lions	W. McBride (17)	A. O'Reilly (6)	G. Hastings (20)	S. Wilson; J Wilkinson (6)	G. Hastings (66)

British & Irish Lions caps and points are not included in the national statistics. Statistics include all full cap matches up to the end of the 2008 Six Nations Championship.

TOP 20 AVERAGE LEAGUE ATTENDANCES IN EUROPEAN FOOTBALL

	CLUB	STADIUM	07/08 AVERAGE
1	Barcelona	Nou Camp	76,243
2	Manchester Utd	Old Trafford	75,691
3	Borussia Dortmund	Signal Iduna Park	72,321
4	Bayern Munich	Allianz Arena	68,412
5	Real Madrid	Santiago Bernabéu	64,426
6	Schalke 04	Veltins Arena	61,334
7	Arsenal	Emirates Stadium	60,070
8	AC Milan	San Siro	56,579
9	Hamburg	AOL Arena	55,752
10	Celtic	Celtic Park	53,573
11	Internazionale	San Siro	52,010
12	VfB Stuttgart	Mercedes-Benz Arena	51,782
13	Newcastle Utd	St James' Park	50,488
14	Marseille	Stade Vélodrome	50,387
15	Ajax	Amsterdam Arena	48,872
16	Eintracht Frankfurt	Commerzbank-Arena	48,082
17	Borussia Mönchengladbach	Borussia-Park	46,739
18	Hertha Berlin	Olympic Stadium	45,693
19	Rangers	Ibrox Stadium	45,617
20	Atletico de Madrid	Vicente Calderón	44,447
Source: www.soccer365.com			

MOST POPULAR DISPOSABLE LIGHTER BRANDS IN THE UK

MANUFACTURER (FOUNDED)	MODELS	TRIVIA
Flamagas (Spain)	Clipper (R)	The Classic CP11R has a round body and a removable flint/spark wheel stick. The manufacturers claim gas content is 3,000 lights. Clippers are manufactured at the company HQ in Barcelona and in Chennai, India.
Ronson (US)	Clearlite / Colourlite / Electrolite; Comet (R)	Ronson was founded by Louis V. Aronson in NYC in 1886. The Clearite is the company's most popular disposable.
Société Bic (France)	Bic Classic; Bic Electronic	Bic is the top-selling lighter brand in North America. The Bic Classic, oval plastic-cased disposable, comes in maxi, mini and slim sizes and was introduced in 1973. The Bic Electronic was introduced in 1991. Five million Bic lighters are sold worldwide every day. Over 15 bn have been produced in total.
Swedish Match (Germany)	Cricket; Poppell (R); Swan (R)	Combined, the three lighter types have a 25 per cent share of the UK lighter market. The company produces over 250 m lighters a year from their factory in Assen, Netherlands.
Tokai (Japan)	Tokai M13 LCS Classic (flint-ignition); Tokai M12 C Classic (piezo-ignition)	Tokai's European plant (Moenchengladbach, Germany) produces over 200 m disposable lighters per year.
Key: (R) = Refillable.		

CONFECTIONERY SOLD IN THE UK

NAME	MAKER	FIRST INTRODUCED	NAME	MAKER	FIRST INTRODUCED
Aero	Nestlé	1935	Maltesers	Mars	1936
After Eight	Nestlé	1962	Mars Bar	Mars	1932
Boost	Cadbury	1985	Milky Bar	Nestlé	1937
Bounty	Mars	1951	Milky Way	Mars	1923
Buttons	Cadbury	1960	Munchies	Nestlé	1957
Caramac	Nestlé	1959	Picnic	Cadbury	1958
Caramel	Cadbury	1976	Reese's Peanut Butter Cups	The Hershey Company	1928
Creme Egg	Cadbury	1971	Rolo	Nestlé	1938
Crunch	Nestlé	1965	Skittles	Mars	1979
Crunchie	Cadbury	1929	Smarties	Nestlé	1937
Curly Wurly	Cadbury	1971	Snickers	Mars	1930
Dairy Milk	Cadbury	1905	Starbar	Cadbury	1974
Double Decker	Cadbury	1976	Starburst	Mars	1960
Drifter	Nestlé	1980	Time Out	Cadbury	1992
Flake	Cadbury	1920	Toblerone	Kraft	1908
Flump	Cadbury	1986	Toffee Crisp	Nestlé	1963
Freddo	Cadbury	1930	Toffo	Nestlé	1939
Fruit & Nut	Cadbury	1928	Tooty Frooties	Nestlé	1963
Fruit Pastilles	Nestlé	1881	Turkish Delight	Cadbury	1914
Fruit Gums	Nestlé	1893	Twirl	Cadbury	1987
Fudge	Cadbury	1948	Twix	Mars	1967
Galaxy	Mars	1960	Walnut Whip	Nestlé	1910

NAME	MAKER	FIRST INTRODUCED	NAME	MAKER	FIRST INTRODUCED
Hershey Bar	The Hershey Company	1894	**Wispa**	Cadbury	1981
Jelly Tots	Nestlé	1967	**Yorkie**	Nestlé	1976
KitKat	Nestlé	1935			
Lion Bar	Nestlé	1976			
M&M's	Mars	1941			

UK Market Stats (2006): Total sales (£4.41 bn); Chocolate confectionery (72.3%); Sugar confectionery (27.3%).

Market Stats Source: www.just-food.com

SCOTTISH LEAGUE CUP CHAMPIONS

	CLUB	LAST WIN	WINS	RUNNERS-UP
1	**Rangers**	2008	25	6
2	**Celtic**	2006	13	13
3	**Aberdeen**	1996	5	7
4	**Hearts**	1963	4	2
5	**Hibernian**	2007	3	6
5	**Dundee**	1974	3	3
5	**East Fife**	1954	3	0
7	**Dundee Utd**	1981	2	4
9	**Partick Thistle**	1972	1	3
9	**Motherwell**	1951	1	2
9	**Raith Rovers**	1995	1	1
9	**Livingston**	2004	1	0

Inception: 1946/1947. Sponsors: no sponsor (1946–1979); Bell's (1979–1984); Skol (1984–1994); Coca-Cola (1994–1999); CIS Insurance (1999–present).
Reached Final: Kilmarnock (5); Dunfermline (3); St Johnstone (2); Ayr Utd (1); Falkirk (1); Morton (1); St Mirren (1); Third Lanark (1).

LARGEST UK TV AUDIENCES

	NAME	VIEWERS (MILLIONS)	DATE	CHANNEL
ENTERTAINMENT				
1	*EastEnders* **(Den and Angie Watts got divorced)**	30.15	25+28/12/1986 (Thu)	BBC1
2	*Coronation Street* (Alan Bradley tried to kill Rita)	26.93	19/03/1989 (Sun)	ITV
3	*Only Fools and Horses* ('Time on Our Hands')	24.35	29/12/1996 (Sun)	BBC1
4	*EastEnders* (Pat ran down a child)	24.30	02/01/1992 (Thu)	BBC1
5	*To the Manor Born* ('A Touch of Class')	23.95	11/11/1979 (Sun)	BBC1
FACTUAL (EXCLUDING SPORT)				
1	**Funeral of Diana, Princess of Wales**	32.10	06/09/1997 (Sat)	BBC1/ITV
2	The Royal Family Documentary	30.69	21/06/1969 (Sat) (BBC) and 28/06/1969 (Sat) (ITV)	BBC1/ITV
3	Apollo 13 Splashdown	28.60	17/04/1970 (Fri)	BBC1/ITV
4	Royal Wedding Ceremony	28.40	29/07/1981 (Wed)	BBC1/ITV
5	Princess Anne's Wedding	27.60	14/11/1973 (Wed)	BBC1/ITV
SPORT				
1	**FIFA World Cup Final 1966: England v West Germany**	32.30	30/07/1966 (Sat)	BBC1/ITV
2	FA Cup Final Replay: Chelsea v Leeds	28.49	29/04/1970 (Wed)	BBC1/ITV
3	Winter Olympics 1994: Torvill and Dean	23.95	21/02/1994 (Mon)	BBC1
4	FIFA World Cup 1998: England v Argentina	23.78	30/06/1998 (Tue)	ITV
5	Heavyweight Boxing: Muhammad Ali v Joe Frazier	21.12	09/03/1971 (Tue)	BBC1

	NAME	VIEWERS (MILLIONS)	DATE	CHANNEL
FILMS				
1	*Live and Let Die*	23.50	20/01/1980 (Sun)	ITV
2	*Jaws*	23.25	08/10/1981 (Thu)	ITV
3	*The Spy Who Loved Me*	22.90	28/03/1982 (Sun)	ITV
4	*Diamonds Are Forever*	22.15	15/03/1981 (Sun)	ITV
5	*Crocodile Dundee*	21.75	25/12/1989 (Mon)	BBC1
Source: BFI/BARB				

CITIES WITH THE MOST SKYSCRAPERS

	CITY	HIGHEST SKYSCRAPER	TOTAL
1	**Hong Kong, China**	2 International Finance Centre (2003) 406.9 m	7,687
2	**New York City, US**	Empire State Building (1931) 381.0 m	5,631
3	**São Paulo, Brazil**	Mirante do Vale (1960) 170.0 m	5,176
4	**Singapore, Singapore**	OUB Centre (1986); UOB Plaza One (1992); Republic Plaza (1995) 280.0 m	3,896
5	**Seoul, South Korea**	Samsung Tower Palace 3 – Tower G (2004) 264.0 m	2,872
6	**Tokyo, Japan**	Tokyo Midtown (2007) 248.0 m	2,769
7	**Rio de Janeiro, Brazil**	Rio-Sul Center (1980) 164.0 m	2,384
8	**Istanbul, Turkey**	Isbank Tower 1 (2000) 181.2 m	2,123
9	**Moscow, Russia**	Naberezhnaya Tower (2007) 268.4 m	2,026
10	**Toronto, Canada**	First Canadian Place (1975) 298.1 m	1,719

'Skyscraper' is defined here as those buildings that were complete with 12 floors or more in 2007. Heights listed are to top of building roof, not to top of spire.

Source: www.emporis.com

UK MEN'S ATHLETICS
NATIONAL RECORDS

EVENT	RECORD	NAME (NATIONALITY)	VENUE	DATE
100 m	9.87 s	Linford Christie (E)	Stuttgart, Germany	15/08/1993
	9.87 s	Dwain Chambers (E)	Paris, France	14/09/2002
200 m	19.94 s	John Regis (E)	Stuttgart, Germany	20/08/1993
400 m	44.36 s	Iwan Thomas (W)	Birmingham	13/08/1997
800 m	1.41:73	Sebastian Coe (E)	Florence, Italy	10/06/1981
1,000 m	2.12.18	Steve Cram (E)	Nice, France	11/07/1981
1,500 m	3.29:67	Sebastian Coe (E)	Oslo, Norway	16/07/1985
1 Mile	3.46:32	Steve Cram (E)	Oslo, Norway	27/07/1985
2,000 m	4.51:39	Steve Cram (E)	Budapest, Hungary	04/08/1985
3,000 m	7.32:79	David Moorcroft (E)	Crystal Palace	17/07/1982
5,000 m	13.00:41	David Moorcroft (E)	Oslo, Norway	07/07/1982
10,000 m	27.18:14	Jon Brown (W)	Brussels, Belgium	28/08/1998
110 m Hurdles	12.91 s	Colin Jackson (W)	Stuttgart, Germany	20/08/1993
400 m Hurdles	47.82 s	Kriss Akabusi (E)	Barcelona, Spain	06/08/1992
3,000 m Steeplechase	8.07:96	Mark Rowland (E)	Seoul, S. Korea	30/08/1988
4x100 m Relay	37.73 s	Jason Gardener (E), Darren Campbell (E), Marlon Devonish (E), Dwain Chambers (E) (GB)	Seville, Spain	29/08/1999
4x200 m Relay	1 m 21.29 s	Marcus Adam (E), Ade Mafe (E), Linford Christie (E), John Regis (E)	Birmingham	23/06/1989
4x400 m Relay	2 m 56.60 s	Iwan Thomas (W), Jamie Baulch (E), Mark Richardson (E), Roger Black (E)	Atlanta, US	03/08/1996

EVENT	RECORD	NAME (NATIONALITY)	VENUE	DATE
4x800 m Relay	7 m 03.89 s	Peter Elliott (E), Garry Cook (E), Steve Cram (E), Sebastian Coe (E)	Crystal Palace	30/08/1982
Discus	66.64 m	Perriss Wilkins (E)	Birmingham	06/06/1998
Hammer	77.54 m	Martin Girvan (NI)	Wolverhampton	12/05/1984
High Jump	2.37	Steve Smith (E)	Seoul, S. Korea	20/09/1992
Javelin	91.46 m	Steve Backley (E)	Auckland, NZ	25/01/2005
Long Jump	8.29 m	Chris Tomlinson (E)	Bad Langensalza, Germany	07/07/2007
Pole Vault	5.80 m	Nick Buckfield (E)	Chania, Greece	27/05/1998
Shot Put	21.92 m	Carl Myerscough (E)	Sacramento, US	13/06/2003
Triple Jump	18.29 m	Jonathan Edwards (E)	Gothenburg, Sweden	07/08/1995
Decathlon	8,847 pts	Daley Thompson (E)	Los Angeles, US	8–9/08/1984

Key: E = English; NI = Northern Irish; W = Welsh.

MEN'S ATHLETICS WORLD RECORDS

EVENT	RECORD	NAME (NATIONALITY)	VENUE	DATE
100 m	9.69 s	Usain Bolt (JAM)	Beijing, China	16/08/2008
200 m	19.30 s	Michael Johnson (USA)	Beijing, China	20/08/2008
400 m	43.18 s	Michael Johnson (USA)	Seville, Spain	26/08/1999
800 m	1:41.11	Wilson Kipketer (DEN)	Köln, Germany	24/08/1997
1,000 m	2:11.96	Noah Ngeny (KEN)	Rieti, Italy	05/09/1999
1,500 m	3:26.00	Hicham El Guerrouj (MAR)	Roma, Italy	14/07/1998
1 Mile	3:43.13	Hicham El Guerrouj (MAR)	Rome, Italy	07/07/1999
2,000 m	4:44.79	Hicham El Guerrouj (MAR)	Berlin, Germany	07/09/1999
3,000 m	7:20.67	Daniel Komen (KEN)	Rieti, Italy	01/09/1996
5,000 m	12:37.35	Kenenisa Bekele (ETH)	Hengelo, Netherlands	31/05/2004
10,000 m	26:17.53	Kenenisa Bekele (ETH)	Brussels, Belgium	26/08/2005
110 m Hurdles	12.87 s	Dayron Robles (CUB)	Ostrava, Czech Republic	12/06/2008
400 m Hurdles	46.78 s	Kevin Young (USA)	Barcelona, Spain	06/08/1992
3,000 m Steeplechase	7:53.63	Saif Saaeed Shaheen (QAT)	Brussels, Belgium	03/09/2004
4x100 m Relay	37.10 s	Nesta Carter, Michael Frater, Usain Bolt, Asafa Powell (USA)	Beijing, China	20/08/2008
4x100 m Relay	37.40 s	Jon Drummond, Andre Cason, Dennis Mitchell, Leroy Burrell (USA)	Stuttgart, Germany	21/08/1993
4x200 m Relay	1:18.68	Michael Marsh, Leroy Burrell, Floyd Heard, Carl Lewis (Santa Monica Track Club, USA)	Walnut, US	17/04/1994
4x400 m Relay	2:54.20	Jerome Young, Antonio Pettigrew, Tyree Washington, Michael Johnson (USA)	Uniondale, US	22/07/1998

EVENT	RECORD	NAME (NATIONALITY)	VENUE	DATE
4x800 m Relay	7:02.43	Joseph Mwengi Mutua, William Yiampoy, Ismael Kipngetich Kombich, Wilfred Bungei (KEN)	Brussels, Belgium	25/08/2006
Discus	74.08 m	Jürgen Schult (GDR)	Neubrandenburg, Germany	06/06/1986
Hammer	86.74 m	Yuriy Sedykh (USSR)	Stuttgart, Germany	30/08/1986
Javelin	98.48 m	Jan Zelezný (CZE)	Jena, Germany	25/05/1996
High Jump	2.45 m	Javier Sotomayor (CUB)	Salamanca, Spain	27/07/1993
Long Jump	8.95 m	Mike Powell (USA)	Tokyo, Japan	30/08/1991
Pole Vault	6.14 m	A Sergey Bubka (UKR)	Sestriere, Italy	31/07/1994
Shot Put	23.12 m	Randy Barnes (USA)	Westwood, US	20/05/1990
Triple Jump	18.29 m	Jonathan Edwards (GB)	Gothenburg, Sweden	07/08/1995
Decathlon	9,026 pts	Roman Šebrle (CZE)	Götzis, Austria	27/05/2001

Records accurate up to the end of the 2008 Olympics

FEMALE SEX TOYS

Anal vibrator	To prevent the danger of complete insertion, these are designed with either a long handle grip, or a wide base.
Ben Wa balls	Hollow metal balls designed for vaginal insertion and can be worn while doing everyday tasks.
Bullet vibrator	Small, bullet-shaped; intended for stimulation or to be inserted into other sex toys (e.g., a dildo) to enable vibration.
Butterfly vibrator	A harness with a vibrating element in the clitoral area which facilitates hands-free clitoral stimulation during intercourse.
Clitoral vibrator (aka vibrating wand)	Incorporating a handle and large rounded end, suitable for clitoral but not internal stimulation. Sometimes closely resembling or identical to, products sold as back massagers.
Dildo	Usually phallic-shaped and made of rubber, glass or metal; non-vibrating and may be used either vaginally, or anally.
Discreet vibrator (aka undercover)	Disguised as everyday objects, e.g., lipstick, mascara tube, nail polish or mobile phone.
Double-ended dildo	A long, flexible dildo designed for mutual penetration of two women, or double penetration of one.
Dual area vibrator (aka Rabbit)	A traditional shape with an attached prong to stimulate the clitoris.
Finger vibrator	A mini-vibrator that fits over the finger like a ring.
G-spot vibrator	Traditionally shaped but curved at the end to make g-spot stimulation easier.
Luxury vibrator	More expensive versions of the traditional shapes, made using precious metals, sometimes with added jewellery, and usually sold in upmarket shops.
Nipple clamp	A light, adjustable-pressure clamp used to stimulate the nipples.
Suction device	To increase sensitivity by engorging the nipples.
Traditional vibrator	Shaped like a penis.
Triple area vibrator	Three pronged, for clitoral, vaginal and anal area stimulation.
Vibrating egg	Egg-shaped design for complete insertion into the vagina.
Vibrating lingerie	Lingerie with a vibrating element in the clitoral area. Remote controlled and can be worn under ordinary clothes.
Waterproof vibrator	Sealed so as to enable use in the bath, shower or hot-tub.

FORMULA 1 GRAND PRIX
AT SILVERSTONE

Location: Silverstone, Northamptonshire. Circuit Length: 5.141 km (3.194 m).

Distance: 59 laps (188.410 miles/303.216 km).

Lap Record: 1 m 18.739 s (Michael Schumacher, Ferrari, 2004, F1).

Current Layout: from 2000 (9th design since 1948).

First Grand Prix Winner: Peter Villoresi (Ita) Maserati (1948).

First F1 World Championship Race Winner: Giuseppe Farina (Ita) Alfa Romeo (1950).

British F1 Winners: Peter Collins (1958), Jim Clark (1963, 1965, 1967), Jackie Stewart (1969, 1971), James Hunt (1977), John Watson (1981), Nigel Mansell (1987, 1991, 1992), Damon Hill (1994), Johnny Herbert (1995), David Coulthard (1999, 2000).

SEASON	F1 WINNER
2000	David Coulthard (UK) McLaren Mercedes
2001	Mika Häkkinen (Fin) McLaren Mercedes
2002	Michael Schumacher (Ger) Ferrari
2003	Rubens Barrichello (Bra) Ferrari
2004	Michael Schumacher (Ger) Ferrari
2005	Juan Pablo Montoya (Col) McLaren Mercedes
2006	Fernando Alonso (Spa) Renault
2007	Kimi Räikkönen (Fin) Ferrari
2008	Lewis Hamilton (UK) McLaren Mercedes

EUROPEAN NATIONAL
FOOTBALL LEAGUES

NATION	NATIONAL ASSOCIATION	TOP LEAGUE	MOST PREVALENT LEAGUE WINNERS (TITLES WON)
Austria	Österreichischer Fußball-Bund (OFB) (1904)	Österreichische Fußball-Bundesliga	Rapid Vienna (32); FK Austria Wien (23)
Belgium	Union Royale Belge des Societes de Football Association (URBSFA) (1895)	Belgian First Division	RSC Anderlecht (29); Club Brugge (13)
Bulgaria	Bulgarian Football Union (BFU) (1923)	Bulgarian A Professional Football Group	CSKA Sofia (31); Levski Sofia (25)
Croatia	Hrvatski Nogometni Savez (HNS) 1912	Prva HNL	Dynamo Zagreb (10); Hajduk Split (6)
Czech Republic	Českomoravský Fotbalový Svaz (ČFS) (1901)	Czech Premier League	Sparta Prague (10); Slavia Prague (2); Slovan Liberec (2)
Denmark	Dansk Boldspil-Union (DBU) (1889)	Danish Superliga	KB (15); Brondby IF (10)
England	The Football Association (The FA) (1863)	The Premier League	Liverpool (18); Manchester United (17)
France	Fédération Française de Football (FFF) (1919)	Championnats Nationaux Ligue I	Saint-Étienne (10); Olympique de Marseille (8); FC Nantes (8)
Germany	Deutscher Fußball-Bund (DFB) (1900)	Deutsche Fußball-Liga Bundesliga	Bayern Munich (21); BFC Dynamo Berlin (10)
Greece	Hellenic Football Federation (HFF) (1926)	Alpha Ethniki	Olympiakos (36); Panathinaikos (19)
Ireland	Football Association of Ireland (FAI) (1921)	FAI Premier Division	Shamrock Rovers (15); Shelbourne (13)
Italy	Federazione Italiana Giuoco Calcio (FIGC) (1898)	Lega Nazionale Professionisti Serie A	Juventus (27); AC Milan (17)
Netherlands	Koninklijke Nederlandse Voetbalbond (KNVB) (1889)	KNVB Eredivisie	Ajax Amsterdam (29); PSV Eindhoven (21)
Northern Ireland	Irish Football Association (IFA) (1880)	Irish Premier League	Linfield (48); Glentoran (22)

NATION	NATIONAL ASSOCIATION	TOP LEAGUE	MOST PREVALENT LEAGUE WINNERS (TITLES WON)
Norway	Norges Fotballforbund (NFF) (1902)	Eliteserien	Rosenborg (20); Fredrikstad (9)
Poland	Polski Związek Piłki Notnej (PZPN) (1919)	Ekstraklasa	Górnik Zabrze (14); Ruch Chorzów (14)
Portugal	Federação Portuguesa de Futebol (FPF) (1914)	Liga de Clubes SuperLiga	SL Benfica (31); FC Porto (23)
Romania	Federatia Romana de Fotbal (FRF) (1909)	Liga I	FC Steaua Bucureşti (23); FC Dinamo Bucureşti (18)
Russia	Football Union of Russia (RFU) (1912)	Russian Premier League	Spartak Moscow (9); CSKA Moscow (3)
Scotland	Scottish Football Association (SFA) (1873)	Scottish Premier League	Rangers (51); Celtic (42)
Spain	Real Federación Española de Fútbol (RFEF) (1909)	La Liga Primera Division	Real Madrid (31); FC Barcelona (18)
Sweden	Svenska Fotbollförbundet (SvFF) (1904)	Allsvenskan	Malmö FF (18); IFK Göteborg (13)
Switzerland	Association Suisse de Football (ASF) (1895)	Swiss Super League	Grasshopper-Club Zürich (27); FC Basel (12)
Turkey	Türkiye Futbol Federasyonu (TFF) (1923)	Premier Super League	Fenerbahçe SK (17); Galatasaray SK (17)
Ukraine	Football Federation of Ukraine (FFU) (1991)	Vyscha Liha	Dynamo Kyiv (12); Shakhtar Donetsk (4)
Wales	Football Association of Wales (FAW)	Welsh Premier League	Barry Town (7); The New Saints (4)

Stats account for league seasons complete up to the end of the 2007/08 season.

GRAND THEFT AUTO GAME FRANCHISE

GAME	PLATFORMS	UK RELEASE	PLAYABLE CHARACTER(S)	SETTING	RADIO STATIONS
Grand Theft Auto	GBC; PC; PS	1997 (PC; PS); 1999 (GBC)	Travis; Kat; Mikki; Divine; Bubba; Troy; Kivlov; Ulrika	Liberty City; San Andreas; Vice City	7
GTA: London Mission Packs	PC; PS	1999	Mick Casey; Maurice Caine; Charles Jones; Johnny Hawthorn; Winston Henry; Rodney Morash; Sid Vacant	London (1961); London (1969)	7
Grand Theft Auto 2	Dreamcast; GBC; PC; PS	1999 (PC; PS); 2000 (Dreamcast; GBC)	Claude Speed	Anywhere City (circa 1999)	11
Grand Theft Auto III	PC; PS2; Xbox	2001 (PS2); 2002 (PC); 2003 (Xbox)	Claude	Liberty City (circa 2001)	9
GTA: Vice City	PC; PS2; Xbox	2002 (PS2); 2003 (PC); 2004 (Xbox)	Tommy Vercetti	Vice City (1986)	9
GTA: San Andreas	PC; PS2; Xbox	2004 (PS2); 2005 (PC; Xbox)	Carl 'CJ' Johnson	San Andreas (1992)	11
GTA Advance	GBA	2004	Mike	Liberty City (2000)	none
GTA: Liberty City Stories	PSP; PS2	2005 (PSP); 2006 (PS2)	Toni Cipriani	Liberty City (1998)	8
GTA: Vice City Stories	PSP; PS2	2006 (PSP); 2007 (PS2)	Victor Vance	Vice City (1986)	9
Grand Theft Auto IV	PS3; Xbox 360	2008	Niko Bellic	Liberty City (2008)	18

Original Pre-Release Title: 'Race 'n' Chase'.

Locations Based on Real Cities: Liberty City = New York City/New Jersey; San Andreas = Las Vegas; Los Angeles; San Francisco; Vice City = Miami.

Developers: most of the games were developed by Rockstar North. The Xbox versions of GTA III, and GTA: Vice City were developed by Rockstar Vienna. Rockstar Leeds co-developed Liberty City Stories, and Vice City Stories. Digital Eclipse developed GTA Advance. Up until 2002, Rockstar North was known as DMA Design.

Perspective: the games had a top-down perspective until 2001. Since the 3D perspective was introduced with GTA III, only GTA Advance has reverted back to the top-down style.

FIFA WORLD CUP AWARDS

TOURNAMENT	FAIR PLAY AWARD	YASHIN AWARD
1978 Argentina	Argentina	-
1982 Spain	Brazil	-
1986 Mexico	Brazil	-
1990 Italy	England	-
1994 US	Brazil	Michel Preud'homme (Belgium)
1998 France	England; France	Fabien Barthez (France)
2002 Japan/Korea	Belgium	Oliver Kahn (Germany)
2006 Germany	Brazil; Spain	Gianluigi Buffon (Italy)

Fair Play Award: Given to teams recognised to have played in a manner that is good for the game. Only teams that qualify for the second round can be considered for the Fair Play award. Winners receive a Fair Play trophy, a medal for each player and official plus a cash award to be used for buying equipment for national youth development.

Yashin Award: Named after the late Russian goalkeeper Lev Yashin. Yashin won 75 caps for USSR between 1954 and 1970. He played his entire career with Dynamo Moscow (1949–1971), and won the USSR Championship five times. He was nicknamed the black spider, and was renowned for his remarkable point-blank reflex saves. In 1953, playing in goals for the Dynamo Kiev ice hockey team, he was part of the team that won the USSR ice hockey championship. In 2000, FIFA named Yashin 'World Goalkeeper of the Century'.

TOP TEN PARODY FILMS
(BY BOX OFFICE TAKINGS)

YEAR	FILM (YEAR)	STARRING	INCLUDING PARODIES OF:	PRODUCTION BUDGET ($ m)	WORLDWIDE BOX OFFICE ($ m)
1999	*Austin Powers: The Spy Who Shagged Me* Jay Roach	Mike Myers as Austin Powers; Heather Graham as Felicity Shagwell; Robert Wagner as Number 2; Rob Lowe as Young Number 2	James Bond [1967–1977]	35	310
2002	*Austin Powers in Goldmember* Jay Roach; Steven Spielberg	Mike Myers as Austin Powers; Beyoncé Knowles as Foxxy Cleopatra; Robert Wagner as Number 2; Michael Caine as Nigel Powers	James Bond [*Goldfinger; You Only Live Twice; The Spy Who Loved Me*]	63	293
2000	*Scary Movie* Keenan Wayans	Anna Faris as Cindy Campbell; Regina Hall as Brenda Meeks; Jon Abrahams as Bobby Prinze	*Scream* [trilogy]; *I Know What You Did Last Summer; I Still Know What You Did Last Summer; Friday the 13th*	19	277
2006	*Scary Movie 4* David Zucker	Anna Faris as Cindy Campbell; Regina Hall as Brenda Meeks; Craig Bierko as Tom Ryan	*The Grudge; War of the Worlds; Saw; Brokeback Mountain; The Village; Million Dollar Baby*	40	179
1991	*Hot Shots!* Jim Abrahams	Charlie Sheen as Lt Topper Harley; Cary Elwes as Lt Kent Harley; Valeria Golino as Ramada Thompson; Lloyd Bridges as Tug Benson	*Top Gun; Dances with Wolves; Gone with the Wind; 9 ½ Weeks; Rocky; Superman*	26	176

YEAR	FILM (YEAR)	STARRING	INCLUDING PARODIES OF:	PRODUCTION BUDGET ($ m)	WORLDWIDE BOX OFFICE ($ m)
2003	*Scary Movie 3* David Zucker	Anna Faris as Cindy Campbell; Regina Hall as Brenda Meeks; Jenny McCarthy as Kate	*The Ring; Signs; The Matrix Reloaded; The Lord of the Rings; Bruce Almighty; The Sixth Sense*	45	155
2001	*Scary Movie 2* Keenan Wayans	Anna Faris as Cindy Campbell; Regina Hall as Brenda Meeks; Christopher Masterson as Buddy	*The Exorcist; Hollow Man; The Shining; The Haunting; Poltergeist; Urban Legend; Hannibal; Cast Away; It*	45	141
1993	*Hot Shots! Part Deux* Jim Abrahams	Charlie Sheen as Topper Harley; Valeria Golino as Ramada Thompson; Lloyd Bridges as Tug Benson	*Rambo; Apocalypse Now; Predator; Missing in Action; Commando*	30	133
1974	*Blazing Saddles* Mel Brooks	Cleavon Little as Sheriff Bart; Gene Wilder as Jim	*High Noon; Destry Rides Again; The Producers; History of the World, Part 1*	2.6	119
1996	*Mars Attacks!* Tim Burton	Jack Nicholson as Art Land; Glenn Close as First Lady Marsha Dale; Pierce Brosnan as Prof Donald Kessler	*The War of the Worlds; Independence Day; Godzilla*	70	101

BDO WORLD DARTS CHAMPIONSHIP

YEAR	CHAMPION	SCORE	RUNNER-UP	PRIZE FUND*
1990	Phil Taylor (Eng)	6–1	Eric Bristow (Eng)	101.2^/24/12
1991	Dennis Priestley (Eng)	6–0	Eric Bristow (Eng)	110.5/26/13
1992	Phil Taylor (Eng)	6–5	Mike Gregory (Eng)	119.5/28/14
1993	John Lowe (Eng)	6–3	Alan Warriner (Eng)	128.5/30/15
1994	John Part (Can) 82.44	6–0	Bobby George (Eng) 80.31	136.1/32/16
1995	Richie Burnett (Wal) 93.63	6–3	Raymond van Barneveld (Net) 91.23	143/34/17
1996	Steve Beaton (Eng) 90.27	6–3	Richie Burnett (Wal) 88.05	150/36/18
1997	Les Wallace** (Sco) 92.19	6–3	Marshall James (Wal) 92.01	158/38/19
1998	Raymond van Barneveld (Net) 93.96	6–5	Richie Burnett (Wal) 97.14	166/40/20
1999	Raymond van Barneveld (Net) 94.65	6–5	Ronnie Baxter (Eng) 94.65	174/42/21
2000	Ted Hankey (Eng) 92.40	6–0	Ronnie Baxter (Eng) 88.35	182/44/22
2001	John Walton (Eng) 95.55	6–2	Ted Hankey (Eng) 94.86	189/46/23
2002	Tony David (Aus) 93.57	6–4	Mervyn King (Eng) 89.67	197/48/24
2003	Raymond van Barneveld (Net) 94.86	6–3	Ritchie Davies (Wal) 90.66	205/50/25
2004	Andy Fordham (Eng) 97.08	6–3	Mervyn King (Eng) 91.02	201/50/25
2005	Raymond van Barneveld (Net) 96.78	6–2	Martin Adams (Eng) 91.35	201/50/25
2006	Jelle Klaasen (Net) 90.42	7–5	Raymond van Barneveld (Net) 93.06	211/60/25
2007	Martin Adams (Eng) 90.30	7–6	Phill Nixon (Eng) 87.09	226/70/30
2008	Mark Webster** (Wal) 92.07	7–5	Simon Whitlock (Aus) 93.92	258/85/30

First Original BDO (Pre-1994) Winner: Leighton Rees (Wal) 92.40 beat John Lowe (Eng) 89.40 in 1978. The total prize money for the tournament was £10,500; the winner received £3,000 and the runner-up received £1,700.

Most Original BDO (Pre-1994) Wins: Eric Bristow (Eng) (5).

First Original BDO (Pre-1994) 100+ Average: Keith Deller (Eng) 100.29 (1985 QF v John Lowe).

Other Original BDO (Pre-1994) 100+ Averages: Phil Taylor (Eng) 100.80 (1990 SF v Cliff Lazarenko; Dennis Priestley (Eng) 102.63 (1992 R1 v Jocky Wilson).

LARGE NUMBERS

1,000,000	Million	10^{36}	Undecillion
1,000,000,000	Billion	10^{39}	Duodecillion
10^{12}	Trillion	10^{42}	Tredecillion
10^{15}	Quadrillion	10^{45}	Quattuordecillion
10^{18}	Quintillion	10^{48}	Quindecillion
10^{21}	Sextillion	10^{51}	Sexdecillion
10^{24}	Septillion	10^{54}	Septendecillion
10^{27}	Octillion	10^{57}	Octodecillion
10^{30}	Nontillion	10^{60}	Novemdecillion
10^{33}	Decillion	10^{100}	Googol

Short-Scale vs Long-Scale: in the nineteenth and most of the twentieth century, the British 'billion' was defined as 1,000,000,000,000. This was the long-scale definition. The difference between long and short-scale is that in long-scale each naming jump after one million is a multiplication of 1,000,000 (i.e., 10^{12} is one billion, 10^{18} is one trillion, 10^{24} is one quadrillion, etc); in short-scale, each jump is a multiplication of 1,000. The US standard has always been short-scale, and in 1974 the UK government opted to officially switch to the short-scale system.

International adoption of short-scale: English-speaking countries generally use the short-scale, as well as Brazil. Bulgaria, Estonia, Indonesia, Iran, Israel, Latvia, Russia, and Turkey all use short-scale, but use the traditional long-scale word (milliard) instead of billion. Most other countries use the long-scale system or their own national version of it.

PDC WORLD DARTS CHAMPIONSHIP

YEAR	CHAMPION	SCORE	RUNNER-UP	PRIZE FUND*
1994	Dennis Priestley (Eng) 94.38	6–1	Phil Taylor (Eng) 90.62	64/16/8
1995	Phil Taylor (Eng) 94.11	6–2	Rod Harrington (Eng) 87.15	55/12/6
1996	Phil Taylor (Eng) 98.52	6–4	Dennis Priestley (Eng) 101.49	61/14/7
1997	Phil Taylor (Eng) 100.92	6–0	Dennis Priestley (Eng) 96.78	98/45/10
1998	Phil Taylor (Eng) 103.98	6–2	Dennis Priestley (Eng) 90.75	71/20/10
1999	Phil Taylor (Eng) 97.11	6–2	Peter Manley (Eng) 93.63	104/30/16
2000	Phil Taylor (Eng) 94.42	7–3	Dennis Priestley (Eng) 91.80	110/31/16.4
2001	Phil Taylor (Eng) 107.46	7–0	John Part (Can) 92.58	124/33/18
2002	Phil Taylor (Eng) 98.47	7–0	Peter Manley (Eng) 91.35	200/50/25
2003	John Part (Can) 96.87	7–6	Phil Taylor (Eng) 99.98	200/50/25
2004	Phil Taylor (Eng) 96.03	7–6	Kevin Painter (Eng) 90.48	256/50/25
2005	Phil Taylor (Eng) 96.14	7–4	Mark Dudbridge (Eng) 90.66	300/60/30
2006	Phil Taylor (Eng) 106.74	7–0	Peter Manley (Eng) 91.72	500/100/50
2007	Raymond van Barneveld (Net) 101.07	7–6	Phil Taylor (Eng) 100.98	500/100/50
2008	John Part (Can) 92.86	7–2	Kirk Shepherd (Eng) 85.10	605/100/50

Key: * = £000's Total Fund/Winner's Prize Money/Runner-Up's Prize Money.

BRITISH DARTS ASSOCIATION (BDO) VS PROFESSIONAL DARTS CORPORATION (PDC)

	BDO	PDC
Sponsors	1978–2003 Embassy; 2004–present Lakeside Country Club.	1994, 1998–2002 Skol; 1995 Proton; 1996 Vernons; 1997 Red Band; 2003 www.ladbrokes.com.
Venues	1978 Heart of the Midland Club, Nottingham; 1979–1985 Jollees Cabaret Club, Stoke-on-Trent; 1986 Lakeside Country Club, Frimley Green, Surrey.	1994–2007 Circus Tavern, Purfleet, Essex; 2008 Alexandra Palace, London.
TV Coverage	1978–present BBC	1994–present Sky Sports
Most Wins	Raymond van Barneveld (Net) 4	Phil Taylor (Eng) 11
Youngest Champion	Jelle Klaasen (Net) 21 y 90 d (2006)	Phil Taylor (Eng) 34 y 148 d (1995)
Oldest Champion	Martin Adams (Eng) 50 y 224 d (2007).	Dennis Priestley (Eng) 43 y 170 d (1994).
Highest Average	Raymond van Barneveld (103.83) 2004 QF v John Walton	Joe Soap (112.45) 2004 R3 v Phil Taylor
Number of 100+ Averages:	16	33
Number of 100+ Averages (not including the player with most 100+ averages)	10 (not including Raymond van Barneveld's)	6 (not including Phil Taylor's)

Players to Have Won BDO (Post-1994) and PDC Titles: John Part (Can) and Raymond van Barneveld (Net).

Nine Dart Finish: only one has ever been scored in any World Darts Championship tournament. It was made by Paul Lim (US) v Jack McKenna (Ire) on 9/1/1990. His method was: 180, 180, followed by the most common nine dart finish outshot, treble 20 (60), treble 19 (57), double 12 (24).

TWENTIETH/TWENTY-FIRST CENTURY UK PRIME MINISTERS

NAME	OFFICE SPAN	PARTY	PLACE OF BIRTH	LIFE SPAN (AGE AT DEATH)	SPOUSE (CHILDREN)
Arthur Balfour	1902–1905 (3 y 145 d)	C	Whittinghame	1848–1930 (81)	n/a
Sir Henry Campbell-Bannerman	1905–1908 (2 y 122 d)	Li	Glasgow	1836–1908 (72)	Charlotte Bruce (-)
H. H. Asquith	1908–1916 (8 y 244 d)	Li	Morley	1852–1928 (75)	Helen (4 s 1 d); Margot (1 s 1 d)
David Lloyd George	1916–1922 (5 y 317 d)	Li	Manchester	1863–1945 (82)	Margaret Owen (2 s 3 d); Frances Stevenson (1 d)
Andrew Bonar Law[2]	1922–1923 (209 d)	C	New Brunswick, Canada	1858–1923 (65)	Annie Robley (4 s 2 d)
Stanley Baldwin	1923–1924; 1924–1929; 1935–1937 (7y 82d)	C	Bewdley	1867–1947 (80)	Lucy Ridsdale (2 s 4 d)
Ramsay McDonald	1924–1924; 1929–1931; 1931–1935 (6y 289d)	L; L; NL	Lossiemouth	1866–1937 (71)	Margaret Gladstone (3 s 3 d)
Neville Chamberlain	1937–1940 (2y 348d)	C	Birmingham	1869–1940 (71)	Anne de Vere Cole (1 s 1 d)
Winston Churchill	1940–1945; 1945–1945; 1951–1955 (8 y 240 d)	C	Blenheim	1874–1965 (90)	Clementine (1 s 4 d)
Clement Attlee	1945–1951 (6 y 92 d)	L	Putney	1883–1967 (84)	Violet Millar (1 s 3 d)
Anthony Eden	1955–1957 (1 y 279 d)	C	West Auckland	1897–1977 (79)	Beatrice Beckett (2 s); Clarissa Spencer-Churchill

NAME	OFFICE SPAN	PARTY	PLACE OF BIRTH	LIFE SPAN (AGE AT DEATH)	SPOUSE (CHILDREN)
Harold Macmillan	1957–1963 (6 y 281 d)	C	Chelsea	1894–1986 (92)	Dorothy Cavendish (1 s 3 d)
Alec Douglas-Home	1963–1964 (362 d)	C	Mayfair	1903–1995 (92)	Elizabeth Arlington (1 s 3 d)
Harold Wilson	1964–1970; 1974–1976 (7 yr 279 d)	L	Huddersfield	1916–1995 (79)	Mary Baldwin (2 s)
Edward Heath	1970–1974 (3 y 259 d)	C	Broadstairs	1916–2005 (89)	n/a
James Callaghan	1976–1979 (3 y 29 d)	L	Portsmouth	1912–2005 (92)	Audrey Moulton (1 s 2 d)
Margaret Thatcher	1979–1990 (11 y 209 d)	C	Grantham	1925–present	Denis Thatcher (1 s 1 d)
John Major	1990–1997 (6 y 154 d)	C	Carshalton	1943–present	Norma Johnson (1 s 1 d)
Tony Blair	1997–2007 (10 y 56 d)	L	Edinburgh	1953–present	Cherie Booth (3 s 1 d)
Gordon Brown	2007– present	L	Glasgow	1951–present	Sarah Macaulay (2 s)

First (De Facto) PM And Longest Period as PM: Robert Walpole (04/04/1721–11/02/1742); 20 y 314 d.

Shortest Period as PM: George Canning (10/04/1827–08/08/1827); 119 d.

Youngest PM: William Pitt 'The Younger' (19/12/1783–14/03/1801; 10/05/1804–23/01/1806); 24 y 205 d.

Most Children: Charles Grey, 2nd Earl Grey (22/11/1830–16/07/1834); 17.

Key: C = Conservative; L = Labour; Li = Liberal; NL = National Labour.

ENGLISH COUNTY CRICKET CHAMPIONSHIPS

YEAR	COUNTY CHAMPIONS	YEAR	COUNTY CHAMPIONS	
1980	Middlesex	1990	Middlesex	
1981	Nottinghamshire	1991	Essex	
1982	Middlesex	1992	Essex	
1983	Essex	1993	Middlesex	
1984	Essex	1994	Warwickshire	
1985	Middlesex	1995	Warwickshire	
1986	Essex	1996	Leicestershire	
1987	Nottinghamshire	1997	Glamorgan	
1988	Worcestershire	1998	Leicestershire	
1989	Worcestershire	1999	Surrey	

A second division was introduced in 2000.				
YEAR	COUNTY CHAMPIONS	RELEGATED FROM 1ST DIVISION	2ND DIVISION WINNERS	PROMOTED FROM 2ND DIVISION
2000	Surrey	Hampshire, Durham, Derbyshire	Northamptonshire	Essex, Glamorgan
2001	Yorkshire	Northamptonshire, Glamorgan, Essex	Sussex	Hampshire, Warwickshire
2002	Surrey	Hampshire, Somerset, Yorkshire	Essex	Middlesex, Nottinghamshire
2003	Sussex	Essex, Nottinghamshire, Leicestershire	Worcestershire	Northamptonshire, Gloucestershire
2004	Warwickshire	Worcestershire, Lancashire, Northamptonshire	Nottinghamshire	Hampshire, Glamorgan
2005	Nottinghamshire	Surrey, Gloucestershire, Glamorgan	Lancashire	Durham, Yorkshire
2006	Sussex	Nottinghamshire, Middlesex	Surrey	Worcestershire
2007	Sussex	Warwickshire, Worcestershire	Somerset	Nottinghamshire

Most Wins (1890–2007): Yorkshire (30+1 shared); Surrey (18+1 shared); Middlesex (10+2 shared); Lancashire (7+1 shared); Kent (6+1 shared); Essex (6); Warwickshire (6); Nottinghamshire; Worcestershire (5); Glamorgan (3); Leicestershire (3); Sussex (3); Hampshire (2); Derbyshire (1). Durham, Gloucestershire, Northamptonshire and Somerset have no country championship titles.

Most Wooden Spoons (1890–2007): Derbyshire (14); Somerset (12); Northamptonshire (11); Glamorgan (10); Nottinghamshire (8); Sussex (8); Gloucestershire (7); Leicestershire (7); Worcestershire (6); Durham (5); Hampshire (5); Warwickshire (3); Essex (2); Kent (2); Yorkshire (1). Lancashire, Middlesex and Surrey have never finished bottom of the county championship.

Highest Ever Team Score: Yorkshire (887) v Warwickshire at Edgbaston, Birmingham (1896).

Highest Post-War Team Score: Lancashire (863) v Surrey at The Oval, Kennington (1990).

Lowest Ever Team Score: Northamptonshire (12) v Gloucestershire at the Gloucestershire Spa Ground, Gloucester (1907).

Lowest Post-War Team Score: Surrey (14) v Essex at the County Ground, Chelmsford (1983).

Schedule: all matches prior to 1988 were scheduled for three days. Between 1988 and 1992, some matches were played over four days. Since 1992 all matches have been scheduled over four days.

Sponsors: 1977–1983, Schweppes; 1984–1998, Britannic Assurance; 1999–2000, AXA ppp Healthcare; 2001, Cricinfo; 2002–2005, Frizzell; 2006–present, Liverpool Victoria.

Current Scoring System: Win (14 pts); Tie (7 pts); Draw (4 pts); Loss (0 pts); 200–249 runs (1 bonus pt); 250–299 runs (2 bonus pts); 300–349 runs (3 bonus pts); 350–399 runs (4 bonus pts); 400+ runs (5 bonus pts); 3–5 wickets taken (1 bonus pt); 6–8 wickets taken (2 bonus pts); 9–10 wickets taken (3 bonus pts). Small deductions (0.5–1pt) may be made for slow over rates and/or poor pitches.

LARGEST DESERTS

	NAME	LOCATION	AREA IN KM² (MILES²)
1	Antarctic	Antarctica	14.0 m (5.4 m)
2	Sahara	North Africa	9.1 m (3.5 m)
3	Arabian	Middle East	2.3 m (0.9 m)
4	Gobi	Mongolia/China	1.3 m (0.5 m)
5	Australian	Australia	1.0 m (0.385 m)
EU	Hálendi	Iceland	79,000 (30,500)
US	The Great Basin	(roughly between Utah and Nevada)	520,000 (200,000)

WORLD PRISON POPULATIONS

	NO. OF PRISONS	NO. OF PRISONERS (2008)	PRISON POPULATION PER 100,000 TOTAL POPULATION	PERCENTAGE OF PRISONERS FEMALE
Australia	124	27,224	130	7.3%
Brazil	1,117	422,590	220	6.1%
China	1,100A	1,565,771	119	4.9%
Denmark	57	3,626	66 (EL)	5.4%
England & Wales	140	82,655 (EH)	152	5.4%
France	185	56,279	91	3.7%
Germany	195	72,656	88	5.3%
Hong Kong	28	11,211	156	19.5% (H)
India	1,328	358,368	32	3.9%
Japan	187	81,255	63	5.9%
Madagascar	77	17,495	91	3.3%
Malawi	28	10,830	79	1.1% (L)
Netherlands	102	19,137	117	9.3% (EH)
Nigeria	228	39,438	29 (L)	1.5%
Northern Ireland	3	1,502	85	3.0% (EL)
Russia	1,051	893,631	633	7.4%
Scotland	16	7,507	145	5.0%
South Africa	237	165,840	347	2.2%
Spain	77	70,130	154 (EH)	8.3%
Switzerland	115	5,715	76	5.5%
Thailand	137	165,316	253	15.1%
UAE	14	8,927	288	11.4%
US	5,069 (H)	2,258,983 (H)	751(H)	9.1%

World Prison Population Total (2007): 9.1 m.

Key: figures from May 2008 (unless stated in upper case).

(H) = highest rate in the world (where recent figures exist, and not including countries with populations less than 1 million);

(L) = lowest rate in the world (where recent figures exist, and not including countries with populations less than 1 million);

(EH) = highest rate in Western Europe (not including countries with a population less than 1 million);

(EL) = lowest rate in Western Europe (not including countries with a population less than 1 million);

A = approximation. Exact figure is unavailable;

B = figures unavailable.

Source: World Prison Brief (Kings College London)

'BIG FOUR' US SPORTS LEAGUE

LEAGUE	NUMBER OF TEAMS	AVERAGE ANNUAL SQUAD MEMBER SALARY (2007)	CONFERENCES
Major League Baseball (MLB)	30	$2.5 m	Atlantic League: East, Central, West; National League: East, Central, West
National Basketball Association (NBA)	30	$4.9 m	Eastern Conference: Atlantic, Central, Southeast; Western Conference: Northwest, Pacific, Southwest
National Football League (NFL)	32	$1.3 m	American Football Conference: East, North, South, West; National Football Conference: East, North, South, West
National Hockey League (NHL)	30	$1.3 m	Eastern Conference: Atlantic, Northeast, Southeast; Western Conference: Central, Northwest, Pacific

RECREATIONAL DRUGS

OFFICAL NAME [CLASS]	AKA	TAKEN	POSITIVE EFFECTS	NEGATIVE EFFECTS
Alcohol [legal for over-18's in the UK]	Booze, drink, liquor	Orally	Pleasant relaxation, 'brings out' personal character.	Impaired judgement, aggression, depression, addiction.
Amphetamine [class B] [class A if injected]	Speed, whizz	Snorted	Heightened alertness, decreased need for sleep.	Increased irritation, desire to continue using.
Barbiturates [class B] [class A if injected]	Barbs	Orally or injected	Sleep-inducing, helps prevent seizures.	Aggression, depression, muscle spasms.
Cocaine hydrochloride [class A]	Coke, Charlie, Blow, Powder	Snorted	Euphoria, excitement, exhilaration, increased confidence.	Skin abscesses, extreme anxiety, restlessness, raised blood pressure, addictive.
Crack cocaine (class A)	Crack, rock	Smoked	Euphoria, excitement, exhilaration. Shorter but more intense high compared with cocaine.	Very addictive.
Ecstasy (3,4-methylene dioxymethamphetamine) [class A]	'E', sweeties, pills, MDMA	Orally	Increased sense of well-being, energy and affection, hallucinations.	Depression, memory loss, anxiety attacks.
Heroin [class A]	Smack, skag, 'H', dope, brown	Smoked, or injected	Numbs pain, increases feelings of calmness and warmth.	Psychological and physical addiction.

OFFICAL NAME [CLASS]	AKA	TAKEN	POSITIVE EFFECTS	NEGATIVE EFFECTS
Ketamine [available under the medicines act]	'K', Special K, Ket, Kitty	Snorted, smoked with marijuana or taken orally	Short-term hallucinations, change in perception ('K-hole'), loss of sense of reality.	Confusion, difficulty in moving, memory lapses, sickness.
Lysergic acid diethylamide [class A]	LSD, Acid	Dissolved on tongue	Hallucinations, alteration of thought processes, intense visions, increased sensation of crossed senses (e.g. 'loud' colours).	Depression, lack of self-control, feelings of terror, paranoia.
Marijuana - Cannabis Resin [class C]	Hash, tack, brown, dope, blow	Smoked	Euphoria, stimulation, tranquillity, greater sensory awareness.	Psychological dependence, feelings of helplessness, fatigue, anxiety.
Marijuana – Grass [class C]	Weed, ganja, blow, chronic	Smoked	Euphoria, stimulation, tranquillity, increased sensory awareness.	Psychological dependence, feelings of helplessness, fatigue, anxiety.
Phencyclidine [class A]	PCP, angel dust, rocket fuel, hog	Snorted, smoked, or taken orally	Detachment, reduced sense of pain, inducement of dreamlike state.	Confusion, anxiety, paranoia, irritability, possible violence.

MOST POPULAR LUXURY LIGHTER
BRANDS IN THE UK

MANUFACTURER (FOUNDED)	MODEL	DESCRIPTION	MANUFACTURER TRIVIA
Alfred Dunhill Ltd (England)	Dunhill Unique	Metal-cased, with a nodding donkey-style lighting mechanism. When introduced in 1924, it was the world's first lighter that could be struck with one hand.	Alfred Dunhill took over his father's saddler business at 21 and diversified into motor car accessories – car horns, lights, dashboard clocks, etc. Dunhill's aim was to sell 'Everything for the car but the motor.'
	Dunhill Rollagas	Slim, rectangular and with a roller flame adjuster located ¾ up the side on the corner. Introduced in 1956.	After retiring from the Motorities business, Dunhill opened a pipe, cigar and tobacco shop among the men's clubs in Duke Street, London.
Colibri (England)	Smitty	Matte black and polished steel outer with integrated carabiner clip.	The golden gun in the James Bond film *The Man with the Golden Gun* was assembled from a Calibri 88 lighter, a cigar case, a fountain pen and cufflinks.
	Lasatron	Ignites when you pass a finger through its laser beam sensor. Battery-powered. Introduced in 1982.	Colibri describe the Lasatron as the first truly space age lighter. The first Colibri lighter was produced in 1928.
Ronson (US)	Premier Varaflame	Metal-cased and uses a flint-levered ignition system. Height is around 50 per cent of width. Introduced in 1957.	In Ian Fleming's books, it's mentioned that the Premier Varaflame is used by James Bond.
S. T. Dupont (France)	miniJet / maxiJet	Slim, broad, lightweight and with a window to show the gas content. Two sizes.	S. T. Dupont was founded in 1872 by Simon Tissot Dupont; it bears no relation to E. I. Du Pont (the world's second largest chemical company). The Ligne 1 was Dupont's first gas lighter.
	Ligne 1	Comes in two sizes - small and large. The roller flame adjuster is on the outer case, not under the hood. Introduced in 1952.	

MANUFACTURER (FOUNDED)	MODEL	DESCRIPTION	MANUFACTURER TRIVIA
Zippo Manufacturing Company (US)	Zippo	Rectangular, metal-cased, windproof lighter. Introduced in 1932.	Invented by George G. Blaisdell. Over 400 m have been produced. Zippo's are manufactured in Bradford, Pennsylvania.

Invention: the first lighter was invented in 1816; it was called 'Dobereiner's Lamp', and was made by German chemist Johann Wolfgang Dobereiner. This early model used hydrogen for fuel (rather than butane or naptha) and used platinum (instead of flint) to ignite the fuel. Lighters Fuelled By Butane: in the 1930s Ronson started making lighters that used butane gas (instead of the traditional naphtha liquid). With butane there was, (a) no need for a wick, (b) the potential to adjust the size of the flame, (c) no pungent odour like naphtha had. Piezoelectric Spark: piezoelectricity was invented in the early 1800s but it wasn't until the late 1950s that it started to be used in lighters. One downside with piezo-ignition lighters is that the higher the altitude, the less likely disposable varieties will strike first time (if at all). Disposable Lighter Market: about £2.5 bn is spent globally on disposable lighters every year. The UK market is worth around £70 m per year.

WORLD TOURISM RANKINGS

RANK	COUNTRY	FOREIGN TOURISTS*
1	France	79.1 m
2	Spain	58.5 m
3	US	51.1 m
4	China	49.6 m
5	Italy	41.1 m
6	UK	30.1 m
7	Germany	23.6 m
8	Mexico	21.4 m
9	Austria	20.3 m
10	Russia	20.2 m

*The official figure is a total number of tourists that arrived in each country in a calendar year. Figures relate to 2006.

Source: United Nations World Tourism Organization (UNWTO).

BRITISH GUITAR BAND
BRIT AWARD WINNERS

YEARS ACTIVE	BAND	BRIT AWARD(S)	STUDIO ALBUMS*	HOME CITY	MEMBERS
1976– present	The Cure	V (1990); G (1991)	12	Crawley, West Sussex	Robert Smith (V/G/K); Porl Thompson (G/K); Simon Gallup (B/K); Jason Cooper (D)
1984– 1992	Fine Young Cannibals	A, G (1990)	2	Birmingham	Roland Lee Gift (V); Andy Cox (G); David Steele (B)
1986– present	Manic Street Preachers	A, G (1997); A, G (1999)	8	Blackwood, Caerphilly	James Dean Bradfield (V/G); Nicky Wire (B); Sean Moore (D)
1989– 2003	Blur	A, G, S, V (1995)	7	Colchester, Essex	Damon Albarn (V); Graham Coxon (G); Alex James (B); Dave Rowntree (D)
1989– 1999; 2007– present	The Verve	A, G (1998)	3	Wigan, Manchester	Richard Ashcroft (V); Nick McCabe (G); Simon Jones (B); Peter Salisbury (D)
1991– present	Oasis	BA (1995); A, G, V (1996); O (2007)	6	Manchester	Liam Gallagher (V); Noel Gallagher (G); Gem Archer (G); Andy Bell (B); Zak Starket (D)
1992– present	Stereophonics	BA (1998)	6	Cwmaman, Glamorgan	Kelly Jones (V/G); Richard Jones (B); Javier Weyler (D)
1993– present	Supergrass	BA (1996)	6	Oxford	Gaz Coombes (V/G); Mick Quinn (B); Rob Coombes (K); Danny Goffrey (D)

YEARS ACTIVE	BAND	BRIT AWARD(S)	STUDIO ALBUMS*	HOME CITY	MEMBERS
1994–present	Muse	LA (2005); LA (2007)	4	Teignmouth, Devon	Matthew Bellamy (V/G/K); Christopher Wolstenholme (B/K); Dominic Howard (D)
1995–1999; 2004–present	Kula Shaker	BA (1997)	3	London	Crispian Mills (V/G); Alonza Bevan (B); Harry Broadbent (K): Paul Winterhart (D)
1995–present	Travis	A, G (2000); G(2002)	6	Glasgow	Francis Healy (V); Andrew Dunlop (G); Douglas Payne (B); Neil Primrose (D)
1996–present	Belle & Sebastian	BA(1999)	7	Glasgow	Stuart Murdoch (V/G/K); Stevie Jackson (G); Chris Geddes (K); Sarah Martin (Vi/K/G); Mick Cooke (T/B); Bobby Kildea (G/B); Richard Colburn (D)
1997–present	Coldplay	A, G (2001); A, G (2003); A(2006)	4	London	Chris Martin (V); Jonny Buckland (G); Guy Berryman (B); Will Champion (D)
1997–present	Kaiser Chiefs	G, R, RA, LA (2006)	2	Menston, West Yorks	Ricky Wilson (V); Andrew White (G); Simon Rix (B); Nick Baines (K); Nick Hodgson (D)

YEARS ACTIVE	BAND	BRIT AWARD(S)	STUDIO ALBUMS*	HOME CITY	MEMBERS
2000–2006	The Darkness	A, G, RA (2004)	2	Lowestoft, Suffolk	Justin Hawkins (V/G); Richie Edwards (G); Dan Hawkins (G); Frankie Poullain (B); Ed Graham (D)
2001–present	Franz Ferdinand	G, RA (2005)	2	Glasgow	Alex Kapranos (V/G); Nick McCarthy (G/K); Bob Hardy (B); Paul Thomson (D)
2002–present	Arctic Monkeys	BA (2006); A, G (2007); A, G (2008)	2	Sheffield	Alex Turner (V/G); Jamie Cook (G); Nick O'Malley (B); Matt Helders (D)
2005–present	The Fratellis	BA (2007)	2	Glasgow	Jon Fratelli (V/G); Barry Fratelli (B); Mince Fratelli (D)

Awards Key: A = Best British Album; BA = Best British Breakthrough Act; G = Best British Group; LA = Best British Live Act; RA = Best British Rock Act; S = Best British Single; V = Best British Video; O = Outstanding Contribution To Music.

Band Members Key: B = Bass Guitar; D = Drums; G = Guitar; K = Keyboard; P = Piano; T = Trumpet; V = Lead Vocals; Vi = Violin. * = 2008 albums included.

'BIG SIX' MAJOR US FILM STUDIOS

MAJOR STUDIO	MAIN SUBSIDIARIES	PARENT COMPANY	US/CAN MARKET SHARE (2006)
Columbia Pictures	MGM, UA, Tristar	Sony	21.1%
Twentieth Century Fox	Fox Faith, Fox Searchlight	News Corp	17.0%
Walt Disney Pictures/ Touchstone	Miramax, Hollywood Pictures	The Walt Disney Company	16.7%
Warner Bros Pictures	New Line Cinema, HBO Films, Castle Rock Entertainment	Time Warner	14.9%
Paramount Pictures	Dreamworks SKG, Go Fish Pictures	Viacom	11.0%
Universal Studios	Focus Features, Rogue Pictures	General Electric	10.9%

BUSIEST UK AIRPORTS
(BY ANNUAL PASSENGER NUMBERS)

	AIRPORT	IATA CODE	INTERNATIONAL PASSENGERS	DOMESTIC PASSENGERS
1	London Heathrow	LHR	62,098,911	5,753,476
2	London Gatwick	LGW	31,142,002	4,023,402
3	London Stansted	STN	21,204,946	2,554,304
4	Manchester	MAN	18,662,468	3,229,255
5	London Luton	LTN	8,427,894	1,491,467
6	Birmingham	BHX	7,592,240	1,541,815
7	Edinburgh	EDI	3,417,891	5,619,309
8	Glasgow	GLA	4,131,512	4,594,575
9	Bristol	BRS	4,608,290	1,275,566
10	Newcastle	NCL	3,948,594	1,675,013

Figures relate to 2007. Source: Civil Aviation Authority

TOP TEN UK PASSENGER AIRLINES
(BY PASSENGERS UPLIFTED)

AIRLINE	FOUNDED	AIRCRAFT IN SERVICE	FLIGHTS	DISTANCE TRAVELLED (KM)	PASSENGERS UPLIFTED	IATA CODE	ICAO CODE	CALL SIGN
British Airways	1974	234 (67 A; 167 B)	265,491	623,270	32,341,360	BA	BAW	Speedbird
EasyJet	1995	125 (94 A; 31 B)	244,102	251,520	30,064,547	U2	EZY	Easy
BMI	1949	62 (26 A; 20 B; 16 E)	125,193	96,197	9,527,396	BD	BMA	Midland
Thomsonfly	1962	48 (48 B)	54,016	117,264	9,499,626	BY	TOM	Thomson
Monarch Airlines	1967	31 (23 A; 8 B)	33,841	72,445	6,106,580	ZB	MON	Monarch
Flybe	1979	88 (15 BA; 33 BO; 6 DE; 34 E)	120,492	61,802	5,850,085	BE	BEE	Jersey
Virgin Atlantic Airways	1984	38 (25 A; 13 B)	21,344	155,406	5,639,957	VS	VIR	Virgin
First Choice Airways	1987	32 (10 A; 22 B)	27,827	79,363	5,576,420	DP	FCA	Jetset
Thomas Cook Airlines*	1999	24 (6 A; 18 B)	23,086	68,667	4,897,860	MT	TCX	Top Jet

AIRLINE	FOUNDED	AIRCRAFT IN SERVICE	FLIGHTS	DISTANCE TRAVELLED (KM)	PASSENGERS UPLIFTED	IATA CODE	ICAO CODE	CALL SIGN
Jet2.com	2002	29 (29 B)	31,809	41,251	3,575,218	LS	EXS	Channex
MyTravel Airways*	1990	25 (22 A; 3 B)	18,343	54,036	3,375,383	VZ	MYT	Kestrel
UK TOTAL		957	1,202,000	1,847,159	128,750,734			

All figures relate to 2007. Key: * = in March 2008 the MyTravel Group was merged into Thomas Cook AG. A = Airbus (Europe); B = Boeing (US); BA = British Aerospace (UK); BO = Bombardier (Canada); DE = De Havilland (UK); E = Embraer (Brazil). IATA = International Air Transport Association; HQ – Montreal, Canada. ICAO code = International Civil Aviation Organization; HQ – Montreal, Canada. Call Sign: ICAO allocates a unique one or two word 'Call Sign' to each airline for use in telephony relating to flight planning – e.g., flight code DP1234 would be referred over the radio as 'Jetset – One – Two – Three – Four'. Flight Code: airlines use their IATA code as the first two letters of each of their flight codes, however if their IATA code contains a number, they use their ICAO code instead – e.g., British Airways' IATA code is BA. Source: Civil Aviation Authority

WORD COUNT DEFINITIONS FOR FICTION

DEFINITION	WORD COUNT
Flash Fiction[1]	1,000 or fewer
Short Story[2]	7,499 or fewer
Novelette[2]	7,500 to 17,499
Novella[2]	17,500 to 39,999
Novel[2]	40,000 or more

[1] As defined by www.duotrope.com.

[2] As defined by the Science Fiction and Fantasy Writers of America (SFWA) to determine categories for their Nebula Awards. Other sources use different definitions; there is no universal standard for all fiction.

VITAL STATISTICS FOR VITAL STATISTICS

Number of Tables	198
Table Body Text Font	Humanist521 BT
Table Body Text Size	Between 7pt & 10pt
Paper	Munken 80gsm
Page Dimensions	198 x 129 mm

LIST OF TABLES

A

B

C

D

V

W

www.summersdale.com